10/07

Financing Your Small Business

D1411365

James E. Burk
Richard P. Lehmann
Attorneys at Law

SPHINX® PUBLISHING
AN IMPRINT OF SOURCEBOOKS, INC.®
NAPERVILLE, ILLINOIS
www.SphinxLegal.com

First Edition: 2006

This publication is designed to provide accurate and authoritative information in regard to the subject matter covered. It is sold with the understanding that the publisher is not engaged in rendering legal, accounting, or other professional service. If legal advice or other expert assistance is required, the services of a competent professional person should be sought.
　　—From a Declaration of Principles Jointly Adopted by a Committee of the American
　　　Bar Association and a Committee of Publishers and Associations

Published by Sourcebooks, Inc.
P.O. Box 4410, Naperville, Illinois 60567-4410
(630) 961-3900
Fax: (630) 961-2168
www.sourcebooks.com

Library of Congress Cataloging-in-Publication Data
Burk, James E.
　Financing your small business : from SBA loans and credit cards to common stock and partnership interests / by James E. Burk and Richard P. Lehmann.
　　p. cm.
　Includes bibliographical references and index.
　ISBN-13: 978-1-57248-553-2 (pbk. : alk. paper)
　ISBN-10: 1-57248-553-1 (pbk. : alk. paper)
　1. Small business--Finance. I. Lehmann, Richard P., 1966- II. Title.

HG4027.7.B8554 2006
658.15'224--dc22
　　　　　　　　　　　　　　　　　　　　　　　　　　　　　　2006030168

Printed and bound in the United States of America
VHG　10　9　8　7　6　5　4　3　2

Acknowledgment

We are grateful for the collaborative support we have received from our professional colleagues, clients, and students, past and present, in writing this book. Specifically, we would like to thank IBI Global for providing a teaching laboratory that enhances human potential and accelerates student learning capacity, and our wives, Katherine and Karen, for providing an environment in which we both can flourish.

With further specificity, we thank Tarby Bryant, Eric Delisle, Burke Franklin, Ike Gadsden, Herb Rubenstein, and Robert Johnson for their contributions. We are especially grateful for the contribution of Jay Winokur in Chapter 2 and Katherine Burk and James Harper III for their editorial work on all of the chapters. We also thank our law partner, Alan Reedy, for his suggestions and revisions that always enhance our work.

James E. Burk
Richard P. Lehmann
Washington, D.C.

Contents

Introduction

The idea for *Financing Your Small Business* came, in part, from the entrepreneurial seminars we have done in the past several years for IBI Global. While serving as faculty instructors, we have encountered literally thousands of students seeking to finance their small business. There have been successes and failures along the way. Many of the so-called *failures* learned from their mistakes and reinvented themselves, becoming stronger and wiser than before.

There are many reasons a small business may seek financing. If you are one of those people with an idea on a napkin, ready to seek fame and fortune, you may need to raise capital before you simply quit your day job and launch your business from ground zero. Among the things you may need at this point are:

- a feasibility analysis to determine the viability of your idea;
- corporate organizational documents (articles, bylaws, minutes);
- a summary business plan (or at least an executive summary);
- federal (and perhaps state) tax identification numbers;
- a corporate bank account; and,
- local licenses (if required).

If you have already started a business by using your own cash (sometimes called *bootstrapping*), you may need to raise additional capital to:

- lease office space;
- purchase office equipment;
- develop a prototype of your product;
- hire a president, chief operating officer (CEO), or chief financial officer (CFO);
- design a logo to establish a branding and marketing program;
- file for trademark or patent protection on intellectual property (IP); and,
- pay yourself a salary.

The list could go on.

We have noticed that some of the books on financing a business focus on the narrower sense of the word—financing through debt. In this book, we address a broader sense of the term to cover both debt *and* equity. You can finance your business by borrowing, selling a part of the company, or a combination of both.

Our goal in writing this book is twofold. First, we want to provide you with a variety of simple techniques and resources to increase your chances of obtaining financing. Second, we want to provide you with the benefit of our experience in this field to help you avoid some of the pitfalls that can derail your business and steal your time.

At various points in the text, we have inserted "How To..." boxes to provide a quick reference to the topics discussed. After all, this book is a *practical* guide to financing your small business.

The chapters that follow suggest resources, as well as a sequence for raising capital for your small business. The rules are not cast in stone, but are instead merely suggested guidelines.

The first topic discussed is what type of company or organization you should form in order to raise capital and the various attributes of those entities. The choices include C corporations, S corporations, limited liability companies (LLCs), limited partnerships (LPs), and sole proprietorships. While you can operate your business as a sole proprietor (that is, no legal entity formed around your business), it may be more difficult for you to attract capital and your personal liability is greater.

Once you have determined the legal entity to use, how and when to draft a business plan for the company is explained, as well as the various parts of a business plan—including the part most investors always read. Then, some of the mistakes that occur in start-up businesses are discussed.

Equity financing is the topic of the next section. Most entrepreneurs recognize the equity categories—common stock, preferred stock, and LLC membership units. There is also a discussion of some hybrid variations on the traditional equity forms of investments. Following the discussion of equity, the book explores the various types of debt instruments of your company that can be offered to investors.

There are pros and cons for a young company to take on debt financing, and Chapter 4 explores some of those circumstances. Information on combinations of debt and equity that have shown some popularity in the current market is provided.

Once you decide on the type of company and the form of the investment, your next step may involve selling securities. In a private placement to qualified investors, federal and state securities laws come in to play. The elements of legal compliance in private securities offerings is discussed in Chapter 5. Most emerging companies raise their initial capital through private placements—not publicly registered offerings. In this book, there are only passing references to public offerings, sometimes called IPOs, since they are rarely available to small companies as a financing alternative.

Once the private placement market has been explored, the book touches on some later stage financing alternatives, including franchising and licensing, combinations of debt and equity, and loans with equity kickers. The current market is seeking more and more investments that combine some degree of liquidity with an equity upside.

The next section introduces the types of investors that look at early stage companies, such as friends, angels, and venture capitalists, how they are different, and what they look for in investments.

When you are pitching your company before potential investors, you need certain skills to effectively present your case and obtain the funding. The mechanics of a good presentation, the use of presentation software, and tips for speakers are explained in Chapter 8.

Next, we discuss the elements of corporate record keeping and selected issues of corporate governance. The impact of corporate governance has recently come to the forefront of public scrutiny with the rash of public company financial scandals.

In the next segment, some guidelines for choosing your professional advisors are provided. Compliance with securities laws can trap the unwary. Thoughtful entrepreneurs are well-advised to choose competent professionals to help them navigate the law and lore of this legal specialty. The guidelines suggested should take some of the mystery and pain out of this process.

Finally, we provide some of our favorite reference sources for further reading and study. The literature and the information available on the Internet sites on this subject is vast. We give you a sampling of both in the reference section and throughout the book. The appendices contain a number of forms that provide a taste of the documentation required for legal compliance.

How to Approach this Book

This book was written with a certain audience in mind—small businesses. The difficulty in maintaining the scope is the fact that some small businesses become bigger businesses with larger and more complex financing needs. If you are a small, family-owned business or want to sell your grandmother's china on *eBay*, it is unlikely you will need to seek venture capital funding or raise capital through a private sale of your company's stock.

The information in this book gives you the ability to finance your business at the earliest level and then move into larger funding strategies if you desire. In that sense, it serves as a reference work that you may return to when the capital needs of your business go to the next level. For example, you might start your business by using your credit card and a loan from your family. At that point, you may not need a business plan. As you ramp up the business to enter a larger market, then you may need to prepare a business plan for either raising money from private sources or to obtain a commercial loan.

If you find your business has a product or service that can address a national market in a unique manner, you may wish to pursue large angel or venture capital funding. In that instance, you need to acquaint yourself with the nuances of a superior business plan aimed at addressing a specific funding audience. You also need to acquire the skills to make a compelling investor presentation.

Use this book as a starting point, from a *how-to* perspective, for various stages of your business financing experience. An extensive reference list of additional works and websites that elaborate on some of the topics started in this book is provided. Most entrepreneurs find they never stop raising capital in their businesses. This book attempts to provide you with a variety of starting blocks from which you can commence your journey.

Even though we are attorneys by profession, the information and the forms contained in this book are provided for general information only and should not be considered legal advice. Each business has its own unique facts and circumstances, so it is always advisable to consult competent professionals for your particular situation.

Chapter

1

Choosing the Form of Your Business

- ▶ Sole Proprietorship
- ▶ Partnership
- ▶ Corporation
- ▶ Limited Liability Company
- ▶ Nonprofit Entities
- ▶ Joint Ventures and Corporate Partnerships
- ▶ Registered Agents
- ▶ Choosing the State in which to Form Your Business
- ▶ Qualifications for Starting a Business

Choosing the correct form of business entity is an important decision when starting a business. Not all entities are suited for raising substantial amounts of *capital* or flexible enough to grow with your changing needs. Most business entities that need to raise capital will organize either as a corporation or limited liability company (LLC) because of the financing options available. With a little forethought and the ability to understand the advantages and disadvantages of the different types of entities, your business will have the capability to achieve your goals.

QUICK Tip

Basic Questions to Ask Yourself when Choosing Your Form of Business:
- How easy is it to set up and operate the entity?
- What kind of capital can I raise in the entity?
- What are the tax advantages and disadvantages of the entity?
- Who is liable for the business debts and obligations?
- What happens if I die or become disabled?

The most common business forms are *sole proprietorships*, *corporations*, *limited liability companies (LLCs)*, and *partnerships*. This chapter explains some of the characteristics, advantages, and disadvantages of each entity, and ends with an explanation of how to form the one you choose.

Sole Proprietorship

A *sole proprietorship* is one person doing business in his or her own name (or under a *fictitious name*) and paying the applicable taxes on his or her personal income tax return. A sole proprietor has unlimited personal liability for the debts and obligations of the business, and cannot sell equity to fund operations or expand the business. As a sole proprietor, you can use debt to finance your operations, but you will be personally liable for the repayment.

Advantages

A sole proprietorship is easy to set up and operate. There are no forms to file with the state, and therefore, no organizational expenses. However, if you are using a fictitious name for the business, a notice should be filed with the county or state in which you are doing business. There are no initial or continuing annual reports to file with the state, and there are no separate income tax forms to file—you simply file a Schedule C with your federal Form 1040 Individual Income Tax Return and applicable state income tax returns. You should keep accurate records of your business income and expenses and make sure to keep those business items separate from your personal expenses.

Employer Identification Number: Even though you are a sole proprietor, you will need to obtain a separate federal *Employer Identification Number* (EIN) for tax withholding purposes if you hire employees to work for you. To obtain an EIN, complete Form SS-4 online at the IRS website, **www.irs.gov**.

Disadvantages

The sole proprietor is personally liable for all debts and obligations of the business. There is no limited liability as there is in a corporation or an LLC. If things go badly, you will be required to pay off creditors. In addition, there is no continuation of the business if you become disabled or die—the business simply goes away. While a sole proprietor may deduct all expenses reasonably attributed to the business from business revenues, all profits are directly taxable to the sole proprietor at individual income tax rates. Finally, since a sole proprietorship has no stock structure, it cannot sell stock to raise capital. The sole proprietor can only incur debt through loans or promissory notes, both of which need to be paid back according to the terms of the loans.

Partnership

Typically, partnerships can be placed into two categories—general partnerships and limited partnerships. One of the advantages these entities have is that they pay no tax at the partnership level. Instead, all profits and losses are passed through to the partners according to their percentage of ownership (in the absence of a special allocation), even if the profits remain in the business to fund continuing operation or expansion. Beyond this basic principle, partnership tax law is a complex subject to understand and is fraught with traps for the unwary.

 **Partnership Tax Returns:** Make certain to consult with a tax professional who is familiar with partnership taxation when forming your partnership and filing the partnership tax return.

General Partnership

A *general partnership* involves two or more people carrying on a business together and sharing the profits and losses. Unless limited by the partnership agreement, each partner has full managerial control over the partnership. In addition, each partner has unlimited *personal* liability for the debts and obligations of the partnership.

To form a general partnership, prepare a written *partnership agreement* to set forth the ownership and responsibilities of the partners. If you require money to fund operations or expand the business, the general partnership can take on new general partners by selling a new partnership interest. Unless otherwise stated, any new partners will have the same rights, responsibilities, and liabilities of the original partners.

Advantages. Partners can combine their expertise and assets for a common goal. Most states do not usually require general partnerships to file organizational documents, unless there is fictitious name filing required. The following states, however, require the filing of a *Statement of Partnership Authority* or similar form for general partnerships.

- California
- Delaware
- District of Columbia
- Hawaii
- Idaho
- Kansas
- Oklahoma
- South Dakota
- Virginia

In addition, a handful of states require the filing of initial and continuing annual reports. General partnerships have higher maintenance costs than a sole proprietorship because they must track assets and liabilities as well as income and expenses. However, they have lower maintenance costs than a corporation because they are not required to have the same governance formalities as corporations. In addition, the business can continue after the disability or death of a partner if there are more than two partners. Partnerships file their federal income tax returns on Form 1065. State income tax filings may also be required, depending on the state in which the partnership is *domiciled* (the state of legal residence).

Disadvantages. A general partnership is potentially a dangerous form of business entity because each partner is jointly and severally liable (meaning together and separately liable) for the debts of the partnership and the acts of other partners within the scope of the business. Thus, if your partner breaches a contract or signs a million dollar credit line in the partnership name, you can be personally liable. All parties share control, and the death of a partner may result in the liquidation of the partnership. It is often hard to get rid of a disgruntled partner.

Alert!

A carefully drafted partnership agreement prepared by an attorney can mitigate the disadvantages inherent in partnerships.

Limited Partnership

A *limited partnership* has characteristics similar to both a corporation and a partnership. The *general partners* have control and unlimited personal liability, but the *limited partners*, who put up money, have their liability limited to the amount of their capital contribution to the partnership (like corporate stock). A limited partnership must have at least one general partner and one or more limited partners.

Advantages. A limited partnership usually only needs to file a one-page document, called a *Certificate of Limited Partnership*, with the state upon formation and pay a fee. In a handful of states, however, the limited partnership is also required to file an initial report and continuing annual reports with the state to update the contact information for the partnership, resident agent, general partners, and in some cases, the limited partners. Capital can be contributed by limited partners who have no control over the business and no liability for its debts or obligations.

A limited partnership may define the term of its existence in its partnership agreement. In addition, the business can continue to operate after the death or disability of a general partner if appropriate survival language is included in the limited partnership agreement.

Just like general partnerships, limited partnerships have higher maintenance costs than a sole proprietorship because they must track assets and liabilities as well as income and expenses. They have lower maintenance costs than a corporation, because they are generally not required to pay taxes (although they must file tax returns on Form 1065) and are not required to hold meetings or keep minutes like a corporation.

Disadvantages. Like a general partnership, your attorney should prepare a limited partnership agreement to set forth the ownership and sharing arrangements of the partners. In a limited partnership, the general partner is personally liable for partnership debts and for the business-related acts of other general partners.

QUICK Tip

Limiting Liability: To limit the general partner's liability, use a corporation or LLC as the general partner.

Limited partners give up most of their control over the business in exchange for limited liability. When limited partners take an active role in the running of the business, they jeopardize their protection from liability and can be held liable as a general partner. Assuming limited partners take no part in management, they enjoy limited liability as in a corporation. Like general partnerships, limited partnerships are subject to the same complex tax rules, so consult with a tax professional familiar with partnership taxation when forming your limited partnership.

In recent years, the *limited liability company* has overtaken the limited partnership as the tax-advantaged vehicle of choice, because everyone involved has limited liability and investors can participate in the decisions of the company.

Corporation

A *corporation* is an artificial legal *person* that carries on business through its officers and directors for the benefit of its shareholders. In most states, one person may form a corporation and be the sole director, officer, and shareholder. The corporation carries on business in its own name and shareholders, officers, directors, and employees are not personally liable for its acts (except in very specific instances). Most entities that intend to raise capital for long-term growth form a corporation. Corporations work well because their structure allows for a wide variety of financing options and there is a *continuity of existence*. When a corporation is young or has few assets, a lender may require the majority shareholder, the directors, or the principal officers of the corporation to personally guarantee a corporate debt.

An *S corporation* is a corporation that has filed Internal Revenue Service (IRS) Form 2553, electing to have all profits and losses pass through to the shareholders under Subchapter S of the Internal Revenue Code rather than being taxed at the corporate level. An S corporation files a federal income tax return on Form 1120-S, but pays no federal or state tax. The profit shown on the S corporation tax return is allocated on a prorated basis according to stock ownership, and is then reported on the shareholders' personal tax returns.

If you plan to raise capital, be aware of a number of restrictions placed upon S corporations. First, an S corporation may only issue one class of stock and it can only have up to one-hundred shareholders. Those shareholders will primarily be individuals, because S corporations cannot be owned by C corporations, other S corporations, many trusts, LLCs, or partnerships. In addition, S corporations may not have any shareholders who are nonresident aliens. If an S corporation were to violate any of these rules, it would lose its S corporation election and be taxed as a C corporation.

A C *corporation* is any corporation that has not elected to be taxed as an S corporation. A C corporation pays income tax on its own taxable income under Subchapter C of the Internal Revenue Code and files a federal income tax return on Form 1120. Thus, when dividends are paid to shareholders, they are taxed twice—once at the corporate level and again by the shareholders. Recent tax law changes favorable to shareholders have, in part, mitigated this tax burden.

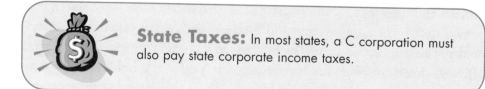

State Taxes: In most states, a C corporation must also pay state corporate income taxes.

Unlike S corporations, C corporations have no restrictions on the number or types of shareholders, and they may also have multiple classes of stock. Classes of stock generally consist of *common stock*, which is voting stock, and one or more classes of *preferred stock*. Preferred stock is generally nonvoting, but usually has first preference to receive declared dividends and a preference in payment in the event of liquidation. When the board of directors of a C corporation defines the preferences of a particular class of preferred stock, the corporation must generally file those preferences with the state prior to issuance of the preferred shares.

HOW TO...Keep Your Corporation Current

- ❑ *Hold the initial directors' meeting to adopt bylaws and appoint officers.*
- ❑ *Keep the state informed if your registered agent moves or changes.*
- ❑ *File your initial and annual reports where required.*
- ❑ *Hold your required annual meetings and document the decisions made at the meetings in the minutes.*

Advantages

Shareholders have no liability for corporate debts and lawsuits. Officers and directors have no personal liability for their corporate acts. Management of the corporation is vested in a *board of directors* that is elected by the shareholders. The board of directors appoints the principal officers of the corporation. Unlike a partnership or an LLC, in which an extensive agreement must be drafted that defines the rights and liabilities of the parties, the board of directors adopt bylaws for the corporation that are based primarily upon state corporate statutes that spell out the rights and liabilities of the shareholders, officers, and directors. Unlike a sole proprietorship, a corporation may enter into contracts and own property in its own name, and capital may be raised by selling stock or taking on debt. The existence of a corporation is usually *perpetual* and it is easy to transfer ownership upon death.

Disadvantages

The start-up costs for forming a corporation are generally lower than forming a partnership or LLC, because of the necessary drafting of a limited partnership agreement or LLC operating agreement. There are usually greater maintenance costs, however, because a corporation has statutory reporting and corporate formality requirements.

Whether you are operating an S or a C corporation, most states require that you file an initial report within thirty to ninety days of formation of the corporation, updating the contact information for the company, its registered agent, officers, and directors. All states require corporations to file some type of annual report updating the same information.

Required corporate formalities include adopting bylaws, holding annual meetings for the directors and shareholders of the corporation, electing directors, appointing officers, drafting resolutions to authorize corporate actions, keeping accurate minutes of meetings, maintaining corporate records, maintaining a registered agent, and paying taxes.

Alert!

If a corporation does not file the required reports or follow the required corporate formalities, it risks losing its corporate charter.

Limited Liability Company

Like a corporation, a *limited liability company* (LLC) is a separate legal entity formed under state law. Rather than being called a corporation, it is called a company, and it has *members* rather than *shareholders*. The document that governs the internal affairs of the company is called an *operating agreement*. Just like a corporation, some states require an initial report to be filed by an LLC within a short period of time after formation, and about half of the states require a report to be filed each year.

An LLC has the characteristics of a corporation in that all members have limited liability. If an LLC has only one person in its membership, it is taxed like a sole proprietorship (Form 1040, Schedule C). If there is more than one member, the LLC is taxed like a partnership, so all items of profit and loss flow through to the members (Form 1065). An LLC may also elect to be taxed like a corporation.

An LLC can be governed like a corporation, with a board of managers and officers, or like a partnership, with a manager running the show. You can also have a *member-managed LLC*, in which all the members have decision-making powers. If you plan to raise capital from investors, however, you would want to have your LLC run by a manager or board of managers, as opposed to a member-managed LLC.

HOW TO...Keep Your Limited Liability Company Current

❑ *Draft an operating agreement to govern the operations of the company. (A sample operating agreement is included in Appendix C.)*
❑ *Keep the state informed if your registered agent moves or changes.*
❑ *File your initial and annual reports where required.*

Advantages

An LLC offers the tax benefits of a partnership with the protection from liability of a corporation. Like a corporation, an LLC offers a business owner protection from the debts, obligations, and liabilities of the business. Unlike a corporation, LLCs are generally not required to have extensive corporate formalities, such as mandatory meetings and minutes. Unlike a limited partnership, members can participate in the operations of the business without jeopardizing their protection from liability.

An LLC is more flexible than an S corporation because it can have different classes of ownership, a flexible management structure, an unlimited number of members, and resident aliens as members. In addition, an LLC may create special allocations of profits and losses for the different classes of ownership. If the company decides they would like to operate as a corporation later on, it can convert to a corporation tax-free under IRS Code Section 351, with the LLC members exchanging their membership units for stock in a corporation.

Disadvantages

Formation costs for an LLC are comparable to a corporation, but because an *operating agreement* needs to be drafted to allocate profits and losses of the LLC among the members and define control, extra costs may be incurred. Another disadvantage of an LLC is that all profits and losses are deemed distributed *pro rata* to members for tax purposes on the last day of the tax year, even though many companies need to retain some funds to meet their current expenses. As a result, some owners can be charged with income they have not actually received. Most well-drafted operating agreements provide for a mandatory *tax distribution* to cover the taxes due on the phantom income. Like a corporation, there is the remote possibility that members of an LLC may be held personally liable for the debts and obligations of an LLC. These cases are rare and are generally the result of the members disregarding the formalities of the entity and committing a fraudulent act that gives rise to personal liability.

Nonprofit Entities

A *nonprofit* can be a corporation, a trust, or an unincorporated association—but a corporation is generally advised. A nonprofit is essentially a regular corporation that has been granted *tax-exempt status* by the IRS and state tax authorities.

The nonprofit corporation known as a Section 501(c)(3) is associated with organizations that are organized and operated for charitable, educational, scientific, or religious purposes. It is formed by filing *articles of incorporation* with the state under the state nonprofit or nonstock corporation act, and then applying to the IRS for recognition of its tax-exempt status on Form 1023.

An advantage for a Section 501(c)(3) nonprofit is that donors get a tax deduction and can even contribute appreciated properties to the nonprofit. There are other types of nonprofit organizations recognized by the IRS, such as trade associations and social clubs, but contributions to them are not deductible as charitable donations.

QUICK Tip

Tax-Exempt Status: In some states—notably, California—you must also apply for state exempt status.

The biggest difference between a nonprofit corporation and a regular corporation is that a nonprofit has no authorized stock, and therefore, no shareholders. However, it is run like a for-profit corporation in that it has a board of directors and officers.

Nonprofit corporations also have a need to raise capital for operations and to fulfill their charitable purposes. Since they have no stock to sell, they generally receive their capital from gifts, grants, and donations. When starting a nonprofit, drafting a business plan can be very helpful. This business plan can be presented to government agencies and to other charitable foundations that grant money or funding to nonprofits. It can also be used to show private donors how their donations are being spent.

While nonprofits have no ownership interests to sell to investors, there are instances in which a nonprofit can raise capital through a *debt offering*. The most typical instance is the use of a church bond for financing construction of a new sanctuary. The bonds, secured by an interest in the building, are retired over time from donations to the church.

Nonprofit corporations have to file initial reports in some states and annual reports in all states. They are also required to file a federal tax return on Form 990, as well as a state nonprofit tax return that many states require. Nonprofit corporations need to observe all of the corporate formality rules of for-profit corporations, including adopting bylaws and keeping corporate minutes. Failure to comply with these rules can result in forfeiture of the corporate charter and personal liability for officers and directors.

HOW TO...Become a Nonprofit Corporation

- ❑ File articles of incorporation with the state in which the organization will be located.
- ❑ Adopt bylaws.
- ❑ Hold an organizational meeting of directors to appoint officers and directors.
- ❑ Apply for a federal tax ID number (Form SS-4).
- ❑ File IRS Form 1023 with the IRS with all applicable schedules.

Joint Ventures and Corporate Partnerships

Relationships among entities can take many forms, such as *joint ventures*, in which two or more companies combine forces to engage in a specific business venture. Businesses form these types of relationships for specific projects in which a combined effort is beneficial, but the parties do not want to merge their businesses or have a long-term relationship.

For example, one company may be in the business of inventing products and another may be in the business of manufacturing and marketing products. An agreement between the two companies can avoid needless duplication of services and allow each company to focus on what it does best.

Joint venture relationships also serve the purpose of cutting costs for a start-up company and essentially form a source of financing. The amount of money you need to raise to invent, manufacture, and market a product is a great deal more than you need just to invent and then outsource the rest. Generally, joint ventures are taxed as partnerships.

Corporate partnering arrangements usually occur when a start-up company receives products or services from an established company in exchange for equity in the start-up or deferred payments, but there can be many variations on this theme.

Specialized Relationships: Other types of relationships between companies could include:
- marketing agreements;
- distribution agreements;
- license agreements;
- R&D agreements;
- manufacturing or supply agreements;
- outsourcing agreements; or,
- facility management agreements.

Always exercise caution when forming a relationship with another company. Not every deal is a good deal, and often the details that you overlook will be the ones that come back to haunt you. Think through the plan before you start, determine what you want to accomplish, and always get the deal in writing. Keep your options open until the deal is done, and do not forget to plan an exit strategy for the partnership.

Registered Agents

Unlike sole proprietorships, all corporations (profit and nonprofit), LLCs, and partnerships that are required to file initial and ongoing paperwork with the state in which they do business must have a *registered agent*. A registered agent is responsible for receiving and forwarding government and legal documents to the company in an accurate and timely fashion. Some examples of documents received and forwarded by registered agents are tax forms from the state and lawsuits (*service of process*) against the company from private litigants. A registered agent is usually an officer or director of the company or a company that performs registered agent services. (See Chapter 9 on Corporate Governance for more information.)

Choosing the State in which to Form Your Business

Where should you form your entity? Does Delaware or Nevada hold some magical power that makes those jurisdictions magnets for many corporate formations? The quick answer is *no.*

Historically, Delaware had favorable corporate laws and a court system set up specifically to deal with corporate disputes. However, most states have caught up substantially with Delaware and have enacted modern corporation law. Nevada's appeal is the lack of corporate tax, and it may—depending on how you set up your company—provide some measure of anonymity for the founders.

However, the best advice is usually to form your entity in the state where you intend to do business. Eventually, if you are doing business in your home state, your friendly tax authorities will come knocking on your door. It is entirely permissible to incorporate in a state different from your home state, but you must qualify your out-of-state (foreign) corporation to do business in your home state. The concept of *doing business* for tax and registration purposes is a vast topic. As a rule of thumb, if a corporation has a fixed place of business, a telephone number, a business license, etc., in a state that is different from the one in which it is registered, then it is doing business in that state. In this situation, the company needs to register and qualify as a *foreign corporation.*

If you form your entity where you intend to do business, you will find it is easier to deal with one bureaucracy as opposed to two and just pay the taxes for one state. Most states require you to register an out-of-state entity with your state and pay additional fees if business is done there.

Staying Focused: In the first few months, as your operations are ramped up, and research and development are conducted on your products or services, you will probably be losing money. Worry about forming multiple companies in multiple states later. For now, keep it straightforward. There are too many other things to worry about—like growing the company.

Qualifications for Starting a Business

Any individual may form a company. Generally, the minimum age is 18. In most states, you are not required to be a resident of the state to form a company. Some states even allow one company to form another company.

Immigration Concerns

Persons who are neither citizens nor legal permanent residents of the United States are also free to organize and run any type of business organization in their own name. The LLC would be the most advantageous, because it allows foreign nationals as owners (unlike an S corporation) and it avoids corporate taxation (unlike a C corporation). Two legal issues should concern foreign persons when starting a business—their immigration status and the proper reporting of the business's foreign owners.

The ownership of a U.S. business does not automatically confer rights to enter or remain in the United States. Different types of visas are available to investors and business owners, and each of these has strict requirements.

A visa to enter the United States may be permanent or temporary. *Permanent visas* for business owners usually require investments from $500,000 to $1,000,000 that result in the creation of new jobs. However, if structured right, there are ways to obtain visas for smaller investments.

 **Visas:** For more information on this area, consult an immigration attorney or visit the United States Citizenship and Immigration Services (USCIS) website, at **www.uscis.gov**.

Temporary visas may be used by business owners to enter the U.S. These are hard to get because in most cases, the foreign person must prove that there are no U.S. residents qualified to take the job.

United States businesses that own real property and are controlled by foreign persons are required to file certain federal reports under the *International Investment Survey Act*, the *Agricultural Foreign Investment Disclosure Act*, and the *Foreign Investment in Real Property Tax Act* (FIRPTA). If these laws apply to your business, consult an attorney who specializes in foreign ownership of U.S. businesses.

Figure 1.1: HOW TO PROCEDURES

Having an understanding of the characteristics of the typical entities used by entrepreneurs and a grasp of the advantages and disadvantages of each is an important first step on your journey. However, it is equally important to know how to get started. The following are checklists of actions to be taken and issues to be considered when starting your entity.

Sole Proprietorship

❑ File or open all accounts, property, and licenses in the name of the owner. (States require the filing of no special forms in starting a sole proprietorship.)

❑ File for a fictitious name (e.g., John Jones doing business as (d/b/a) Phoenix Car Wash) with the state or county, if necessary.

❑ Apply for a federal Employer Identification Number if you are going to have employees.

General Partnership

❑ Prepare a written Partnership Agreement to spell out rights and obligations of the parties.

❑ Some states (previously mentioned on page 5) require registration, but most do not.

❑ Most accounts, property, and licenses can be in either the partnership name or that of the partners.

❑ File a fictitious name statement if you are doing business in the name of the partnership.

Limited Partnership

❑ Draft and file a one-page Certificate of Limited Partnership with the state, along with the appropriate filing fees.

❑ Draft and sign a complete Limited Partnership Agreement (agreement should be signed by all partners).

❑ Have an attorney organize a limited partnership and prepare the Limited Partnership Agreement because of the complexity of partnership taxation. (The Limited Partnership Agreement is a private document and is not filed with the state.)

❑ If you offer to sell units of limited partnership interests to investors, the Limited Partnership Agreement should be part of the disclosure documents.

Corporations

❑ File the Articles of Incorporation with the state, along with the appropriate filing fees. The articles set forth the name of the company, its authorized capital structure (how much common and preferred stock a corporation can issue), establishes an address for the company, and identifies a registered agent.

❑ After filing the articles, an organizational meeting is held. At the first meeting, bylaws are adopted, directors and officers are appointed, stock is issued, and other formalities are adhered to in order to avoid the corporate entity being set aside later and treated as though it never was formed.

❑ Licenses, bank accounts, and vendors are taken in the name of the corporation.

❑ States require ongoing annual filings that list the officers, directors, and stock structure of the company.

❑ The annual report is usually due in March or April of each year, and is subject to penalties and interest if filed late.

❑ Corporations are also required to keep ongoing corporate governance records (minutes).

❑ The bylaws are a private document and are not filed with the state.

Limited Liability Company

❑ File Articles of Organization with the state, along with the appropriate filing fees. (The Articles of Organization establish the name and address of the company, identifies the registered agent, and defines the term of the company. Most states allow an LLC to have a perpetual existence like a corporation.)

continued

❑ An LLC is generally not required to have much in the way of corporate formalities.

❑ Licenses, bank accounts, and vendors are taken in the name of the company.

❑ Most states require an LLC to have a governing document called an Operating Agreement. Drafting an Operating Agreement is highly recommended even if it is not required by state law.

❑ The Operating Agreement is a private agreement among the members of the company and is not filed with the state. (However, if you sell membership units to investors, the Operating Agreement should be included as part of the disclosure documents, because the investors are becoming new members of the company.)

Figure 1.2: BUSINESS COMPARISON CHART[1]

	Sole Proprietorship	General Partnership	Limited Partnership	Limited Liability Company	Corporation (S or C)	Nonprofit Corporation
Liability Protection	No	No	For Limited Partners	For All Members	For All Share-holders	For All Members
Taxes	Pass Through	Pass Through	Pass Through	Pass Through	S Corps. Pass Through; C Corps. Pay Taxes	None on Corp.; Employees Pay on Wages
Minimum Number of Members	1	2	2	1	1	3 in Most States
Different Classes of Ownership	No	Yes	Yes	Yes	S Corps. No; C Corps. Yes	No Ownership; Diff. Classes of Membership
Survives After Death	No	No	Yes	Yes	Yes	Yes
Best For	One Person, Low-Risk Business or No Assets	Low-Risk Business	Low-Risk Business w/Silent Partners	All Types of Business	All Types of Business	Charitable, Educational, Religious, Scientific

Figure 1.3: BUSINESS START-UP CHECKLIST[2]

Make your plan

❑ Obtain and read all relevant publications on your type of business

❑ Obtain and read all laws and regulations affecting your business

❑ Calculate whether your plan will produce a profit

❑ Plan your sources of capital

❑ Plan your sources of goods or services

❑ Plan your marketing efforts

Choose your business name

❑ Check other business names and trademarks

❑ Reserve your name and register your trademark

Choose the business form

❑ Prepare and file organizational papers

❑ Prepare and file a fictitious name document (if necessary)

❑ Prepare and file with the state the initial report of officers and directors (if necessary)

Choose the location

❑ Check competitors

❑ Check zoning

Obtain necessary licenses

❑ City

❑ County

❑ State

❑ Federal

Choose a bank

❑ Checking

❑ Credit card processing

❑ Loans

Obtain necessary insurance

❑ Workers' Compensation

❑ Automobile

❑ Liability

❑ Health

❑ Hazard

❑ Life or disability

File necessary tax registrations

❑ Obtain federal EIN by filing Form SS-4

❑ Obtain state tax identification number (if necessary)

Set up a bookkeeping system

❑ Keep track of receipts

❑ Hire an accountant

❑ Keep separate accounts for personal and business

Chapter 2

Business Strategy, Planning, and Feasibility Analysis

This chapter addresses the need to develop a business strategy—and eventually a business plan—to enhance your chances of receiving financing. In some cases, a comprehensive business strategy, properly articulated, will be the difference between obtaining financing or not.

Strategy

A *strategy* is a plan of action specifically designed to achieve a predetermined goal. Business strategy requires an executive approach to defining and solving the marketing, design, production, and financial problems that may prevent you from achieving your goal. However, creating your basic strategies may not require a time-consuming and arduous process, just as communicating your strategy does not require writing a very lengthy and complex book.

Recognizing Success: You know you have created and communicated effective strategies when your audience understands three things.
1. The current state of your business—your origin.
2. Your long-term (typically five-year) goals for the business—your destination.
3. How you will travel from origin to destination and solve the problems you know you will encounter along the way.

Developing Strategy

If you go to the Business and Economics Department at any large bookstore, you may find hundreds of books written on strategy. Many of them are well-written and effective. A few such titles are listed in the recommended reading list in this book. The following ideas originate with Jay Winokur, a financial management consultant and chief financial officer for hire. His unique perspective comes from extensive work with large, multinational corporations and with emerging companies.

Business Vision

You can describe what the business is that you want to build, but you must also understand what makes it the right business for you. Determine the skills and experience it takes to make the business successful. Which of those critical factors are among your greatest talents? Which of those factors are also the tasks you love to do, twenty-four hours a day, seven days a week? The business that is right for you fits your individual expertise and your personal motivators.

Personal Values

Examine your personal values in order to set meaningful goals and objectives for your business. High-growth, high-reward, high-risk enterprises are not for people who value security, stability, and tranquility. The prospect of working eighty-hour weeks may not appeal to those who have lifestyle and family considerations. Issues concerning political, religious, philosophical, and economic beliefs will have a major impact on company policies, goals, and strategies. Acknowledge what is important to you so that you can build your values into your business.

Goals

When you understand what your business is and how you fit with it, you can set goals. Given the market opportunities and your personal values, how large could your company become? How profitable? What is the time frame for accomplishing all this? How will you and the company's other stakeholders benefit from these accomplishments?

Market Definition

Market issues make the difference between success and disaster. Identify a problem and identify the specific groups of people who have the problem. How much pain do they feel? The greater the pain, the greater the value of an effective solution. How does the market currently solve this problem? Every possible solution—including ignoring the problem—represents your competition.

Business Model

This *business model* does not refer to the wheelbarrow-sized pile of financial projection spreadsheets that your favorite number cruncher produces. Instead, it refers to how your company operates. It includes the extent to which the people on your management team are full-time employees, part-time employees, or consultants. It includes whether you manufacture your own products—domestically or elsewhere—or contract it out. It includes whether your salespeople are employees or outside representatives. It includes your marketing approach—how you advertise, attend trade shows, and use direct mail and email, infomercials, telemarketers, and other aspects of your business. Not all of these decisions are made at start-up; however, the issues and possible alternative solutions should be identified.

Figure 2.1: FACTORS THAT INDICATE SUCCESS

Experience shows that there is a list of fifteen specific economic factors that lead toward strong business models. Few, if any, businesses incorporate all fifteen, but observation suggests that the more you incorporate, the better your chances for success.

1. An established, identifiable, segmental market.

2. The market perceives its need for your proprietary benefits, providing you with a true strategic advantage.

3. Repeat buyers who generate continuous revenue.

4. Penetrable distribution channels, so you can easily build the bridge to your end users.

5. Dependable supplies of inputs (material, labor, capital, etc.) and a reliable production process.

6. High margins to absorb operating expenses and provide profit.

7. Good cash flow, such as customer deposits or supplier trade terms.

8. Limited product liability. (You do not want product mistakes to bankrupt you.)

9. Slow product obsolescence. (You want to avoid high rates of technological change, physical perishability, or fashion fad.)

10. Limited entrenched direct competition. (Would you really want to go head-to-head against *IBM, Microsoft, General Motors,* or *Exxon/Mobil?*)

11. Intellectual property protection to build a secure wall around your market.

12. Exit potential or other wealth creation. (Very few companies have successful IPOs. Select a wealth creation strategy that is prevalent in the industry.)

13. Legal simplicity.

14. Minimal government interference. (Avoid highly regulated situations.)

15. Build a company that requires appropriate levels of investment. (Be responsive to investors' sweet spots.)

Resources

So far, you have articulated your vision, acknowledged your values, set your goals, defined your market, and determined your economic and business model. The next strategic focus is on the resources you require to put the enterprise in motion and grow it through each of your milestones.

There are three types of resources—people, facilities and equipment, and capital. You already know the skills and experience sets that are necessary to make your business successful. Your management team and board of advisors will guide you in determining the methods of staffing your start-up. They will plan the growth of your organization so that you have the appropriate quantity of skilled and experienced managers and employees to support your growth. Your team will also determine the selection and timing of facilities, production equipment, office equipment, computer systems, and other assets necessary for everyone in your organization to do their part. Finally, your financial advisors will help you determine the amount and types of funding you need to finance your growth.

Organizational Structure

As part of the planning process, you will need to determine which type of entity best supports the achievement of your goals. Input from your management team, as well as legal and other advisors, will help in the decision-making process. See Chapter 1 for more guidance on choosing the best type of entity to form.

Business Plan

A *business plan* is a blueprint of what your business is and what you want it to become. The business plan describes a serious problem suffered by individuals or organizations. It shows how your solution to that problem is *much* better—not just marginally better—than those that already exist. The plan shows how you will implement your solution, grow your company, and create ownership value.

Generally, business plans take two forms—one is the plan you write to raise capital, and the other is the plan that represents ongoing evolution of your business. You will find that both forms must be updated frequently to incorporate your latest progress and achievements.

This section focuses on the plan you write to crystallize your business strategies and raise capital. Numerous resources exist in print and online to assist you in writing a business plan. These sources range from business plan software like BizPlanBuilder (**www.jian.com**) to the Small Business Administration's website at **www.sba.gov**, to classic works such as the *Venture Capital Handbook* by David Gladstone.

Later in this book, the use of the *private placement memorandum* (PPM) to raise capital for your business is discussed. The PPM is a somewhat stylized disclosure document, prescribed by federal and state securities laws. The PPM serves a different function than the business plan. The PPM is a legal *retail document* and the business plan is a strategic *wholesale document*. In other words, when you go to individual investors to raise capital, you use the PPM as your offering document. When you approach larger investors, sometime called *angels* and *institutional investors*, including banks or financing institutions, they are more likely to ask for your business plan. (See Chapter 7 for details.)

A business plan allows you to address the essential issues of your new business, such as the unique benefits and competitive advantages of your products or services, your market opportunity and marketing plan, and how you intend to capture a defensible share of the market. The financial statements (income statement, balance sheet, and cash flow analysis) accompanying the plan will give you, your management team, and potential investors a roadmap of the next three to five years of your business. Your financial projections should not exceed five years, as too much can change in that amount of time. Three years is generally sufficient. What matters is that you select a reasonable time frame during which you can achieve your stated goals.

Feasibility Analysis

Many entrepreneurs have not thoroughly considered whether the business they are proposing is commercially feasible in the marketplace—some experts call this a *feasibility analysis*. Marvelous ideas are born each day, but many are simply not commercially viable. One of the benefits of initially creating your strategies and writing your own plan is discovering exactly what business you are in and how it will deliver both emotional satisfaction and financial reward to you. The feasibility analysis is a relatively brief version of the financial model that you will eventually develop to create economic scenarios. It indicates the broad operating parameters—product volume, prices, margins, operating expenses, and resources—under which you will achieve your financial goals. Your team will examine and interpret the analysis to determine the feasibility of operating within those guidelines.

Structuring Your Business Plan

Before discussing the contents of a business plan, it needs to be clear that a business plan is a management tool—it is not a legally required document. If you have an existing business and intend to continue that business without specific plans for expansion or other significant change, then you may not yet need a business plan. If you are going to register with eBay to sell your grandmother's china online, you may never need a business plan (although you do need your grandmother's permission or that of her estate).

A business plan should be a living document that evolves with the business and is constantly a work in progress. Business planning is a constant process, not a brief project. Internally, the business plan is a useful management tool when it is continually updated to reflect the marketplace. It should not be treated as a paperweight. Externally, the business plan often secures bank financing and attracts private or institutional investors. When your company is more mature, a business plan may serve as a basis for a strategic alliance, a merger, or an acquisition.

Assuming the business has been determined to be generally feasible, turn to the specifics of the plan. A general outline for a business plan follows.

Figure 2.2: GETTING INVESTOR ATTENTION

Investors want to know some very fundamental information. Do not be intimidated by the questions that follow. Very few beginning businesses will have all of these questions fully answered from the start. However, sophisticated investors get hundreds of business plans to read. Your task is to write a business plan that is *sticky*—a plan that piques the interest of an investor to look further at your business.

❑ What is your business?

❑ What is the market for the product or service?

❑ How big is the market for the product or service?

❑ Have you segmented the market into digestible pieces?

❑ What is the revenue model (i.e., how does the business identify and sell to its customers)?

❑ What have you done to develop the business model?

❑ Have you identified all the resources you need to support the revenue model?

❑ How does the business make money?

❑ Why is this product or service unique?

❑ What qualities give it a competitive advantage over existing products or services?

❏ How is it better, faster, and cheaper than other choices available to your customers?

❏ What tangible assets does the company own?

❏ What intellectual property (trademarks, patents, trade secrets) does the company own?

❏ Who are the people in management and what are their backgrounds?

❏ What does the investor get for the investment?

❏ How much will the business be worth?

❏ How long will it take to be profitable?

❏ What is a reasonable risk assessment?

Cover Sheet and Table of Contents

The *cover sheet* should contain the name of your business, CEO, and contact information (including the address, phone, fax, and email for both). If you have a spiffy logo, the cover page is a good place to introduce it. The next item should be a *table of contents* of the major topics contained in the business plan.

QUICK Tip

Tab It: Some reviewers like to have the various sections of your business plan tabbed for easy reference.

Executive Summary

The executive summary is the most important part of the business plan because it is the part read first and determines whether the reader goes any further. The executive summary gives a brief synopsis of:

- the company's strategy for success;
- the company's unique business proposition;
- how your business proposition offers a competitive advantage;
- the market you are addressing;

- a description of the product and services offered;
- the management team's qualifications;
- key financial data and a statement of funds required; and,
- a statement of how you will either pay the funds back or how the investors will receive a return on their investment.

All of these brief topic descriptions will be expanded in the business plan. The executive summary should be brief—usually no more than two pages. Typically, the executive summary is the section written last, after the whole business plan is completed.

Statement of Purpose or Mission

This is where you articulate the vision of the company and its management. Some writers have called this the distinctive *value proposition* of the company—the formula you have devised that delivers goods and services to your customers better than the competition does.

Description of the Business

In this section, you give the history of the business entity. For start-ups, the following information is recommended:

- name of the business;
- legal form of the business (corporation, LLC, partnership, etc.);
- state of organization;
- when it was organized;
- location of the business;
- brief description of the owners/founders; and,
- stage of development of the business—conceptual, start-up, emerging, or mature.

Description of the Products or Services Offered

Describe your products and services and show how they are related to your mission. What is your business? Be clear. Many business plans do not begin to discuss the actual business of the company until the middle of the plan. Most investors will not be that patient. Tell it up front and tell it in plain language. If the product is highly technical, save the details for inclusion in an appendix. Keep the discussion on a strategic level. The potential financers are probably not yet interested in tactical details.

Management Team

On equal footing with the products and services offered is the credibility of the management team of the company. Investors say that the three most important factors for success in business are management, management, and management. In this section, you will be providing a synopsis of the management team and its members' qualifications. You can include full résumés in an appendix. Investors, especially sophisticated ones, would prefer an *A* management team and a *B* idea to a *B* management team and an *A* idea.

QUICK Tip

Differentiating the As from the Bs: What differentiates the A team from the B team is a history of solid success and accomplishment. It proves the existence of skills and experience that can mean the difference between success and failure. Do not merely state that the marketing executive spent decades with a Fortune 500 company. Instead, specify the revenue growth and profitability results achieved in products and divisions for which the executive was responsible.

Many start-up ventures have difficulty attracting an experienced management team before their business has been tested in the marketplace. One way to offset any lack of depth on the management team is to establish a board of advisors and populate it with persons well-known in the business and professional community. Often, advisors become more interested in the business and can be recruited to join the management team. Alternatively, they may introduce you to qualified management candidates.

Marketplace and the Competition

The marketplace and competition section helps you understand and define your market, the demographics and psychographics of your target customers, your competitor's products or services, and your business risks.

Describe the target market for your product or service and the trends in your industry. For example, your market may be consumers between 25 and 40 years of age in the Rocky Mountain states or the upscale furniture industry in Chicago. Drill down to the specific market niche that fits your situation.

How large is your niche? Investors look for products that have scalable markets; that is, niches capable of expanding with the acceptance of the product in the marketplace.

How large a share of the market can you capture, and over what time? Who are the people who will buy from you? Why will these customers buy from you and not your established competitors?

Describe your competition as specifically as possible and do not ever state that you have no competition no matter how unique your product or service. It is said that the only companies that have no competition are those that have no customers.

Marketing and Sales Plan

The *marketing and sales plan* section of your business plan includes your advertising, promotion, pricing, profitability, selling tactics, distribution, public relations, and strategic business relationships. It answers the question, *What marketing vehicles will you use in your business—advertising in print and broadcast, direct mail, product brochures, trade shows, public relations?* You should also discuss how your product would be sold, including your distribution channels and methods.

Financial Information

The financial information section addresses your ability to make money in your proposed business. Your company's capital requirements and the profit and wealth potential are analyzed and demonstrated here. Include any financial history as well as your forecasts in the financial statements. Normally, your projection should forecast at least three years out. Remember that financial projections are only as good as the underlying assumptions, which must be uniformly applied to the cash flow statements, income statements, and balance sheets. Once you have completed the financial statements, review the business plan and make sure the language and examples in your plan are supported by and consistent with the financial statements. Some of the assumptions you will wrestle with are revenues, marketing expenses, research and development costs, general and administrative expenses (*G&A*), inventory, accounts receivable, property and depreciation, debt and interest expense, and cash. Do not shirk from this task. It will cause you to seriously analyze, perhaps for the first time, the financial essence and feasibility of your business proposition.

One venture capitalist, when asked about his internal review of business plans, said, "[we] take their projected revenue, cut it in half, double the expenses and then see if it still makes sense."

Avoid the use of *hockey stick* financial projections—financial statements that skyrocket during the last year or two of the planning period. It is probably not reasonable to assume that the level of marketing, production, and other resources can grow fast enough to accommodate the hockey stick. It is also unreasonable to assume large sales volume during the first year when your business is still in a conceptual or start-up stage.

Use a Number Cruncher: Some business plan software allows you to prepare financial projections. If you get easily lost in the numbers, this may be a good time to hire an experienced financial executive to help you engineer your business.

Time Frame and Benchmarks

You may wish to provide a section that shows the *benchmarks* or significant developments in the life of the company, and the projected time frame in which these events will occur. For example, *at the end of month three—*

develop a prototype; at the end of month six—solicit manufacturing bids and file for patent protection; etc.

Funding Request

The *funding request* is a statement of how much money you need, why you need it, how you are going spend it, and how the investor is going to be rewarded. In the case of a loan request, the return to the lender is the amount borrowed plus interest. In the case of an equity investment, an exit strategy (IPO, acquisition, merger, sale of the company, or stock redemption) is required. Determine what the typical wealth creation event is for your industry and how business values are determined.

Appendices

The advantage of having a shorter business plan is that you can include more lengthy materials in the appendices. At a minimum, include the full résumés of management. You can also insert articles on your product or the industry trends, test results, marketing studies, or any other information that supports the main plan.

You will need a cover letter when forwarding your plan to someone for review. For a start-up company, a summary business plan of approximately ten to fifteen pages may work for you. Most beginning companies do not have an extensive history of operations, and therefore, do not initially need a twenty- to forty-page plan.

Figure 2.3: QUESTIONS TO ASK

Burke Franklin, President of Jian Tools for Sale, Inc. and the creator of BizPlanBuilder software, suggests questions to ask in formulating your business plan.[3]

❏ What type of business do you have?

❏ What is the purpose of this business?

❏ What is the key message or phrase to describe your business in one sentence?

❑ What is your reason for starting your own business?

❑ What is your product or service?

❑ Can you list three unique benefits of your product?

❑ Do you have datasheets, brochures, diagrams, sketches, photographs, related press releases, or other documentation about your product or service?

❑ What is the product application?

❑ What led you to develop your product?

❑ Is this product or service used in connection with other products?

❑ List the top three objections to buying your product or service immediately.

❑ When will your product be available?

❑ Who is your target audience?

❑ Who is your competition?

❑ How is your product differentiated from that of your competition?

❑ What is the pricing of your product versus your competition?

❑ Are you making any special offers?

❑ What plans do you have for advertising and promotions?

❑ How will you finance company growth?

❑ Do you have the management team needed to achieve your goals?

You can also include this template as an initial summary for bankers or investors. You should have the answers to these questions readily available when seeking a loan or investors for your new venture. Some of these answers may be appropriate to include in a cover letter for the company and may accompany the executive summary document.

Consultants vs. Do-It-Yourself

You are encouraged to write your own business plan—at least the initial draft. If you are not experienced in this process, use software to assist you. Entrepreneurs need to answer the fundamental questions. What business are you really in? How does it make money and build value? From those questions flow the ways and means of entering the marketplace and how much it is going to cost.

However, you can hire a consultant to help you polish your plan. Many entrepreneurs use an accountant to assist with the financial analysis and projections. Remember, the soundness of financial projections is largely dependent upon the underlying assumptions. Using estimates that are based on sound experience, relevant knowledge, and thorough research will give credible and realistic results.

In expressing financial projections, you may wish to present a conservative version and one or more optimistic versions, or worst case, expected case, and best case scenarios. This can show the investor that your conservative version is viable and more favorable conditions generate better results.

 **Make Realistic Projections:** Projections have a funny way of coming back to haunt you if you do not meet investor expectations. Be as certain as you can that you can make the numbers.

What the Experts Say

The most frequent complaint among venture capitalists and other business plan reviewers is that the plan does not clearly explain both the opportunity and risks. This comment is equally applicable to the executive summary, since that is the portion of the business plan that is read first and determines whether the reader will read further into the plan.

Close on the heels of lack of clarity is the use of unrealistic or *hockey stick* projections supported by *weak assumptions*. Unrealistic, in this instance, means unrealistically high. Weak assumptions are those not supported by the economic realities of the marketplace. Many times, the concern is that the assumptions are too simplistic.

There is a marked tendency on the part of entrepreneurs to treat their product or service as unique in the marketplace. Thus, one will read claims that no competition exists. Conduct thorough research to discover direct as well as indirect competitors. Oddly, some entrepreneurs believe it is advantageous to provide filtered information to reviewers and omit a thorough competitive analysis or other information that might detract from their business model. For the sophisticated reviewer, omissions and mistakes do not generate a high degree of confidence in the plan or in management. Many investors want to be on the second wave of companies entering a field or market space; thus, the existence of competition, accurately described, can actually provide an element of risk reduction. They know that competition exists in every market and that the later market entrants often have the best chance at success.

A business plan must establish the existence of a sustainable competitive advantage, yet many business plans are weak on market analysis. One reason for this weakness is that the cost of obtaining comprehensive market data can be very high. A low-cost, high-value alternative is to get your market research from the Internet. The advantages of the Internet cannot be overemphasized. Compare it to doing market research at the public library just a few years ago.

While the uniqueness of the product or service is helpful, the proven ability of the management team is even more important. It is common for business plans to overstate management's strengths or to provide an inadequate discussion of the management team. Sophisticated investors will not invest in the best product or service if there is a lack of confidence in management or an unwillingness to cede control to professional management if necessary.

There is also a tendency to overvalue companies. The days of sky-high valuations of the 1980s and 1990s are over. *Valuation* is an art, not a science—especially in early stage companies. Your best defense is to be able to identify valuable aspects of your business and attach a realistic valuation. Learn how investors in your industry or geographic area determine company value. In a nonrevenue company, focus on *intellectual property* (IP), management, and benchmarks achieved to date.

Amazingly, a number of companies fail to include their contact information in the materials they send or present to investors. A good place to include that information is on the front cover of the business plan and in the executive summary.

HOW TO...Get Their Attention with Your Business Plan

❑ *Have a snappy executive summary.*
❑ *Have your contact information clearly stated.*
❑ *Keep the initial plan short—ten to twelve pages.*
❑ *Talk about your business and revenue model first.*
❑ *Describe the market and show how your product is unique in that market.*
❑ *Present a management team with a history of successes.*
❑ *Present conservative financial projections.*
❑ *Do not argue about valuation—yet.*

Summary

None of the ideas in this chapter are all-encompassing, and not all of the items apply to every business. The information should spark your imagination while giving a context in which to analyze the business. Take your ideas, information, and research and develop a plan that makes investors take notice. Use the executive summary to give your potential investors what they want and to get them interested in learning more.[4]

An example of such a summary appears on the following pages.

Figure 2.4: SAMPLE EXECUTIVE SUMMARY

Headquarters
DigiBelly, Inc.
3251 Progress Dr.
Ste.-A
Orlando, FL 32826
Phone:
407.210.2102
Fax:
407.207.7348

CEO
Eric B. Delisle
ceo@digibelly.net
www.digibelly.com

Corporate Facts
Employees: 15
Ownership: Private
Offices: Florida
Stage: Product
        Launch
 - Proven Solution
 - Customers
 - Reseller Base
 - University
Partner

Industry
Web-Based
Business Software

Business Summary

Many businesses still DO NOT have a website. This has not changed since 1999. Non-tech business owners are bewildered by the options available and have no confidence in making good decisions regarding their IT needs while at the same time feel very strongly they MUST get digital to be competitive. DigiBelly, Inc. is becoming an essential bridge for non-technical business owners to cross the "Digital Divide."

Combining deep knowledge of state-of-the-art Web technology, process automation and superior delivery capability, DigiBelly helps customers minimize cost and obtain useful business tools while providing the hand-holding this market desires.

The way AOL enabled the ordinary person to get on the Internet, DigiBelly is enabling the ordinary businessperson to get digital. The past three years, the company has built and tested its systems, marketing strategies, and market acceptance, and as of 2003 is ready to launch its first retail product, DigiBuildIt.

Company Highlights

- **Deep Knowledge**—DigiBelly executives and developers have designed and implemented web based solutions for companies such as Tupper Ware, Governors Office of the State of Arizona, US Airways, Musclemag.com, Hooters, Red Lobster, Olive Garden, and Top Secret Level systems at Lockheed Martin.

- **Compelling Customer Value Proposition**— DigiBelly delivers a customized website with features such as automated content management, user management, browser-based one-click site editing, database integration, and award winning ecommerce capabilities with one-on-one customer interaction at a cost benefit 4-5x less expensive than competing solutions.

continued

Law Firm
Burk & Reedy Law
Firm, LLP
Washington DC &
Los Angeles
Securities Law

Investors
Angel Investors
DigiBelly
Executives
$1.2 Million
Raised to Date

**Amount
Financing
Sought**
$2.5 Million
Preferred Series B.
Fixed 2X Dividend
on investment paid
from 5% Gross
Revenue starting
Month 13 plus
automatic conver-
sion 1 to 1 to com-
mon stock.

Use of Funds
Infrastructure,
Sales & Marketing

**Profitability
Expected**
Q3 – Q4, 2004

- **Expanding Market Opportunities**—Past and continuing investments in Web presences and online commerce; lower costs of entry; more devices on the Net; easier integration between front- and back-end systems continue to fuel market growth.

To reach customers (both individuals and businesses), businesses around the world are continuing to invest in getting onto the Web. Ten million businesses had websites in 2000; 25 million will by 2005*. Today, less than 70% of small businesses have websites. In five years, more than 80% will.

- **Value-added Solutions Create Switching Barriers**—While the company wins customers by leveraging market knowledge to deliver a great price, it assures long-term relationships by providing value-added marketing solutions and continued integration with back-end business critical systems. This creates a dependency on the entire implementation far beyond a basic website.

- **University of Central Florida Resources**—DigiBelly is supported by UCF with contacts, PR, technology transfer opportunities and resources. DigiBelly has already participated in winning a $600K National Science Foundation Award with UCF.

- **DigiBelly Partner Program**—DigiBelly has also developed a technology infrastructure to support a grass roots, referral based marketing effort where traditional marketing dollars are directed back to the customer base that refers additional customers to the program. Additionally, the program acts as a customer service buffer with people helping people with their technology needs.

- **DigiBelly New Business Service**—DigiBelly has also developed a unique method of starting and nurturing a relationship with all types of businesses through its New Business Program. The test bed resulted in 75% + appointment setting rates on pure cold calls and a 42%+ closing sale on the first visit

Key Relationships
University of Central Florida
Time Warner Telecom
IBI Global

Prominent Clients
Tupper Ware - Orlando
1002 Productions – Nashville
CENTECOM – Orlando
InvestorBeware.org – NYC

Demand
"It was much easier than I thought. We have 8,000 agents that need this!"
Alex Conti
Northwestern Mutual

Market Perspective
"I believe many of the companies we meet need this kind of solution. This should be a great partnership."
Ray Maxwell
Time Warner Telecom

with an average sale of $450+. All in a win/win solution for the business owners and DigiBelly.

Solution Highlights

- **DigiBuildIt.com**—Enables a non-technical user to create and manage rich content directly on their website entirely through their Web browser in a WYSIWYG manner without installing or learning new software. The cost of a custom solution with these features would cost $25,000+ to develop by a Web development firm.

With advanced automation DigiBelly can develop the solution at a cost of roughly $300-$400 in less than 3 hours per site including setup, customization, and training the client to use the tools for making changes themselves. DigiBelly has sold a number of sites at $4,500 per site providing both excellent savings to the client and excellent profit margins to DigiBelly and has met little price resistance at this pricing level.

- **Built on Content Management Base**—Other solutions have template automation and a few even have WYSIWYG editing, however none are built on a Content Management System in this price range. Microsoft's Content Management Server costs $49,000 per CPU.

DigiBelly's Site Manager enables the setting of dated site content that turns pages on and off AUTOMATICALLY by date, allows the management of multiple users with varying degrees of permissions, password protected pages by member and much more.

- **New Solutions in Development in 2005**

- **WebOffice.com**—DigiBelly will provide an entire virtual office online integrating many necessary business processes such as ecommerce, communications modules, market research, and much more.

- **Artificial Intelligence Knowledge Management**—DigiBelly's long-term strategy has

continued

very little to do with the world of building websites. As 2003 progresses DigiBelly will begin to announce its plans and products for its developments in the AI business space.

Management Team

- Eric B. Delisle, Chairman and CEO (Meridian, CFI)
- Tom Hagood, MBA, COO (Fmr. Proj. Mgr. For International Space Station)
- Greg Badgewell, VP Sales (General Motors and Westgate Resorts)
- Bret Pirquet, MBA, CFO (Wells Fargo, Jasmin.com)
- Shera Kelly, Operations Manager (Bell South)
- Jim Eddy, CTO (Switch & Data, CitiGroup/Travelers)

Board of Directors

- Eric B. Delisle, Chairman & CEO
- James E. Burk, Esq. (Burk & Reedy, LLP—WDC/LA Securities Law Firm)
- Nicholas Zaldastani (Zaldastani Ventures, Saba, Oracle)
- John Lawrence Allen, Esq. (NYC Securities Fraud Attorney—Investor Beware)

Financial Projections
Financial Summaries in thousands (000's)

Revenue

Y1	$2,289
Y2	$14,276
Y3	$36,908
Y4	$47,981
Y5	$62,375

Cost of Sales

Y1	$180
Y2	$515
Y3	$872
Y4	$1,047
Y5	$1,256

SG&A (w/o COS)

Y1	$3,182
Y2	$9,646
Y3	$16,739
Y4	$21,814
Y5	$27,957

Net Income Before Tax

Y1	$(1,073)
Y2	$4,114
Y3	$19,297
Y4	$25,120
Y5	$33,162

Chapter 3

Equity Financing

- Ownership
- Corporation Equity
- Warrants
- Limited Liability Company and Limited Partnership Equity
- Raising Capital in Stages

Equity is an ownership interest in a company. In a corporation, it typically takes the form of *common stock* or *preferred stock*. In a limited liability company, equity ownership is called a *membership unit* (or *membership interest*). In a general or limited partnership, it is termed a *partnership interest*.

The difference between raising capital by selling an ownership interest in your company and by the incurring of debt is that the first is a nonrepayable capital contribution and debt is a legally binding promise to repay the amount borrowed with interest. Debt has to be paid back, usually on a prescribed schedule, and negatively impacts the balance sheet (the *debt-to-equity ratio*). Equity, on the other hand, does not have to be paid back. In return, you have given away a portion of the ownership of your company. This is not all bad, however, because it allows your company to grow.

Beginning businesses that need to raise capital should consider the sale of equity for a number of reasons. The terms of equity financing are more flexible than debt financing and they have a positive effect on the company's balance sheet. In addition, investors understand that they are entering into a long-term investment and are less likely to expect immediate returns on their investment. Last, but not least, cash flow can be retained by the company for expansion of the business operations, conducting research and development, and obtaining assets, such as intellectual property, rather than servicing a debt.

Raising money from investors can be a daunting task that will require a substantial commitment of time. It can become a second, full-time job apart from developing the products and services that you hope to sell someday.

Determining what is attractive to investors is an art more than a science, and everyone will have an opinion on what works best at any one time. This chapter informs you of the types of ownership interest that can be used in the various business organizations.

Ownership

Equity financing involves selling a percentage of ownership in the company to an investor. The advantage of equity financing is that the company does not incur a debt obligation that must be repaid. As the company makes a profit, the investors may be paid dividends and their ownership interest will increase in value. The biggest disadvantage of equity financing is that every time you sell ownership, your percentage of ownership is diluted or decreased. Depending on the stage of funding and the amounts involved, you may have to give up varying degrees of control of your company.

If things go badly for a company and its assets are liquidated, equity investors are paid back after debt holders. Equity investors realize this going in and therefore usually consider a company's *debt-to-equity ratio*—the amount of debt a company has versus the amount of equity or paid-in capital. If a company has too much debt, it may not be able to meet its obligations to pay back debt from revenues, which could result in a foreclosure. On the other hand, if a company has sold too much equity, the return on investment might take a long time. It is all a balancing game.

Understanding Your Repayment Schedule: It is time and money well spent to forecast how much capital you will need to fund the company and also how long you anticipate it will take to pay lenders back or give investors a return or an exit.

The type of equity securities that a company issues to founders and investors will depend, in part, on the amount of capital needed to be raised and the number and type of investors needed. If the company does not need large amounts of capital to accomplish its goals, one form of securities may be all that is needed. If the company needs to raise a significant sum of cash, creating different classes of securities could be advisable.

Corporation Equity

The equity of a corporation is called *stock*. Typically, you will hear the stock in a corporation referred to as *shares of stock*. A corporation may sell its stock to investors to raise capital for expansion and operations, and once an investor has purchased stock in a corporation, he or she becomes an owner of part of that corporation. The ownership of stock is *perpetual*, meaning that there is no maturity date for the stock, and the investor may own the stock until the corporation decides to buy them back or until the investor decides to sell them. Shares of stock of a corporation have a number of terms associated with them.

Authorized stock is the total amount of stock that a corporation possesses. When a corporation is formed, it must state the amount of its authorized stock in its articles of incorporation. That language will read something like the following.

> *The number of shares that the corporation is authorized to issue is 15,000,000, 10,000,000 of which are common shares at a par value of $0.001 and 5,000,000 of which are preferred shares at a par value of $0.001. Authority shall be vested in the board of directors to change the class, the number of each class of stock and the voting powers, designations, preferences, limitations, restrictions, and relative rights of each class of stock.*

By stating its authorized stock, the corporation determines the size of its universe, and it lets investors know where their investment fits into the company. For example, they want to know if the 10,000 shares they are buying represent 1% or 10% of the company. *Par value* is a nominal value arbitrarily assigned to the shares and bears no relationship to the market value that changes over time.

The next term you need to know is *issued stock*. Issued stock is the amount of authorized stock that currently is or has been in the hands of the founders, or sold to investors since the beginning of the corporation. Once stock has been issued, it will always be regarded as issued, regardless of its current status (i.e., whether someone currently owns it or if it has been repurchased by the corporation). Closely related to issued stock is the term *outstanding stock*. Outstanding stock is stock that has been sold or issued that is currently in the hands of the founders and investors.

Treasury stock are those shares that had been issued but have subsequently been returned to the corporation through a redemption, purchase, or other liquidity event. These shares are back in the *treasury* of the corporation. The corporation may elect to reissue the shares at a later date or it may retire the shares.

To determine the amount of treasury stock, use the following formula:

Issued stock – Outstanding stock = Treasury stock

Figure 3.1: THE LIFE OF A SHARE OF STOCK

To gain an understanding of the terms just described, an example is helpful. Anderson Industries, Inc. is founded with 10,000,000 authorized shares with a par value of $0.001. The founders want to maintain majority control of the corporation, so they issue 5,000,000 shares amongst themselves, for which they pay the par value, or $5,000 (5,000,000 × $0.001 = $5,000). At this point, there are 5,000,000 issued and outstanding shares, which is 50% of the authorized shares. The ownership structure looks like this:

	Authorized stock	Issued stock	Outstanding stock	Treasury stock
Founders		5,000,000	5,000,000	0
Investors		0	0	0
Totals	10,000,000	5,000,000	5,000,000	0

Next, the board of directors of Anderson Industries, Inc. decides that the corporation needs to raise $1,000,000 for operations, and they determine that a fair market value for the shares to be sold will be $1.00 per share. (Do not get too bogged down with how they are going about raising capital or what the value of the shares is here—the finer points of valuation and raising capital are discussed in later chapters). The ownership structure now includes the investors and looks like this:

	Authorized stock	Issued stock	Outstanding stock	Treasury stock
Founders		5,000,000	5,000,000	0
Investors		1,000,000	1,000,000	0
Totals	10,000,000	6,000,000	6,000,000	0

continued

Once the 1,000,000 shares are sold to investors, there are 6,000,000 issued and outstanding shares, or 60% of the authorized shares. Investors will be concerned with two ratios here: the amount of issued and outstanding shares they own in relation to the number of authorized shares, and the amount of shares they own in relation to the total number of issued and outstanding shares in the corporation.

In this example, the investors own 10% of the authorized shares (1,000,000 of the 10,000,000 authorized shares) and they own 16.6% of the issued and outstanding shares (1,000,000 of the 6,000,000 issued and outstanding shares). These values can be expressed like this:

	Percentage of Authorized stock	Percentage of Issued stock
Founders	50.0% (5,000,000 of 10,000,000)	83.4% (5,000,000 of 6,000,000)
Investors	10.0% (1,000,000 of 10,000,000)	16.6% (1,000,000 of 6,000,000)
Totals	60.0% (6,000,000 of 10,000,000)	100.0% (6,000,000 of 6,000,000)

Over the years, the corporation becomes successful and the board of directors decides to redeem the shares it has sold to investors for $5.00 per share, so it creates a plan of redemption and offers it to all of the investors. A number of the investors decide to redeem their shares and the corporation buys back 750,000 of the shares it had sold. At this point, there are still 1,000,000 issued shares, 250,000 of which are outstanding shares and 750,000 are treasury shares. Now the ownership structure looks like this:

	Authorized stock	Issued stock	Outstanding stock	Treasury stock
Founders		5,000,000	5,000,000	0
Investors		1,000,000	250,000	750,000
Totals	10,000,000	6,000,000	5,250,000	750,000

With a good grasp of the terms associated with the status of shares of stock, a description of the types of shares that you will typically see in a corporation, their function, and their attributes, is discussed in the following pages.

Common Stock

C corporations can sell equity in two basic forms—common stock and preferred stock. Common stock is voting stock. Typically, it is issued to the founders of a corporation shortly after formation in exchange for the founder's time and expertise, or perhaps the assignment of intellectual property or other assets. Some common stock may be sold to initial investors and issued to officers, directors, and consultants as incentives. Common stock may also be given as stock options that may be exercised at a higher price at some future date.

Dividend Rights. Dividends are declared by the board of directors from available after tax earnings and profits. In most states, the company cannot pay a dividend if it would impair the capital of the corporation, which means, in layman's terms, you cannot pay a dividend unless you have earnings and profits. Directors can be held personally liable under some laws if they impair the capital of a corporation. A board of directors is not under any obligation to declare a dividend at any time. They merely have the right to declare one. The practical reality is that most beginning corporations do not pay dividends and may never pay dividends until they are fully mature. In 2002, Microsoft Corporation paid the first dividend in its history.

Alert!

Common stock can receive dividends, but if there is any outstanding preferred stock that has a dividend preference, it will be entitled to receive dividends first.

Voting Rights. Holders of common stock are typically entitled to one vote per share on all matters to be voted on by the shareholders. When holders of common stock vote for directors, the directors with the greatest plurality win. Most states allow common stockholders to *cumulate* (combine) their votes, if such voting is allowed by the articles of incorporation. The use of cumulative voting should be discouraged, because it concentrates unequal voting power in a few shareholders and can be a negative to new investors.

Liquidation Rights. In the event of a liquidation or dissolution of the corporation, holders of common stock are entitled to share in all assets remaining after creditors and any preferred stockholders are fully repaid. Unfortunately, if liquidation or dissolution of the corporation occurs, it means that things are not going well and probably have not been going well for quite some time. So, there may not be much left in the way of assets to distribute to common stockholders.

Redemption Rights. Redemption is the purchase of issued and outstanding stock by the corporation. There is no inherent right of shareholders to redeem their shares unless it is part of a contract with the corporation. The company can attach a right of redemption to a particular class of common shares, and this could create an attractive exit strategy for certain common shareholders. However, a company can voluntarily offer redemption to some or all of its common shareholders. If a right of redemption is part of a stock offering, the company may wish to create a *sinking* or *reserve fund* to have the after-tax money available to fund the redemption in the future.

Redemption can be at the option of the company, the stockholder, or both. There are a variety of methods to set the redemption price—a fixed price per share, a multiple of the purchase price, market value determined by an appraisal, and other methods. In setting the time for the redemption event, the longer the hold period of the stock, the greater the redemption price.

Preemptive or other Preferential Subscription Rights. *Preemptive rights* entitle a current shareholder to purchase additional shares in the event of an ownership percentage dilution due to subsequent rounds of stock offerings. The use of preemptive rights or other preferential subscription rights is not recommended because they can discourage additional investors. By granting a shareholder the right to purchase additional shares of stock when the corporation offers stock to outside investors, funding is often delayed because the stock has to be offered to existing shareholders first.

Nonvoting Common Stock. Nonvoting common stock can also be used in a stock incentive plan. Such a plan may reward employees with shares in the company as part of their compensation package. In this manner, the company can share ownership with its employees and still maintain voting control.

You may use nonvoting common in both an S corporation and a C corporation when the voting shareholders do not want to grant voting rights to other shareholders. Family-controlled corporations are another instance where the family members maintain control by issuing nonvoting common stock.

QUICK Tip

The S Corporation: One of the limitations of an S corporation is that it is allowed only one class of stock. However, S corporations do allow the issuance of non-voting common stock in addition to issuing voting common stock.

Preferred Stock

Preferred stock is the second kind of equity available for sale by a corporation. It entitles its holders to certain preferences that differ from common stock. Investors like preferred stock because dividends are paid before common stock, and if the company is liquidated or dissolved the preferred stockholders have a preference to the liquidation proceeds ahead of common stock.

The board of directors of a corporation is typically authorized in the articles of incorporation to create multiple series of preferred stock. It is allowed to determine the rights, preferences, and privileges of any series of preferred stock, and the number of shares constituting any such series. Pursuant to this authority, the board of directors will adopt a resolution at a board meeting designating a series of preferred stock. The board will then file the preferences with the state through an amendment to the articles of incorporation or a designation of preferences, depending upon the laws of the state of incorporation.

The language would read something like this.

RESOLVED, that the number of shares that the corporation is authorized to issue is 15,000,000 shares, 10,000,000 of which are common shares and 5,000,000 of which are preferred shares, and

RESOLVED FURTHER, that 750,000 of the 5,000,000 authorized preferred shares are hereby designated as Series A Preferred Shares, and RESOLVED FURTHER, that the voting powers, designations, preferences, limitations, restrictions of Series A Preferred Shares are as follows: [Details of the preferences would appear here].

When amending the articles of incorporation, the board of directors sets forth the proposed amendments in a resolution (like described) and submits it to the shareholders for approval. In most cases, the chairman or president calls a special meeting of the shareholders and the shareholders vote to ratify the amendment to the articles. If there are few shareholders, all shareholders sign a *unanimous written consent* and no meeting is necessary.

Preferences for preferred stock can include the following.

Dividend Rights. Shares of preferred stock will either have a cumulative or noncumulative right to dividends. A cumulative dividend accumulates from year to year if it is not paid. For example, if a corporation promises to pay a cumulative dividend of ten cents per share every year to each holder of preferred stock, and the corporation was unable to pay one year because it had no available earnings and profits, the dividend would cumulate the next year, so that the corporation would owe twenty cents per share. A noncumulative dividend does not accrue when unpaid, and it does not roll over to the next year. If dividends are not declared during the year, no dividend is due. Investors realize this, too, and often will want cumulative dividends. It is all about bargaining power.

Dividends are calculated by applying a rate percentage to the face value or the purchase price of a share of stock at the time a dividend is declared. In a privately held company, the face value is what the investor paid for the preferred stock. If there was an 8% dividend rate and the face value was $1.00 per share, the dividend would be $0.08 per share multiplied by the number of preferred shares owned. Whether or not the company declares dividends to shareholders will depend upon a number of factors, including the capital requirements and the financial condition of the company.

Voting Rights. In exchange for their preferential treatment for dividends, preferred stockholders will usually give up their right to vote on corporate matters, except when it pertains to changes to the preferences of the stock they are holding. They will most likely want to be part of the decision-making process if their preferences are going to change. They may also want a voice if the corporation wants to create a series of preferred stock that is senior in preference to their series of preferred stock.

If an institutional buyer, an angel, or a venture capitalist is funding the company, they want a designation of an entire series of preferred stock. The stock structure of venture deals usually involves preferred stock that votes and converts to common stock in a variety of circumstances. In addition, the venture funder may demand representation on the board, which is generally helpful because of their experience and contacts.

Liquidation Rights. Holders of preferred stock will normally be entitled to receive a certain dollar amount per share (plus declared but unpaid dividends) before any distribution or payment is made to holders of common stock in the event of a dissolution, liquidation, or wind-up of the corporation.

If the corporation liquidates, dissolves, or winds up, and the assets of the corporation are insufficient to permit full payment of the amount promised to the preferred stockholders, the holders would then be entitled to a ratable distribution of the available assets and the common stockholders would get nothing.

Alert!

A consolidation, merger, or sale of all or substantially all of the assets of a corporation is generally not considered a liquidation, dissolution, or winding up for these purposes.

Conversion and Redemption Rights. Preferred stockholders are sometimes granted the right to convert their shares into shares of common stock of the corporation. Conversion rights can be voluntary or compulsory. The preferred shareholder can exercise voluntary conversion anytime. Compulsory conversion usually occurs on the happening of an event, such as a public offering or merger.

When the time comes to convert, the *conversion ratio* is the paramount concern. The conversion ratio is the formula by which you calculate the number of shares of common received by surrendering a certain number of preferred shares. The most straightforward conversion formula is one share of preferred stock for one share of common stock. Other formulas call for a third party appraisal at the time of conversion, which can be expensive. The conversion rate should be subject to adjustment from time to time if any of the following events occur:

- the company splits or combines its common stock or issues dividends to common stock;
- the corporation issues other convertible securities at a lower price or with a conversion rate less than the then-current conversion rate for the issued and outstanding preferred stock; or,
- the corporation sells its common stock at a price less than the then-current conversion rate of the issued and outstanding preferred stock.

There are a number of different formulas used to safeguard the interests of an investor when calculating how to convert convertible securities. These are called *antidilution provisions* and the corporation needs to pay particular attention to these provisions when negotiating with an institutional investor.

As a starting point, look at this typical conversion scenario:

$$\frac{\text{original share price}}{\text{conversion price}} \quad X \quad \begin{array}{c}\text{number of shares of}\\ \text{preferred stock}\\ \text{to be converted}\end{array} \quad = \quad \begin{array}{c}\text{common stock}\\ \text{to be received}\\ \text{on conversion}\end{array}$$

Under this scenario, the original share price and the conversion price would be equal and essentially the investor would be converting at a ratio of one to one. But what happens if the corporation sold a bunch of convertible preferred stock at $2.00 per share and subsequently had to lower their valuation based upon changes in the economic landscape? The corporation would probably have a tough time selling additional shares at $2.00 per share and would probably have to enter into what is called a *down round* of financing, in which the price per share is lower than had previously been offered.

Existing investors do not like down rounds because their ownership in the corporation is diluted. Essentially, their investment is worth less. That is when antidilution provisions come into play.

The first and most harsh antidilution provision is called a *full-ratchet conversion*. A full-ratchet looks at the price per share paid by the investor and compares it to the price paid later on by other investors and compares the two. If the first investor paid $2.00 per share and later investors paid $1.00 per share, the first investor with full-ratchet protection could convert at a 2 to 1 ratio. This is harsh because it applies even if the corporation went out and sold just a few shares at $1.00 per share.

The second and more preferable antidilution provision is called a *weighted-average conversion*. A weighted-average takes into account sales prices just like the full-ratchet, but it also takes into account how many shares were sold at the lower price in proportion to the total outstanding shares of the corporation.

What the investor is trying to accomplish through these antidilution formulas is to safeguard their position in the corporation. If the investor bought their securities at $2.00 per share and the corporation needs to sell securities in a future round at $1.00 per share because the corporation's valuation will not support a $2.00 per share price, the investor wants some assurance that they will not be left holding the bag. They want some assurance that when it comes time to convert, they will get more shares for their money because of the subsequent lower valuation of the corporation.

The corporation will also want to maintain *automatic conversion rights* if the corporation merges with or into any other corporation, if it sells or transfers substantially all its assets, or in the event of an underwritten public offering. Essentially, the corporation wants to have the option to convert everybody over to common stock if a big deal is coming down the pike and it makes a whole lot more sense to be selling apples as opposed to apples, oranges, pears, and mangos.

Redemption can go hand in hand with conversion. A series of stock may be redeemable, in whole or in part, at the option of the corporation upon the happening of a specified event such as a public offering or the sale of the corporation's assets. So, the investor can either convert to common stock or have their shares redeemed by the corporation.

Preemptive or other Subscription Rights. Just as with common stock, preemptive or other preferential subscription rights are discouraged. If an investor already has some antidilution protection, it is unnecessary to add preemptive rights to the package.

Other Types of Stock

In addition to common and preferred stock, there are endless variations and hybrids a creative business attorney can design to reflect ownership in your company. For example, some companies have nonvoting common stock, others have convertible preferred stock that converts into common stock at the option of the holder or when certain events occur (i.e., a public offering) or both.

Warrants

An often overlooked source of equity financing is the issuance of *warrants*. A warrant is a contractual right to acquire some shares of a corporation at a specified price for a specified period of time. It is similar to a stock option, but warrants are issued to investors while stock options are issued to employees, officers, and directors.

Warrants are often issued to investors as part of the sale of securities as a *sweetener* or *kicker* to an offering of securities. For example, an investor purchasing 5,000 shares of common stock at $1.00 per share would receive a warrant to purchase an additional 5,000 share of common stock at a strike price of $1.00 per share for a three-year period.

> **QUICK Tip**
>
> Warrants and the Right to Purchase: The holder of a warrant is not obligated to purchase the shares in the future—they just have the right to purchase them. If the warrant holder fails to exercise the warrant, it expires.

The company must be careful to comply with federal and state securities laws when using warrants. Since the investor will buy the additional shares under the warrant (if they buy them at all), at some point in the future, it is considered a separate offering of securities.

Limited Liability Company and Limited Partnership Equity

As you may recall, limited liability companies (LLCs) and limited partnerships (LPs) are pass-through tax entities. This means that they file tax returns but do not pay any income tax. Instead, the net income and losses of the company flows through to the equity holders (members or limited partners) and is reported on their individual tax returns.

> **Alert!**
>
> Partnership (pass-through entities) tax law is complex, so check with your attorney and accountant every step along the way.

To understand how a pass-through tax entity works, it is helpful to define certain terms. The first term is *allocation*. Net income and losses of pass-through tax entities are allocated among the equity holders in predetermined percentages. Those percentages can correspond directly with the percentage of ownership of the company or they could be different. The latter is called a *special allocation* that can be used to accelerate an investment return to investors. The second term is *distribution*. After the net profits and losses have been allocated to the equity holders, some or all of the net profits can be distributed to them.

The difference between allocation and distribution is important because an equity holder will pay taxes at the end of the year based upon the amount of net income *allocated* to them and not on the amount that is actually *distributed* to them. All operating agreements and limited partnership agreements should have a provision allowing the managers to distribute sufficient monies to pay the taxes on all allocated but undistributed sums for a particular tax year.

A number of factors determine how much of the net profits that have been allocated to the equity holders will actually be distributed. The most important factor is the need to retain funds for use in the operation and expansion of the business. A company may need to retain a portion of the net profits and use them for the operation of the business rather than to raise more capital from new investors. The basic point, however, is that net profits do get distributed eventually. This is a big advantage over a corporation in which common stockholders may have to wait years before seeing any return on their investment. For this reason alone, pass-through tax entities are an attractive investment vehicle.

The complex partnership tax laws that underlie LLCs and LPs allow for a greater amount of flexibility when it comes to creating an attractive return for investors. The company can allocate a disproportionate amount of the net income or loss to investors. For example, investors may only hold 10% of the equity, but they could be allocated 50% of the net profits to create an accelerated return on their investment.

While LLCs and LPs are treated the same for tax purposes, there are differences in the way each is structured and the way in which equity is offered to investors.

Limited Liability Company Equity

The equity of a limited liability company (LLC) is called a *membership unit* (or *interest*). Unlike a limited partnership, every member of an LLC may participate fully in the management of the company. When an LLC is formed, it may elect to be managed by a manager or managers or by the members themselves. As a practical matter, if an LLC is looking to raise capital from investors, it will more than likely be run by a manager or group of managers.

Limited liability companies are ideally suited for businesses that are looking to focus on the delivery of a few products or services that will produce distributable cash. Also, keep in mind that an LLC can convert to a corporation in a tax-free exchange known as a Section 351 exchange if the needs of the company change in the future.

An LLC is different than a corporation because it does not have to state a maximum amount of membership units. There can be an infinite number of membership units. However, as part of the planning process to make an LLC attractive to investors, the managers of the LLC will often define a maximum amount of membership units that the LLC can issue in the operating agreement.

A number of factors need to be taken into account when deciding the maximum number of membership units in an LLC, including the total amount of money that the company anticipates raising from investors and the valuation of the company.

Figure 3.2: AN LLC EXAMPLE

Three people meet through a local business networking event. One is a designer of custom jewelry, the second has experience in managing a company, and the third has marketing experience. The three decide to pool their talents to create a line of custom jewelry and market it to wholesale jewelry dealers.

After meeting with an attorney, the three decide to form an LLC in which they will serve as managers. Each person will have an equal amount of decision-making responsibility and equal amounts of membership units in the company. After filing Articles of Organization with the state corporation commission, they work with their attorney to draft an Operating Agreement for the company.

As part of the Operating Agreement, they designate different classes of membership units to be divided among the founders, investors, and principals of the company (managers, officers, directors, employees, and consultants). The different classes of membership units will have vastly differ-

continued

ent attributes. The class reserved for the founders will have voting rights, while the class to be issued to the investors and principals of the company may not. In addition, the allocation of net income will be weighted heavily in favor of the investors at first and then gradually even out over time.

The managers then work with their attorney, accountant, and a business plan writer to draft a business plan and financial projections. The cost estimate for designing, manufacturing, and marketing the jewelry comes in at $350,000. Based on a number of factors, the company can justify a valuation of $1,000,000. Therefore, if the company were to set a maximum limit of 10,000,000 membership units and then sell 3,500,000 membership units at $0.10 per unit, it would raise enough capital to achieve its goals.

The membership units will be split up into three classes:

- 6,000,000 Class A membership units will be reserved for issuance to founders and managers;

- 500,000 Class B membership units will be reserved for issuance to officers, directors, employees, and consultants; and,

- 3,500,000 Class C membership units will be reserved for issuance to investors.

Obviously, the Class A membership units would be issued to the founders first. Over time, some Class B membership units would be issued as incentives (much like stock options in a corporation) to officers, directors, employees, and consultants. Class C membership units would be sold to investors.

A sample breakdown of the three classes of membership units would probably look like this:

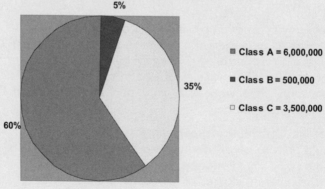

Sample Equity Ownership of an LLC

- Class A = 6,000,000
- Class B = 500,000
- Class C = 3,500,000

Holding 60% or 6,000,000 of the 10,000,000 maximum authorized membership units will ensure that the founders retain decision-making control over the company for quite some time. Issuing up to 5% or 500,000 membership units as incentives will help establish the culture that the officers, directors, employees, and consultants are valuable members of the team and provide incentive for them to do a good job. Setting aside 35% or 3,500,000 will ensure that the company has enough breathing room to be able to raise the additional capital it will need to set up and expand its operations.

Most often, an LLC will structure a graduated reduction in the percentage of net profits allocated to investors. For example, even though the investors as a group will only own 35% of the equity, they could be allocated 60-80% of the net profits until they have been allocated an amount equal to their investment in the company. Thereafter, the investors could be allocated an amount that corresponds directly with their percentage of ownership of the company. There are obviously innumerable variations on this theme that will most likely be driven by how fast investors expect a return on their investment and how large those returns should be.

Limited Partnership Interests

The equity of a limited partnership is called a *limited partnership interest.* Limited partnership interests are typically designed and marketed to passive investors whose monetary returns are dependent upon the efforts of the general partner. Most investors in limited partnerships invest because of the passive nature of the investment. They neither want nor desire to make decisions for the partnership. In fact, unlike an LLC, if a limited partner takes too much control of the operation of the business, they run the risk of incurring personal liability just like a general partner.

The *Revised Uniform Limited Partnership Act*, which has been adopted by a majority of states, lists a number of activities that a limited partner *can* engage in without triggering personal liability. Some of those activities include:

- being an officer, director, or shareholder of a corporate general partner;
- consulting with or advising the general partner on business matters;

- voting on dissolution of the partnership;
- voting on the sale or mortgaging of partnership assets;
- voting on the incurrence of unusual indebtedness;
- voting on the admission or removal of general or limited partners;
- voting on transactions involving potential conflicts of interest; and,
- all other matters required by the partnership agreement.

Limited partnerships are well-suited for investment ventures that are looking for a handful of high net worth investors, like real estate investments. The general partner will solicit the interest of a few investors, form the limited partnership, and have the limited partnership agreement drafted. The investors will then be brought on board by signing the limited partnership agreement and contributing capital to the venture.

Just like LLCs, limited partnerships do not have to state a maximum amount of authorized capital. The limited partnership agreement usually limits the number of limited partnership interests to be sold to investors.

Typically, the net income and losses of a limited partnership will be split between the general partner and limited partners, with a disproportionate amount being attributed to the limited partners at the beginning and leveling out later on.

Allocation of the net income and losses of the limited partnership are typically split between the general partner and limited partners. In the scenario, the three founders formed a corporation that served as the general partner and they also contributed capital as limited partners. However, a general partner is under no obligation to contribute any capital to the venture.

Because the three founders are serving as officers of the corporation, which is the general partner, they will be entitled to receive compensation from the share that is allocated to the general partner. Because they also hold 200,000 limited partnership interests, they will be entitled to their percentage of the share that is allocated to the limited partners.

The three founders will not run into trouble and risk incurring personal liability, because they are allowed, as officers and directors of corporation that serves as the general partner, to have decision-making power.

Figure 3.3: THE LP EXAMPLE

Three people are interested in purchasing a piece of commercial real estate for investment, but they do not have enough cash to obtain financing. After consulting with an attorney, they decide to form a limited partnership. The three of them intend to share equally in the decision-making power for the limited partnership, but are concerned about being personally liable for the debts and obligations of the limited partnership. Therefore, the three of them form a corporation in which they are the directors and officers, and appoint that new corporation as the general partner of the limited partnership.

After filing a Certificate of Limited Partnership with the state corporation commission, they work with their attorney to draft a Limited Partnership Agreement. The three of them together contribute $200,000 to the venture. In order to obtain financing, they calculate that they will need to raise an additional $800,000 from the sale of limited partnership interests.

The Limited Partnership Agreement sets the maximum amount of limited partnership to be sold at 1,000,000 and issues the first 200,000 limited partnership interests to the three founders who contributed the first $200,000. The limited partnership then works with their attorney to draft a Private Placement Memorandum to offer $800,000 in limited partnership interests under Rule 506. (see Chapter 5.) The limited partnership interests are offered to investors at $1.00 per unit of interest, with a minimum purchase of $50,000. Sixteen investors later, the limited partnership has the capital it needs to obtain its financing.

Just like an LLC, the limited partnership can allocate the net income and losses of the partnership any way it wants to. Typically, since the limited partners are putting up all of the capital, they will receive the lion's share of the profits and losses initially. After some time, the allocations can be adjusted.

QUICK Tip

Protect Yourself with Redundancy: Spell out your allocation amounts and schedule in both the limited partnership agreement and the private placement memorandum.

If the limited partnership was going to acquire multiple properties with the same financing, serious thought might be given to raising its capital through a series of offerings.

Raising Capital in Stages

When you start your company, you may end up having to give away a healthy portion of your company in exchange for little money because you have nothing more than a good idea. As your successes grow, however, you will be able to justify a higher price for the equity of your company. This is why young companies should raise capital in stages and accomplish certain goals with the money they raise.

Figure 3.4: SELLING IN STAGES

An inventor came to an investor with a great idea for some software that would also be a video game. For this venture, the inventor needed to write and build the software, test market it, adapt the software to the video game formats that are out there, and finally, manufacture, market, and distribute the software. To accomplish these goals, it would take quite a chunk of money, so the investor broke it down: raise some capital to write and build the software. Raise more capital to test market and adapt the software to video game software formats. Then, raise some final capital to manufacture, market, and distribute the whole thing.

All along the way, the successes of the company justified higher share prices for each of the three rounds of capital raising. Consequently, the company ended up selling off less of its equity than if it had tried to raise it all at once.

Chapter **4**

Debt Financing

An alternative to financing through equity is *debt*. The advantages of using debt are:

- the time to secure debt financing is usually shorter than equity;
- the cost of the money (principal and interest) is readily measurable;
- documentation costs for the transaction will probably be less than an equity transaction; and,
- the equity of the company is not diluted by new ownership.

The disadvantages to debt are:

- unlike equity, the company has to pay back debt;
- the company must carry debt on its balance sheet as a liability, which may make it less attractive to some investors;
- if the cash flow of the business is tight, debt service can put an undue strain on the finances;
- in many small businesses, commercial lenders require the principals to personally guarantee the debt and possibly pledge personal collateral; and,
- some lenders require rather onerous record keeping by the borrower, such as quarterly and annual financial statements—possibly audited—and impose restrictions on certain business transactions without the lender's consent.

Bank Loans

One of the most common types of financing is bank loans. In order to obtain a bank loan for a new business, you may need to present a business plan or a loan proposal, which are similar documents.

The advantage of seeking a bank loan may be that you or your family has a preexisting relationship or history with a bank that makes the process easier. In any event, a bank will focus on several things in reviewing your loan application.

First, they will want to know about your business (the business plan), how much money you need, and how you intend to spend it. Equally important is demonstrating to the bank how your business intends to pay the loan back and over what time period. Financial projections are most helpful at this time.

Banks are in the business of loaning money—that is one of their main profit centers. Your task is to demonstrate to them that you are creditworthy and that the revenues from your company are likely to pay back the loan in a timely manner. You demonstrate your ability to pay back the loan through your financial projections. If you already have a history of running a profitable business, a historical financial statement coupled with a financial projection could win the day.

Unless you have substantial assets in your company and healthy annual revenues, banks are likely to look to the creditworthiness of the owners of the business. In other words, you and your partners' credit histories will be checked and you may be required to submit a personal balance sheet.

Keep in mind that it is a crime to submit false information to a bank—tell it like it is without unnecessary embellishment.

In the case of a start-up business, many banks will require, as a condition of the loan, that each of the founders (and possibly their spouses) guarantee the loan. The demand for personal guarantees may also surface when you are signing a lease for your company office or plant. If you have to sign a personal guarantee, see if the bank will agree to remove it after some reasonable period. Commercial landlords tend to be more open to the eventual removal of personal guarantees than banks, but it never hurts to ask.

Banks charge interest for loans, which is deductible as a business expense to the borrower. Interest rates vary among banks and can be influenced by the type of loan made and the perceived credit risk of the borrower. You should explore the various types of bank loans available to your business to see what fits. For example, a line of credit allows you to draw funds when needed and only pay interest on outstanding balances.

Yearly Paybacks: In the case of a line of credit, you may be required to pay out of the line (i.e., pay back all balances) once a year in order to renew it.

An installment loan is usually for a certain sum that you pay back in payments of principal and interest, similar to your home mortgage. Many business loans have a *floating* interest rate that adjusts with changes in a standard index, such as the *prime rate*.

Some banks may require that you provide security or collateral for any business loan. If your business does not have equipment or receivables, they may require you to put up your house and other personal property to guarantee the loan. If that is not enough, you and your partners, directors, and possibly principal shareholders will most likely have to sign personally on the loans as previously discussed.

If your company is writing a business plan and a bank loan is in the picture, you may wish to specifically address the issues the lending bank will consider in making a loan. As a practical matter, you will probably have trouble getting a loan as a start-up if you cannot demonstrate an ability to repay the loan from revenues. You should probably enlist the aid of your accountant to make certain that you tell your story in believable numbers.

You will also help your case by having substantial clients or orders in the wings to demonstrate imminent revenues. It also helps if you have invested your own money in the venture, as this demonstrates your commitment to the business and its success. In venture circles that is known as having *skin in the game*. Pledging *collateral* is another way to put skin in the game.

Another useful approach is to plan your presentation to the bank, preferably on your own turf, so that key employees are included in making portions of the presentation. If you are in a position to reduce or cut your own salary for some period of time, that will also impress the bank—they do not relish your seeking a loan to pay your own salary.

Larger, institutional banks are not the only game in town when seeking loans. Smaller, community banks are generally more connected with local people and may be more flexible. Innovative officers in small banks will try to *syndicate* or farm out portions of loans to other small banks to increase their lending limit.

You should not necessarily stop with banks as the sole source of lending. Many venture funds, larger companies like *GE Capital*, and brokerage houses have bank-like divisions that could be a source of debt capital or some combination of debt and equity. *American Express* has a small business division called *OPEN: the Small Business Network* (**www.americanexpress.com**) that can grant needed lines of credit for small businesses.

HOW TO...Get a Bank Loan

❑ *Prepare a business plan targeted to a lender rather than an investor.*
❑ *Present believable financial statements and projections that demonstrate that the company will have sufficient cash flow to service the debt and meet its operational budget.*
❑ *Interview the lender prior to submitting the package and find out exactly what type of presentation and information is expected.*

Small Business Administration (SBA)

The *Small Business Administration* (SBA) (**www.sba.gov**) has a number of loan programs for small companies. Its basic *7(a) loan guarantee program* is perhaps the best known. The program is designed for small businesses that cannot otherwise obtain a loan. The actual loans are delivered through commercial banks, with the bulk of the loan principal being guaranteed by the SBA. The maximum loan under this program is $2 million, but most of the loans placed are for less. More information on the 7(a) program is available at **www.sba.gov/financing/sbaloan/7a.html**.

Another SBA program is the 504 loan program, which provides long-term, fixed-rate financing to small businesses to acquire land, buildings, or equipment. The 504 program cannot be used for working capital or inventory. The loans are delivered through *certified development companies* (CDC), which are private, nonprofit corporations designed to contribute to the economic development of their communities. A private lender has a *senior lien*, and the CDC issues an SBA guaranteed debenture for up to 40% of the loan amount. The debenture is secured by *junior lien*. The owner must contribute at least 10% of the equity. The maximum SBA debenture is $1 million, which can go to $1.3 million in some cases. More information on the 504 loan program can be found at **www.sba.gov/financing/sbaloan/cdc504.html**.

The SBA has a microloan 7(m) program in which a small business can get a short-term loan of up to $35,000. This loan can be used for working capital, inventory, furniture, supplies, and the like. Microloans are delivered through specially designated intermediary organizations, usually nonprofits with experience in lending. More information on the microloan program can be found at **www.sba.gov/financing/sbaloan/microloans.html**.

In addition, there are other, more specialized programs at the SBA that address the needs of women, minorities, veterans, and Native Americans. More on these loans and other special interest topics can be found at **www.sba.gov/financing/index.html**.

The SBA has a surety bond program for contractors and other special purpose programs that include an alliance with the Export-Import Bank to promote export trade, *employee stock option ownership plans* (ESOPS), and lines of credit under the CAPlines program. Information on the SBA programs can be found at **www.sba.gov/financing/index.html** and the Ex-Im Bank information is at **www.exim.gov/products/work_cap.html**.

Several misconceptions about the SBA programs seem to surface now and then. The SBA programs are not grants or free money. They are generally loans that constitute legitimate debt and that need to be repaid. It is generally believed that a business has to be a start-up or in distress to apply. Neither of these statements is true. The SBA is not a bailout agency. It finances healthy businesses that need bridge financing or an extended term loan.

The SBA: The SBA is an often-overlooked resource for more established businesses that need to grow or acquire new facilities.

Credit Cards

Many entrepreneurs use *credit cards* to initially finance their business. If you go this route, you need to treat the credit card debt as an installment loan and pay it back as soon as possible. You should also shop around to get the best rates—credit card interest can be steep.

Establish guidelines for credit card borrowing. For example, do not borrow any money you cannot repay in ninety days. Make sure to keep accurate financial records that separate your personal expenses from business expenses. A good strategy is only to use credit cards for the purchase of a long-term asset like a computer, or for something that will quickly generate cash, like buying inventory to fill an order. Do not use credit cards to pay expenses that are not generating revenue.

Home Equity Lines

In the initial start-up phase of the business, other direct sources of financing include *home equity lines*. The home equity line is essentially asset-backed borrowing. You could do the same thing with the business if it had assets to pledge. To obtain a home equity loan, you apply to a bank or financing institution and the loan is secured by a lien on your home, usually a second mortgage.

Retirement Funds

You can always use self-directed IRA accounts of investors as a source for financing. Owners of self-directed plans can make investments in private companies. However, there are certain *disqualified persons* who cannot engage in prohibited transactions with the IRA. Common occurrences of IRA prohibited transactions are (1) purchasing investments that will benefit the IRA holder (as opposed to the IRA itself) and (2) using the IRA as security for a loan. An example of the direct benefit example is having the IRA purchase a vacation home for your family. Disqualified persons include the IRA holder, his or her spouse, ancestors and lineal descendants of the IRA holder and spouse, and any corporation, partnership, trust, or estate in which the IRA holder has a 50% or greater interest. In calculating the percentage ownership of the IRA holder, the IRA attribution rules apply so that the interest of spouses, ancestors and lineal descendants are included. In some circumstances, investors can utilize their 401(k) plans to invest in private companies.

Consult with a tax professional before making any investments from retirement accounts. If your investor is having trouble convincing your custodian to make an investment with their retirement account, you can set up a new self-directed account with a company like Trust Administration Services Corporation (**www.trustlynk.com**) that specializes in self-directed retirement funds. Other sources for self-directed plans are **www.lincontrust.com** and **www.pensco.com**.

Life Insurance Borrowing

You may also consider borrowing against your life insurance policy, assuming that you have the kind of whole life policy that builds cash value. The interest rates are less than credit cards, and the loan will stay in place as long as you continue to pay the premiums. If you die while the loan is outstanding, the benefits of your policy will be reduced.

Financial Brokers

You will undoubtedly cross paths with financial headhunters or brokers during your quest for financing. These individuals or companies usually work for a commission and typically want a portion of your company's equity as part of their fee. You should exercise caution when employing a financial broker, since they are generally not licensed like stock brokers, attorneys, and accountants, and there is little public information available on them.

Always insist on references and do a thorough job of due diligence on the brokers. Avoid paying up-front fees if possible. If travel expenses are required, approve them on a case-by-case basis. Avoid signing an exclusive agreement with the broker, but if you must, have the period of exclusivity expire after thirty to sixty days if no meaningful results are forthcoming. In all events, make certain that the broker is not paid their fee unless financing actually occurs. Make sure you have the absolute right to decline any financing offered for any reason.

Alert!

Many brokers will try to convince you that your business plan needs *upgrading* to an *investor-grade* business plan before they can present it, and that will cost you several thousand dollars for the makeover. If you have a solid business plan with CPA-blessed financials, politely decline the offer.

Reverse Mergers

The subject of *reverse mergers*, where a company merges into a publicly traded shell company, is well beyond the scope of this book. Any start-up company would be well-advised to avoid a reverse merger until they have raised several rounds of financing—and maybe not even then. While there are successful reverse mergers, the field is strewn with wrecked companies that have insolvable regulatory problems. Caution is advised. Make certain you consult with competent professionals before undertaking this route.

Factoring

Factoring, also known as *receivables financing*, is a popular form of raising capital. While it is not for everyone, it can be useful if your business has a large volume of receivables. Essentially, a factoring company advances to your company the value of a percentage of your receivables, less a fee, and assumes the responsibility to collect the factored receivables.

When you factor your receivables, you usually end up with between 50% and 90% of their value, depending upon the creditworthiness of your clients and your company's collection history. When the factor collects the receivable, it forwards the balance to you less a fee that can range from 2%–7%. The advantage of factoring is immediate cash flow to the business without a long-term debt obligation. The disadvantage is that the process is fairly costly.

 **Factoring Guides:** A source for factoring companies can be found in *Edwards Directory of American Factors*, Edwards Research Group, Inc., Newton, MA (**www.edwardsresearch.com**). This factor guide is usually available at public libraries as well.

Revenue Participation/Royalty Financing

Revenue participation or royalty financing occurs when an investor buys a percentage of a future revenue stream of the company. This type of financing can be risky for the investor if there are no sales revenues or revenues do not occur for a time. When sales do occur, payment to the investor comes before any other expenses of the company, regardless of profitability.

In the current market of hybrid securities, a revenue or royalty component, coupled with some equity participation by way of warrants, can be an attractive option to investors seeking both cash flow and equity participation. A version of royalty or revenue participation can be structured within a class of preferred stock or LLC membership units. The tax and legal aspects of this creative form of financing are complex, and careful planning with your legal and accounting team is advised.

Merchant Banking

Historically, merchant banks have not been commercial banks that accept deposits, but private banks with access to *private equity funds*. That said, many of the traditional lending banks have ventured into the private equity market in the past few years. With a little research, you may be able to uncover a source of equity financing from your bank. Larger banks have been investing in private equities for quite a while, and now small banks are getting in the game with some banks syndicating the investments with other small banks. It is unlikely your local branch officer will know much about these programs, and you may need to do a bit of digging to get to the right person in the bank. If you have a preexisting relationship with the bank, you will probably get answers a lot quicker.

In addition to the private equity groups of commercial banks, there are other private equity nonbanking groups, such as insurance companies, hedge funds, large and small angels, private equity funds, and other institutional investors who invest in early stage companies. Like an entrée into venture capital, an introduction to the group, especially from a person who has previously raised money from that sector, is extremely helpful.

SBIC Financing

The Small Business Administration (SBA) also sponsors an equity investment program known as the *Small Business Investment Corporation* (SBIC), which is a series of privately owned investment funds licensed by the SBA. Essentially, the SBIC program is a public-private partnership designed to flow venture dollars in to emerging companies. With the SBA contribution, the SBIC funds can vastly leverage their private investor dollars. Essentially, they are SBA-sponsored venture funds that may or may not have a debt element.

Between FY 1994 and 2002, the SBIC funded 8% of the venture market investments for a total of 23.7 billion dollars—and this figure represents only the financings that contain equity features. 2.7 billion dollars was funded in FY 2002 alone. A large percentage of fund dollars go to low and moderate income businesses in more diverse parts of the country than the investments of conventional venture funds. Information on the SBIC program can be found at **www.sba.gov/INV**, as well as a list of SBIC sponsored funds in your area.

Private Debt

A company can raise capital by offering a debt instrument to investors as opposed to an equity instrument. For example, the company could offer secured or unsecured promissory note obligations payable over time at a competitive interest rate. Private company debt, particularly the unsecured variety, is considered risky, and an above-market interest rate is necessary to attract private investors or lenders.

Be sure to check the state usury laws before setting the interest rate.

Many start-up companies offer a convertible promissory note in their early seed rounds. The convertibility feature of the note allows the holder (lender) to convert the amount due for principal and interest to an equity interest in the company. The conversion rate would be the amount at which equity interests in the company will be offered to new investors or at a discount to make the investment more attractive. If you use convertible notes or any debt instrument to raise early money, you should organize the entity first and have the note be issued by the entity rather than you personally.

Combining Equity and Debt Financing

Recently, there have been some offerings that combine both debt and equity in order to give the investors some liquidity in a debt instrument and a possible upside for growth with an equity component. One method is to use unsecured promissory notes that give the lender the option to convert all or a portion of their investment into an equity interest in the company, usually at a discount below any current offering price of the company's stock. Using any method that involves the sale of securities by the company means federal and state securities laws *must be* observed. Chapter 5 discusses some of the issues surrounding securities offerings.

Several years ago, it was common to see real estate development loans containing a provision that allowed the lender to participate in the equity or income potential (or both) of the underlying real estate project. Your company can offer a debt instrument coupled with equity or income participation as an inducement to invest. The LLC format is particularly suited to this type of investment because of the flexibility of the partnership taxation rules. Again, these are fairly complex offerings that require carefully drafted documents as well as compliance with the securities laws. As you enter the arena of hybrid debt instruments, a do-it-yourself approach is not advisable.

Chapter 5

Securities Law

Compliance with federal and state securities laws is a serious consideration for every company. Learning what you can and cannot do under the securities laws is a valuable tool in your arsenal of knowledge. Every time your company issues or sells securities, the transaction must comply with federal securities laws and the securities laws of the state in which it is sold. Doing it right the first time can mean the difference between survival and failure of your business.

Understanding Securities Laws

What is a *security?* Basically, securities have been held to exist in any case in which a person provides money to someone with the expectation that they will derive a profit through the efforts of that person. This can apply to any situation in which someone buys stock in or makes a noncommercial loan to your business. The company that sells securities is known as the *issuer.*

There are basically two types of securities offerings—*public* and *private.* The private placement offering is the means used by most new businesses to raise their initial capital. It is far less costly than a public offering, and is not subject to the review process of the *Securities and Exchange Commission* (SEC) and the state agencies. The sale is accomplished through the use of an offering document known as a *private placement memorandum* (PPM), which is prepared by an attorney who specializes in securities law. When you sell equity in your company (common stock or preferred stock, limited partnership interests, or LLC membership units), you must comply with the federal and state laws regulating the sale of securities.

Brief History of Securities Laws

The states got into the act first. Massachusetts enacted a law in the 1850s that regulated the sale of railroad stock. In 1911, Kansas adopted the first securities statute with a broad application to protect the welfare of its citizens from unscrupulous promoters of securities. A handful of states followed suit. There were constitutional challenges to these states regulation of securities that were defeated in 1917, which opened the way for the wholesale adoption of state regulatory controls. Today, each state has some form of securities regulation.

State securities laws were a great starting point in protecting investors from fraud and abuse, but something more was needed. Congressional hearings into the cause of the Great Depression uncovered that one-half of the total sales of securities during the 1920s proved to be worthless due to massive fraud, abuse of trust, and lack of disclosure standards. State regulation was largely ineffective due to lack of resources and the fact that people committing these crimes were moving from state to state to avoid getting caught.

One of the first things President Roosevelt did when he got in to office was to urge Congress to adopt legislation controlling the issuance and sale of securities. One of the first pieces of New Deal legislation was the *Securities Act of 1933 (33 Act)*, which created the Securities and Exchange Commission (SEC) and instituted a process for federal registration of securities and an administrative process to review securities offerings.

Curiously enough, while other New Deal legislation created federal bureaucracies that supplanted state services, the creation of this new federal review mechanism of securities also left in place the existing state securities laws. This concurrent jurisdiction over securities created, in many cases, a dual registration process at the federal and state level that still exists today.

Since 1933, issuers of securities either had to register their securities or qualify for an *exemption* from registration. Securities registration is an expensive and time-consuming process. Rather than filing a public registration, most small companies use an exemption from registration provided, in part, by *Regulation D* of the *33 Act*.

The Rise of Rule 506 of Regulation D

In 1982, the SEC adopted Regulation D, which provided three exemptions from registration under the *33 Act*—Rules 504, 505, and 506. If the guidelines are followed, these rules collectively provide a *safe harbor* to sell securities in a private transaction without having to file a registration statement with the SEC.

In 1996, Congress passed the *National Securities Market Improvement Act* (NSMIA). NSMIA brought some semblance of uniformity to the widely variant state exemptions from registration. It created a federal preemption over state registration for what it called *covered securities*. Essentially, it provided that Rule 506 offerings were to be recognized as valid exemptions in all states, thus preempting state securities law for this type of offering.

Today, virtually all young companies will issue their securities in accordance with Regulation D. Rule 506 is a popular choice because of its acceptance by all of the states.

Rule 506 provides that an offering of securities will be exempt from registration if it meets the following requirements.

- There can be no more than thirty-five purchasers who are not accredited in any given offering, but there can be an unlimited amount of accredited purchasers.
- Each purchaser who is not an accredited investor either alone or with their purchaser representative(s) must have such knowledge and experience in financial and business matters that they are capable of evaluating the merits and risks of the prospective investment, or the issuer reasonably believes immediately prior to making any sale that such purchaser comes within this description.
- Certain financial and nonfinancial disclosure requirements must be met by the company.
- Financial disclosures include financial statements for up to two years, and in some cases they must be audited, depending upon the amount of the offering, and the balance sheet must be dated within 120 days of the start of the offering.
- There can be no general advertising or general solicitation of potential purchasers.
- Resale limitations on the securities must also be disclosed.
- Notice of the sale of securities (Form D) under Rule 506 must be filed with the SEC no later than fifteen days after the first sale of securities. (Form D is a statistical reporting form that is not, at present, reviewed by the SEC.)

Accredited Investors

An issuer typically determines an investor's accredited status by having the investor answer written questions regarding his or her accredited status.

Regulation D defines an *accredited investor* as a person or business entity meeting the following qualifications.

- Any individual with an individual net worth, or joint net worth with that person's spouse, of $1,000,000, *or* with an individual income of $200,000 ($300,000 with that person's spouse).
- An officer, director, or general partner of the company issuing the securities.
- A nonprofit company with total assets in excess of $5,000,000 that was not formed for the specific purpose of acquiring the securities offered.
- A bank, saving and loan association, broker, dealer of securities, insurance company, investment company, or any employee benefit plan with assets exceeding $5,000,000.
- Any trust with total assets in excess of $5,000,000 that was not formed for the specific purpose of acquiring the securities offered.
- Any entity in which all of the equity owners are accredited investors.

Nonaccredited Investors

Nonaccredited investors are everybody else who falls below or comes outside the qualifications of an accredited investor. Accredited investors are determined by a quantitative test, while nonaccredited investors are determined by a qualitative test. You have to be a bit more careful with nonaccredited investors. The issuer has to make certain that a nonaccredited investor has enough knowledge and experience in financial and business matters to be capable of evaluating the merits and risks of the prospective investment. The issuer must reasonably believe, immediately prior to making any sale, that such purchaser comes within this description.

In addition, although it is not a requirement under Rule 506, the financial capability of the investor should not be ignored. The issuer should provide disclosures that this is a high-risk investment and obtain an assurance that the investor is capable of losing their entire investment.

For purposes of Rule 506, there can be no more than thirty-five nonaccredited investors purchasing securities in any offering. An issuer can, however, count certain groups of investors as one investor. Multiple purchasers who are counted as one purchaser for the thirty-five count include:

QUICK Tip

Accredited vs. Nonaccredited Investors: Accredited investors are assumed to have knowledge and experience in financial matters. With nonaccredited investors, you have to find out. Typically, you ask the investor a series of written questions regarding their financial and business experience.

- any relative, spouse, or relative of the spouse of a purchaser who has the same principal residence as the purchaser;
- any trust or estate in which the purchaser owns, either alone or together with related persons, more than 50% of the beneficial interest;
- any business entity majority-owned by the purchaser either alone or with (1) related persons as described in the first bullet or (2) a trust or estate as described in the second bullet; and,
- persons or business entities that are, or the issuer reasonably believes to be, accredited investors.

Nonaccredited investors who do not have such knowledge and experience in financial and business matters may rely on a *purchaser representative* to evaluate the investment to make them capable of evaluating the merits and risks of the prospective investment.

HOW TO...Determine the Status of Your Investor

Part of a private placement document is a **subscription agreement**, which all investors must complete. There are questions in the subscription agreement that determine whether the purchaser is an accredited or nonaccredited investor. In some smaller offerings, investors complete an **investor letter**.

Disclosure Requirements

The guiding principle behind all offerings of securities, whether public or private, is full disclosure of all material facts concerning the company and the offering. This is so an investor can make an informed investment decision. It is always advisable to err on the side of inclusion in terms of disclosure.

All disclosures must be in writing and made available to each purchaser at a reasonable time prior to the purchase of the securities. Each investor must have the opportunity to ask questions and receive answers concerning the terms and conditions of the offering. The investor may request any additional information that the issuer possesses, or can acquire without unreasonable effort or expense, that is necessary to verify the accuracy of the information provided in the disclosure document. Essentially, every investor must have equal access to information. An issuer should not rely upon *ad hoc* conversations with individual investors to convey all of the information necessary to provide full disclosure. For these reasons, it is important to draft a clear and concise document containing all material information. That document is referred to as a *private placement memorandum* (PPM).

Private Placement Memorandum

The PPM is intended to be an all-inclusive document providing specific information on the company, its business, its management, the risks involved in the investment, and a description of the securities offered. Much like a business plan, it is imperative that the principals of the company participate in the process of drafting a disclosure document to ensure the accuracy and completeness of the information. In addition, an understanding of the private offering exemption rules is essential, because if you violate any of the rules you could get into trouble with the SEC or state securities administrator.

Figure 5.1: THE PRIVATE PLACEMENT MEMORANDUM

The information in the PPM should include the following.

- A summary of the offering, containing a synopsis or snapshot of the information that will be discussed in detail throughout the rest of the document, including (but not limited to):

  - the name, address, and telephone number of the company;

  - the date of the offering document;

  - a description of the securities being offered;

  - a description of any minimum dollar amount that has to be invested by an investor;

  - any minimum dollar amount that must be raised in the offering before the funds are spent by the company;

  - the total amount of money being raised;

  - any escrow requirements of the offering; and,

  - the resale or transfer restrictions of the securities.

- A cover page that contains information about any commissions paid to selling agents or finders (where allowed by law) and disclaimers about the high risk nature of the investment and the fact that the securities have not been recommended or approved by any federal or state securities commission and are being offered under an exemption from registration.

- A table of contents to provide a road map for the document.

- A description of the company, including the name of the company, date, state of incorporation, street address, telephone number, and contact person.

- A description of the factors that the company considers to be the most substantial risks to an investor (risk factors) in this offering. This includes all the facts and circumstances that otherwise make the offering high risk or speculative. The following are possible risk factors that will have to be tailored to the company's unique situation—some will be applicable and others will not:

  - the limited operating history of the company;

  - the potential fluctuation of operating results;

- the intensity of competition in the market or industry;

- the company's business model (if unique);

- the dependence on key personnel of the company;

- the dependence on third-party vendors for goods and services;

- the need to hire and retain skilled personnel;

- the timing of positive revenue generation;

- the need for additional capital;

- applicable government regulations that affect the company;

- the need to expand operations;

- the need to obtain and maintain intellectual property protection;

- any conflicts of interest that exist among the company and officers, directors, or key employees;

- the fact that this is a high-risk investment—that the investors may lose their entire investment;

- the heavy reliance on the plans and concepts of management;

- the arbitrary determination of the offering price of securities—the fact that no independent valuation of the company was conducted;

- the resale and transfer restrictions of the securities imposed by the limited offering exemption rules;

- the fact that no dividends are anticipated in the near future;

- if there are no escrow provisions, the funds raised in the offering may be used immediately by the company;

- the lack of an independent review of the information in the offering—the investor must rely upon the company for the accuracy of the information;

- that the securities have not been registered with or approved by any federal or state securities commission;

- that any forward-looking statements in the document are based on assumptions made by the company; and,

- that the financial projections in the document are based on assumptions made by the company.

continued

- Description of the business of the company, including:
  - what the company does and proposes to do, including what products or goods are or will be produced, or services that are or will be rendered;
  - how these products or services are to be produced;
  - how the company intends to carry out its activities;
  - the industry and competition of the company;
  - the company's marketing strategies;
  - any firmly written orders for products or services;
  - the number of employees and anticipated employees;
  - any real property and intellectual property that the company owns or has rights to;
  - the extent to which the company operations depend on patents, copyrights, trade secrets, know-how, or other proprietary information, and the steps undertaken to protect this intellectual property;
  - whether the company's business, products, or properties are subject to government regulation, indicating the nature and extent of regulation and its effects on the company;
  - the names of any subsidiaries and which, if any, are included in the financial statements; and,
  - the material events in the development of the company, including any mergers or acquisitions during the past five years—or for whatever lesser period the company has been in existence—and any pending or anticipated mergers, acquisitions, spin-offs, or recapitalizations.
- If the company was not profitable during the last fiscal year, list the events or milestones that—in management's opinion—must or should occur in order for the company to become profitable, and the manner in which the company will achieve these milestones. Also, state the probable consequences to the company if delays occur.
- Description of the offering price factors and indicate:
  - what the net, after-tax earnings were for last year;
  - the offering price of securities as a multiple of earnings if the company had profits;

- what the *net tangible book value* of the company (the total assets minus total liabilities) is (if the net tangible book value is substantially less than the offering price, explain the reasons for the variation);
  - the details of all other securities offerings in the last twelve months;
  - what percentage of the outstanding shares of the company investors will own after this offering; and,
  - what the post-offering value of the company will be.
- Description of what the funds raised in this offering will be used for, including such categories as:
  - legal and professional consultants;
  - intellectual property protection;
  - research and development;
  - marketing and advertising;
  - repayment of debt;
  - acquisition of assets;
  - salaries and benefits;
  - insurance;
  - lease or purchase expenses;
  - travel and entertainment;
  - inventory;
  - working capital (office expenses, telephone, etc.); and,
  - expenses of the offering.
- Indicate whether the company anticipates having cash flow or liquidity problems in the next twelve months, or is subject to any unsatisfied judgments, liens, or settlement obligations.
- State whether the proceeds of the offering will satisfy the company's cash flow requirements for the next twelve months or whether it will be necessary to raise additional funds.
- Describe the capitalization of the company from the most recent balance sheet date, with any adjustments since then, and also as adjusted for the sale of securities now being sold.

continued

- Describe the securities, indicating:

  - the attributes of the securities being offered, including the type (common, preferred, promissory notes, etc.), voting rights, dividend rights, liquidation preference, conversion rights, redemption rights, etc.;

  - any other outstanding securities; and,

  - whether there is any debt or other class of securities that have the right to be paid before the securities now being sold.

- Describe who will be selling the securities. Typically, securities offered through private placements are offered by the officers, directors, and key employees of the company. The company may, however, employ a licensed selling agent or finder (where allowed by law).

- Describe any compensation to selling agents or finders, if the selling agents or finders will be held harmless for any mistakes they might make, and if there is any kind of business or personal relationship between the selling agent or finder and the company.

- Describe the resale or transfer restrictions to which the securities are subject.

- Identify any escrow agent that will be used to hold the securities if there is a minimum amount to be raised in the offering. The escrow agent holds the money until the minimum amount is raised. If the minimum amount is not raised, the escrow agent returns all monies to the investors, with or without interest, as provided in the PPM.

- Explain the resale restrictions of any presently outstanding securities and when those restrictions will expire.

- If the company has paid dividends, made distributions, or redeemed any of its securities in the past five years, describe when and how much.

- Describe the officers and key personnel of the company, indicating:

  - the employment, education, business or personal bankruptcy, and litigation history of all officers for the past five years, and

  - any details of any key man life or other insurance policies on the officers and key personnel. *Key man* insurance is used for business purposes, usually to reimburse a company for the loss it sustains when an important member of the company dies.

- Describe the directors of the company, indicating:
  - ◆ the number of directors and any special election or voting trust arrangements for the election of directors;
  - ◆ the employment, education, business or personal bankruptcy, and litigation history of all directors for the past five years; and,
  - ◆ any details of any key man life or other insurance policies on the directors.
- Provide information on the principal owners of the company (those who directly or indirectly own 10% or more of the presently outstanding common or preferred stock) and how much they paid for their stock.
- Describe the management relationships, transactions, and remuneration, and:
  - ◆ describe any conflicts of interest that the officers, directors, and key personnel have;
  - ◆ describe if any of the officers, directors, key personnel, or principal stockholders are related by blood or marriage;
  - ◆ provide details if the company has made loans to or is doing business with any of its officers, directors, key personnel, or principal stockholders, or if they have guaranteed or co-signed any of the company's debt or other obligations;
  - ◆ list all salaries and compensation to the officers, directors, and key personnel for the past and upcoming year, and describe any employment agreements the company may have;
  - ◆ list any outstanding stock purchase agreements, stock options, or warrants; and,
  - ◆ if the business is highly dependent upon the services of certain key personnel, describe noncompete or nondisclosure agreements the company has with them.
- Describe any past, pending, or threatened litigation or administrative actions that have had or may have a material effect upon the company's business, financial condition, or operations, including any litigation or action involving the officers, directors, or key personnel.
- If it is anticipated that any significant tax benefits will be available to investors, discuss them as they relate to the offering.

continued

- Describe any other material factors that could affect the company or its business, or that are necessary to make any other information in this document not misleading or incomplete.

- For companies that have a significant operating history, include a management discussion and analysis of certain relevant factors, such as:

  - if the company's financial statements show losses from operations, the causes and what steps the company has taken or will take to address these causes;

  - any trends in the company's historical operating results;

  - if the company is selling products and had significant sales last year (state the existing gross margin as a percentage of sales and the anticipated gross margin for the next year of operations);

  - any foreign sales, domestic government sales, and anticipated changes; and,

  - any strategic alliances, corporate partnerships, or special marketing arrangements.

- Appendices to the PPM should include:

  - subscription documents;

  - financial statements of the company (balance sheet and income statement);

  - financial projections (if used);

  - operating agreement (in the case of an LLC); and,

  - any other documents and agreements material to the offering.

HOW TO...Begin Drafting a Private Placement Memorandum

Work closely with an attorney that specializes in securities law to draft your PPM. To begin the process, organize and provide copies of the the following documents to your attorney:

- ❏ *articles of organization and operating agreement for an LLC;*
- ❏ *articles of incorporation and bylaws for a corporation;*
- ❏ *minutes of board of directors and shareholder meetings for a corporation;*
- ❏ *business plan and financial projections;*
- ❏ *financial statements (for two years or from inception);*
- ❏ *a list of how you intend to spend the money raised in the offering (use of proceeds);*
- ❏ *any promissory notes or debt instruments the company has entered into;*
- ❏ *joint venture agreements or contracts with strategic partners (companies depended on to make, sell, or distribute products or services);*
- ❏ *any employment and work made for hire agreements;*
- ❏ *documentation of any litigation the company is involved in;*
- ❏ *any real and material personal property owned by the company;*
- ❏ *documentation of any intellectual property (patents, trademarks, or copy rights);*
- ❏ *any intellectual property assignments, licenses, or agreements pertaining to copyright, trademark, trade secret, or patent filings, including vendor agreements; and,*
- ❏ *all significant contracts or agreements.*

No General Advertising or General Solicitation of Securities.

In a private placement, the company or anyone acting on behalf of the company may not offer or sell the securities through any form of general advertising or solicitation. Two examples of these types of prohibited activities are set forth in Regulation D.

1. Any advertisement, article, notice, or other communication published in any newspaper, magazine, or similar media or broadcast over television or radio.

2. Any seminar or meeting whose attendees have been invited by any general solicitation or general advertising.

General solicitation is allowed for registered (public) offerings, but not for private placements. By their nature, private placements must be sold to a limited number of investors. If the company or its principals have a pre-existing relationship with those persons to whom the offering is made, then prohibitions against general solicitation do not apply.

Consequently, an investor meeting could be held to discuss the offer, as long as the attendees were not solicited through general advertising and the company or its principals had a preexisting relationship with the attendees.

Do not post a PPM on your company's website. Allowing unrestricted access to your PPM on the Internet is a proven way of receiving a warning letter from the enforcement division of the SEC or your state securities administrator. It is viewed as a violation of the prohibition against general solicitation and advertising. You can post your PPM on the Internet if (1) the offering is to accredited investors only who have completed an investor questionnaire and (2) they have been prescreened by the company prior to being given access to the PPM. Access to the PPM should be password-protected with a record kept of all persons to whom access is granted. Registered offerings, which are not subject to the general solicitation rules, can be sold through the Internet under certain circumstances.

HOW TO...Sell Securities in a Private Placement

❑ Prepare a private placement memorandum with appropriate appendices and a subscription agreement.
❑ File a Form D with the SEC and then file with each state in which a purchaser lives.
❑ Filing fees may be charged in any of the states, and they may require a U-2—consent to service of process—be filed.

Limitations on Resale of Securities. Securities purchased in a private placement offering are restricted securities. They cannot be freely transferred or resold. A restrictive legend should be included in the PPM and on the actual certificate for the shares being purchased that states:

> *The securities represented hereby have not been registered under the Securities Act of 1933, as amended (the Act) and may not be offered, sold, or otherwise hypothecated unless and until registered under the Act; or in the opinion of counsel, in form and substance satisfactory to the issuer of these securities, such offer, sale or transfer, pledge, or hypothecation is in compliance with the Act.*

Under Rule 144, a one-year holding period is the minimum required period for resale of restricted securities subject to certain volume restrictions. After two years, the security may be traded without limitation unless you are an officer, director, or more then 5% shareholder. In that case, you continue to be subject to the volume restrictions of Rule 144 until you no longer occupy any of those positions for more than ninety days. This information is relatively useless to shareholders of nonpublic companies, since there is no market for their securities anyway. The restrictions of Rule 144 only apply to brokerage trades of securities (sales in the public markets). You can sell or transfer restricted securities in a private (nonbrokered) transaction as long as there is a private sale exemption available.

The issuer must take reasonable steps to inform investors that they are purchasing restricted securities, that they are acquiring the securities for their own purposes, and that they are not buying the securities with the intention of reselling or transferring them. Normally, the investor makes these representations in the subscription documents or in the investor letter.

The Sale of Securities and the Issuer Exemption

Once you have decided to sell securities in your company, you can sell them yourself under what is called an *issuer's exemption* or you can engage a licensed broker-dealer to sell for you. Federal and state securities laws require people who sell securities to be licensed unless an exemption from licensure exists.

Federal securities rules permit any partner, officer, director, or employee of an issuer of the securities to make and accept offers to purchase securities, as long as that person:

- is not disqualified from selling securities for another reason;
- does not receive commissions or other remuneration based directly or indirectly on the sale of the securities;
- is not a broker or dealer, or an associated person of a broker or dealer of securities, at the time of the offering or within twelve months preceding the offering of securities;
- primarily performs, or is intended to primarily perform, at the end of the offering, substantial duties for or on behalf of the issuer otherwise than in connection with the transaction of securities; and,
- does not participate in selling an offering of securities for any issuer more than once every twelve months.

Most states have a comparable provision to the federal issuer's exemption.

If the company engages a licensed broker-dealer, they customarily enter into a placement agreement that sets forth the terms of the selling engagement. Broker-dealers are licensed with the *National Association of Securities Dealers* (NASD) and with the states in which they conduct business.

Some companies enlist individuals or companies to act as finders of potential investors. Finders are under the same limitation as issuers in that they can only approach people with whom they have had a preexisting relationship. Finders can only refer leads to the company and cannot offer the securities or discuss the offering with any prospective investor. If finders receive referral fees based upon a percentage of the amount raised, they run the risk of being regarded as unlicensed brokers under federal and state securities laws.

Alert!

The legitimate use of a finder depends upon the law of the state where the investor resides. Some states allow a limited use of finders, while others are stridently opposed to finders. Check with that state's securities administrator and work with an attorney experienced in securities law before using a finder.

Integration of Offerings

One of the limitations with a Rule 506 offering is that you are limited to thirty-five nonaccredited purchasers in any one offering, and you cannot get around this limitation by creating multiple offerings, of smaller portions. When two or more offerings are substantially similar, the SEC treats them as a single *integrated* offering and applies the thirty-five person limitation to the combined offerings. The following are the factors to consider when deciding whether two offerings will be integrated.

- Are the different offerings part of a single plan of financing?
- Are the offerings offering the same type of security?
- Are the offerings made at or about the same time?
- Is the same type of consideration to be received in both?
- Are the offerings made for the same general purpose?

The best way to avoid having two offerings integrated is to either offer substantially different types of securities in subsequent offerings that are close together in time or wait six months between offerings. The six month rule—no securities sold six months before or six months after—is another *safe harbor provision*. If you meet the time requirements of the safe harbor rule, you do not have to consider the factors mentioned and you are free to offer a similar or identical security.

If your company seeks to raise several million dollars in a private placement, holding to the thirty-five nonaccredited limitation can become problematic. As a possible strategy, the company could stage the total capital raise in phases, six months apart, to avoid integration. Integration is only an issue with the number of nonaccredited investors since Regulation D allows an unlimited amount of accredited investors. If, for example, your second or third round is sold to accredited investors only, the issue of integration does not arise.

Offering different types of securities is another viable solution. For example, sell common stock in your first offering. Close that offering and then open a second offering selling a class of preferred stock.

QUICK Tip

Avoid Integration Problems: The best way to avoid integration is to wait six months between rounds of raising capital. Alternatively, sell a different security, such as preferred stock after common stock, or a debt instrument so the two offerings are very different from one another.

State Securities (Blue Sky) Laws

Blue sky laws is the term given to the myriad state regulations that are written to protect investors. The term *blue sky* originated in the early 1900s when a Supreme Court justice declared his desire to protect investors from speculative ventures that had "as much value as a patch of blue sky." In the United States legal system, there are federal and state statutes that regulate the sale of securities. With the one possible exception, both federal and state securities laws must be considered in an offering.

When selling a security in a private placement, the company must find an exemption at both the federal and state level. Some state exemptions mirror federal exemptions, and other state exemptions are unique to the state. Exemptions are not mutually exclusive, such that an offering may be able to claim multiple exemptions.

State securities laws regulate the sale of securities within their borders. When determining which state securities law applies, look to the state in which the purchaser resides. It makes no difference whether you sell a security to a Texas resident while attending a meeting in California—Texas blue sky laws apply.

Exemptions from registration of securities vary among the states, but there is some common ground. Most state exemptions allow for ten purchasers during any twelve-month period, if the seller reasonably believes the buyer is purchasing for investment (as opposed to wanting to resell the securities) and no commission or other remuneration is paid for soliciting any buyer. Most states set a dollar limit on these exemptions and require a disclosure document to be drafted, and as always, antifraud provisions apply. Also, these state transactional exemptions are not mutually exclusive, so you may qualify for one or more at the same time. Check with your state securities administration or an attorney experienced in securities offerings before undertaking any offering of securities.

Notice Filings of Securities

The *National Securities Market Improvement Act of 1996* preempted state registration provisions for transactions that are exempt from registration under Rule 506 of Regulation D of the Securities Act of 1933, but allowed the states to preserve notice filing requirements that are substantially similar to the Rule 506 requirements.

Notice of a Rule 506 offering is accomplished by completing and filing Form D, *Notice of Sale of Securities Pursuant to Regulation D*, which gives the contact information of the company selling the securities and the details of the offering, to the Securities and Exchange Commission (SEC) in Washington, D.C., and filing a copy of the Form D with each state in which a sale of securities is made. Naturally, the states charge a fee for this notice filing that varies from state to state.

Most states also require the filing of Form U-2, *Uniform Consent to Service of Process*, which designates the state securities administrator as the person to contact for any complaints lodged against the company selling securities.

A few states also require Form U-2A, *Uniform Corporate Resolution*, to be filed stating that a corporation's board of directors authorized the sale of the securities.

The following is a comprehensive list of the forms and fees required by the SEC and each state for notice filings under Regulation D, Rule 506. With the exception of Hawaii and New York, all notice filings are made after the first sale of securities in the state. If no sales are made, then no filing is required.

Alert!

Both federal and state statutes change frequently, particularly filing fee amendments, so it is advisable to check for current information before filing any document.

Figure 5.2: **SECURITIES AND EXCHANGE COMMISSION**

Federal

File one original and four copies of Form D no later than fifteen days after the first sale of securities. There is no filing fee.

Alabama

File Form D, Form U-2, and the Offering Documents with the Alabama Securities Commission along with a *certified or cashier's check* for $250 made out to State Securities Commissioner of Alabama no later than fifteen days after the first sale of securities in the state.

Alaska

File Form D and Form U-2 with State Appendix with the Department of Commerce and Economic Development, Division of Banking, Securities and Corporations along with a check for $600 made out to State of Alaska no later than fifteen days after the sale of securities in the state. The notice filing must be renewed every twelve months.

Arizona

File Form D with the Arizona Corporation Commission, Securities Division along with a check for $250 made out to Securities Division, Arizona Corporation Commission no later than fifteen days after the first sale of securities in the state.

Arkansas

File Form D with the Arkansas Securities Department along with a fee of ⅒ of 1% of the maximum aggregate offering price at which the securities would be offered in Arkansas, with minimum and maximum fees of $100 and $500, respectively, in the form of a check made out to Arkansas Securities Department no later than fifteen days after the first sale of securities in the state.

California

File Form D, Form U-2, and the statement, "This filing is pursuant to Rule 506 and §18(b)(4)(d) of the Securities Act of 1933," with the California Department of Corporations along with a check for $150 made out to California Department of Corporations no later than fifteen days after the first sale of securities in the state.

Colorado	Even though it is not required to make a notice filing in Colorado unless the issuer makes more than ten sales in Colorado, it is strongly recommended that a notice filing be made with the first sale of securities just to let them know that you are making sales in Colorado under Rule 506. File Form D and a cover letter with the Colorado Department of Regulatory Agencies, Division of Securities along with a check in the amount of $75 made out to the Colorado State Treasurer.
Connecticut	File Form D and Form U-2 with the Department of Banking, Securities and Business Investments Division along with a check in the amount of $150 made out to the Connecticut State Treasurer no later than fifteen days after the first sale of securities in the state. In addition, file Connecticut Sales Agent/Broker/Dealer Licensing Questionnaire.
Delaware	File Form D with State Appendix and Form U-2 with the Secretary of State no later than fifteen days after first sale of securities in the state. There is no notice filing fee in Delaware.
District of Columbia	File Form D and Form U-2 with the Division of Securities, Department of Insurance and Securities Regulation along with a check for $250 made out to DC Treasurer no later than fifteen days after first sale of securities in the District.
Florida	There is no notice filing requirement in Florida if you are an issuer-dealer or if it is a limited offering defined as no more than thirty-five nonaccredited purchasers with no advertising.
Georgia	File Form D and Form U-2 with the Georgia Office of Secretary of State, Securities and Business Regulation along with a check in the amount of $250 made out to the Secretary of State no later than fifteen days after the first sale of securities in the state.
Hawaii	File Form D with State Appendix, Form U-2, and Form U-2A with the Hawaii Department of Commerce and Consumer Affairs along with a

continued

check or money order in the amount of $200 made out to the Commissioner of Securities, State of Hawaii not later than ten days after the first *offer* of securities in the state.

Idaho

File Form D and Form U-2 with the Idaho Department of Finance along with a $50 check made out to the Idaho Department of Finance no later than fifteen days after the first sale of securities in the state.

Illinois

File Form D with the Illinois Secretary of State, Securities Department along with a check in the amount of $100 made out to the Secretary of State of Illinois no later than fifteen days after the first sale of securities in the state.

Indiana

File Form D and Form U-2 with the Indiana Office of Secretary of State, Securities Division no later than fifteen days after the first sale of securities in the state. There is no notice filing fee in Indiana.

Iowa

File Form D with State Appendix and Form U-2 with the Iowa Division of Insurance, Securities Bureau along with a check or money order in the amount of $100 made out to the Insurance Commissioner of Iowa no later than fifteen days after the first sale of securities in the state.

Kansas

File Form D with the Kansas Office of Securities Commissioner along with a check or money order in the amount of $100 made out to the Securities Commissioner of Kansas no later than fifteen days after the first sale of securities in the state.

Kentucky

File Form D and Form U-2 with the Kentucky Department of Financial Institutions along with a check in the amount of $250 made out to Kentucky State Treasurer no later than fifteen days after the first sale of securities from or into Kentucky.

Louisiana

File Form D, Form U-2, and Form U-2A with the Louisiana Commissioner of Securities along with a check in the amount of $300 made out to the Louisiana Commissioner of Securities no later than fifteen days after the first sale of securities in the state.

Maine	File Form D with State Appendix and Form U-2 with the Maine Securities Administrator along with a check in the amount of $300 made out to Maine Securities Administrator no later than fifteen days after the first sale of securities in the state.
Maryland	File Form D and Form U-2 with the Maryland Office of Attorney General, Division of Securities along with a check in the amount of $100 made out to the Office of the Attorney General no later than fifteen days after the first sale of securities in the state.
Massachusetts	File Form D with the Massachusetts Secretary of the Commonwealth, Securities Division along with a check (no personal checks) or money order made out to the Commonwealth of Massachusetts according to the following schedule no later than fifteen days after the first sale of securities in the state.

Less than $2,000,000 = $250
$2,000,000–$7,500,000 = $500
More than $7,500,000 = $750

Michigan	File Form D and Form U-2 with the Michigan Department of Consumer and Industry Services, Corporation, Securities and Land Development Bureau along with a check or money order in the amount of $100 made out to the State of Michigan no later than fifteen days after the first sale of securities in the state.
Minnesota	File Form D and Form U-2 with the Minnesota Department of Commerce along with a check or money order in the amount of $50 made out to the State Treasurer no later than fifteen days after the first sale of securities in the state.
Mississippi	File Form D with State Appendix with the Mississippi Office of Secretary of State, Business Services Division along with a check or money order in the amount of $300 made out to the Secretary of State no later than fifteen days after the first sale of securities in the state.

continued

Missouri	File Form D and Form U-2 with the Missouri Office of the Secretary of State along with a check or money order in the amount of $100 made out to the Director of Revenue, State of Missouri no later than fifteen days after the first sale of securities in the state.
Montana	File Form D and Form U-2 with the Montana State Auditor's Office, Securities Department along with cash or negotiable instrument in the amount of $200 for the first $100,000 of initial issue or portion thereof in Montana, based on the offering price, plus $\frac{1}{10}$ of 1% of any excess over $100,000, with a maximum fee of $1,000 made out to the Montana State Auditor, Securities Commissioner no later than fifteen days after the first sale of securities in the state.
Nebraska	File Form D and Form U-2 with the Nebraska Department of Banking and Finance, Bureau of Securities along with a corporate check or money order in the amount of $200 made out to Department of Banking and Finance no later than thirty days after the first sale of securities in the state.
Nevada	File Form D with State Appendix with the Nevada Secretary of State, Securities Division along with a cashier's check, certified check, or money order in the amount of $300 made out to the Secretary of State no later than fifteen days after the first sale of securities in the state.
New Hampshire	File Form D with State Appendix, Form U-2, and Form U-4 (if no broker-dealer is used) (just pages 2, 3, and 4 and original signature, no CRD # required) with the New Hampshire Secretary of State along with a check in the amount of $500 made out to the State of New Hampshire no later than fifteen days after the first sale of securities in the state.
New Jersey	File Form D and Form U-2 with the New Jersey Department of Law and Public Safety, Division of Consumer Affairs along with a check or money order in the amount of $250 made out to the State

of New Jersey, Bureau of Securities no later than fifteen days after the first sale of securities in the state. Form U-2 should appoint the Chief of the Bureau of Securities as the Attorney for Service of Process.

New Mexico

File Form D with State Appendix and Form U-2 with the Regulation & Licensing Department, Securities Division along with a check in the amount of $350 made out to the Securities Division, State of New Mexico no later than fifteen days after the first sale of securities in the state.

New York

Prior to any offer or sale of securities in or from New York:

1. New York State Department of Law. File an original NY Form 99, a copy of Form U-2 (if an out of state issuer), and a copy of State Notices form with the New York Department of Law along with a certified check or money order according to the following schedule made out to the New York State Department of Law:

> Less than $500,000 = $500
> More than $500,000 = $1,200

2. New York State Department of State. File a copy of NY Form 99, an original Form U-2 (if an out of state issuer), and an original State Notices form with the New York State Department of State along with a certified check or money order in the amount of $75 made out to the New York State Department of State and a certified check or money order in the amount of $35 made out to the New York State Department of State for the filing of the Form U-2.

North Carolina

File Form D and Form U-2 with the Department of the Secretary of State, Securities Division along with a certified check or money order in the amount of $350 made out to the Office of the Secretary of State no later than fifteen days after the first sale of securities in the state.

continued

North Dakota	File Form D and Form U-2 with the North Dakota Office of Securities Commissioner along with a check (no personal checks) in the amount of $100 made out to North Dakota Securities Commissioner no later than fifteen days after the first sale of securities in the state.
Ohio	File Form D with State Appendix with the Ohio Department of Commerce, Division of Securities and Form U-2 with the Ohio Secretary of State along with a check or money order in the amount of $100 made out to the Division of Securities no later than fifteen days after the first sale of securities in the state.
Oklahoma	File Form D, Form U-2, and Form U-2A with the Oklahoma Securities Department along with a check in the amount of $250 made out to the Oklahoma Securities Department no later than fifteen days after the first sale of securities in the state.
Oregon	File Form D with State Appendix with the Oregon Department of Consumer & Business Services, Division of Finance and Corporate Securities along with a check in the amount of $225 made out to the Department of Consumer & Business Services no later than fifteen days after the first sale of securities in the state.
Pennsylvania	File Form D with the Pennsylvania Securities Division along with a check in the amount of $500 made out to the Commonwealth of Pennsylvania no later than fifteen days after the first sale of securities in the state.
Rhode Island	File Form D and Form U-2 with the Rhode Island Department of Business Regulation, Securities Division along with a bank draft or certified check in the amount of $300 made out to the Department of Business Regulation—Securities Division no later than fifteen days after the first sale of securities in the state.
South Carolina	File Form D and Form U-2 with the South Carolina Office of the Attorney General, Division of Securities

along with a certified check, or cashier's check in the amount of $300 made out to the Attorney General of South Carolina no later than fifteen days after the first sale of securities in the state.

South Dakota   File Form D and Form U-2 with the South Dakota Department of Commerce and Regulation, Division of Securities along with a check, certified check, or postal money order in the amount of $200 made out to the Division of Securities no later than fifteen days after the first sale of securities in the state.

Tennessee   File Form D with State Appendix, Form U-2 and a copy of the offering documents with the Tennessee Department of Commerce and Insurance, Division of Securities along with a check in the amount of $500 made out to the Department of Commerce and Insurance no later than fifteen days after the first sale of securities in the state.

Texas   File Form D with State Appendix and Form U-2 with the Texas Securities Board along with certified check, cashier's check, or money order in the amount of $\frac{1}{10}$ of 1% of total offering (maximum fee of $500) made out to the State Securities Board no later than fifteen days after the first sale of securities in the state.

Utah   File Form D with State Appendix and Form U-2 with the Utah Department of Commerce, Division of Securities along with a check in the amount of $60 made out to the Division of Securities no later than fifteen days after the first sale of securities in the state.

Vermont   File Form D with State Appendix and Form U-2 with the Vermont Department of Banking, Insurance, Securities and Health Care Administration along with a check or money order in the amount of $1.00 for each $1,000 of the aggregate amount of the offering, with minimum and maximum fees of $400 and $1,250 made out to Treasurer of State of Vermont no later than fifteen days after the first sale of securities in the state.

continued

Virginia	File Form D with State Appendix and Form U-2 with the Virginia State Corporation Commission, Division of Securities and Retail Franchising along with a check or money order in the amount of $250 made out to the Treasurer of Virginia no later than fifteen days after the first sale of securities in the state.
Washington	File Form D and Form U-2 with the Washington Department of Financial Institutions, Securities Division along with a check in the amount of $300 made out to the State Treasurer no later than fifteen days after the first sale of securities in the state.
West Virginia	File Form D and Form U-2 with the West Virginia State Auditor, Securities Division along with a check or money order in the amount of $250 made out to State Auditor no later than fifteen days after the first sale of securities in the state.
Wisconsin	File Form D with State Appendix with the Wisconsin Department of Financial Institutions, Securities Division along with a check in the amount of $200 made out to Office of Commissioner of Securities no later than fifteen days after the first sale of securities in the state.
Wyoming	File Form D and Form U-2 with the Wyoming Secretary of State, Securities Division along with a check in the amount of $200 made out to Secretary of State no later than fifteen days after the first sale of securities in the state.

Rule 504 and 505 Offerings

Federal Regulation D actually contains provisions for three types of limited offerings in Rules 504, 505, and 506. Rule 504 contains an exemption for an offering up to $1,000,000 in securities by an issuer during any twelve month period. No specific disclosures are required, but the company is still subject to the antifraud rules. In addition, purchasers do not have to meet any sophistication test and there is no limitation on the number of purchasers. Rule 504 also allows a limited solicitation of investors; however, most states do not permit solicitation without first registering the offering in the state so the relaxation of this solicitation rules at the federal level is of little practical use.

While no specific disclosures are required under Rule 504, it is better practice to provide full disclosure to investors to avoid later misunderstandings. Unlike Rule 505 and 506, for which states adopted similar rules, the states did not adopt rules similar to Rule 504—so the exemption at the state level is of limited use unless the company files a full state registration or uses a SCOR offering. Typically, a Rule 504 offering would, in the absence of a state registration or SCOR compliance, have to rely on limited state exemptions, such as the ten or under rule, found in most state blue sky statutes.

Rule 505 offerings are limited to $5,000,000 in any twelve-month period. A disclosure document is required if you sell to any nonaccredited investors and you are required to provide financial statements to investors. You are also limited to thirty-five nonaccredited investors and an unlimited number of accredited investors, but there are no defined purchaser qualifications.

While there are no qualifications required for purchasers under Rule 505, it is the best practice to ensure that all nonaccredited purchasers meet the qualifications established under federal Regulation D—that they have such knowledge and experience in financial and business matters that they are capable of evaluating the merits and risks of the prospective investment.

When the National Securities Market Improvement Act came along in 1996, Rule 506 became the dominant and preferred choice among companies offering securities under an exemption from registration because of the standardized disclosure standards and uniform notice filing procedures, and Rule 504 and 505 offerings declined because their perceived advantages were outweighed by their disadvantages.

SCOR Offerings

Most states have adopted a shortened registration form for limited offerings being registered at the state level called the *Small Corporate Offering Registration* form (SCOR). The SCOR offering is the response of the states to the federal Rule 504 offering.

A SCOR offering, which is conducted pursuant to Rule 504 at the federal level, allows companies to raise up to one million dollars by selling securities to the general public, and the disclosure and registration requirements are encompassed in one document, Form U-7, in a question-and-answer format. The offering price for securities in a SCOR offering must be at least $5.00 per share, which precludes most small companies from conducting a SCOR offering.

Figure 5.3: STATES ADOPTING SCOR REGISTRATION

The following states have either adopted the SCOR registration program or recognize and accept Form U-7 filings under a state offering exemption.

Alaska	Missouri
Arizona	Montana
Arkansas	Nevada
California	New Hampshire
Colorado	New Jersey
Connecticut	New Mexico
Delaware	North Carolina
District of Columbia	North Dakota
Florida	Ohio
Georgia	Oklahoma
Hawaii	Oregon
Idaho	Pennsylvania
Illinois	Rhode Island
Indiana	South Carolina
Iowa	South Dakota
Kansas	Tennessee
Kentucky	Texas
Louisiana	Utah
Maine	Vermont
Maryland	Virginia
Massachusetts	Washington
Michigan	West Virginia
Minnesota	Wisconsin
Mississippi	Wyoming

To conduct a SCOR offering, an issuer must obtain the approval of each state where it intends to selles securities, which is sometimes a lengthy process. To alleviate some of this burden, some states have banded together into regional review groups, in which one state will take the lead on reviewing a SCOR offering and the rest of the states in the region acknowledge the lead state's approval once it is granted. In addition, Alabama, Nebraska, and New York have not adopted the SCOR offering.

The use of SCOR offerings has not been as widespread as was intended. This may be because of the lack of uniformity in the states' review processes. SCOR was designed to create a simplification of the small issue registration process, but the disclosure requirements of the Form U-7 and review process belies that admirable goal. Any registration of a SCOR offering requires a review by one or more state securities administrators, which increases the time and effort it takes for an issuer to make an offering.

QUICK Tip

Put Form U-7 to Work for You: While the promise of simplified state registrations under SCOR may not have lived up to their intended potential, the Form U-7 SCOR offering form is an excellent checklist and guide for reference when drafting a disclosure document for any offering of securities.

Regulation A Offerings

Regulation A offerings are small public offerings—limited to $5,000,000 during any twelve-month period. In addition, Regulation A offerings allow an unlimited number of investors, permit general solicitation of investors, and have no qualification standards for investors. The Form U-7, which was developed for use with SCOR offerings, may also be used for a Regulation A offering.

You are required to file a registration statement with the SEC that includes two years of unaudited financial statements. Regulation A offerings are reviewed by the SEC like any other public offerings, and must be cleared or declared effective by the SEC before they can be sold. The SEC review process could take three to six months from the date of filing, and therefore, increases the costs to the company and amount of time associated with starting to raise capital.

Follow-up and Closing an Offering

Once you have made a sale of securities to an investor, there are essential record keeping requirements. The following are some guidelines for keeping accurate records of your securities offering.

❑ When a sale of securities appears imminent, check the notice filing requirements of the state in order to have timely filings.

❑ Open a separate file on each investor. In that file, place the completed subscription documents, copies of the check you received from the investor, and any correspondence with the investor.

❑ Check the subscription documents for completeness and make certain they contain all of the information requested. Also, be certain they have been signed in all appropriate places. In particular, make sure the investor has noted whether they are an accredited investor.

❑ When you have accepted the subscription, sign it in the appropriate place, keep the original document, and send a photocopy and the investor's stock certificate (or LLC membership unit certificate) to the investor. You should also send a welcome letter.

❑ Keep a master list of investors, including the names, addresses, Social Security numbers, dates and amounts of purchases, number of shares or units purchased, and whether the investor is accredited or nonaccredited.

❑ End the offering of securities on a specific documented date and close it out.

❑ Send periodic reports to the investors including financial reports.

Your shareholder database can be an important source of referrals for accredited investors. If you keep investors informed about the progress of the company and they are satisfied with their investment, you can return to them for further offerings.

Chapter 6

Licensing and Franchising

▶ **Licensing**

▶ **Franchising**

▶ **Business Opportunities**

There are ways of growing your business that use neither equity nor debt financing. Those methods include licensing your product or franchising your operation. The manner in which to engage in these activities is beyond the scope of this book, but some background is useful as you plan for the future.

Licensing

Some businesses develop a proprietary product, but do not necessarily want to pursue manufacturing and distribution for that product. In that case, your company may wish to pursue a licensing opportunity for the product. In the licensing scenario, you or your company would grant a license to the licensee for a period of years with a royalty back to you or your company. Licensing royalties can be based upon gross or net revenues, an amount per unit, or other variations. When you license your intellectual property, you do not transfer your ownership rights, just the rights to commercially exploit the property.

Once you grant a license, you are giving up some degree of control over your property and how it will be brought to market. You should perform due diligence on the prospective licensee to determine their financial history and success in bringing products to market. Licensing can get your product to market quicker, but that must be balanced against your loss of quality control and dependence on the skills of third parties.

Licensing agreements can be drafted either broadly or narrowly, depending upon the desires of the parties and their relative bargaining strengths. For example, the license may cover a specific geographical territory or only apply to one of the several applications of the product. This cautionary approach is particularly applicable in the case of merchandise and character licensing, in which the license is granted to a manufacturer of consumer goods for using a recognized trademark or copyright, for example, in the merchandising of the Disney characters. Care must be taken in drafting license agreements that closely resemble franchises because you may be dealing with a *hidden franchise* that can lead to many legal headaches.

Technology licenses typically join the inventor/licensor with the company/licensee that has the financial resources and marketing clout to bring the product to market. A technology transfer agreement may transfer the intellectual property rights with the understanding that the rights can come back or revert to the licensor if the licensee fails to meet its obligations and objectives set forth in the agreement.

License to Success: Licensing is ultimately a way to finance your product to market without having to raise your own capital. Many successful companies have used licensing as their entire revenue model, and have never manufactured or distributed products on their own.

Franchising

Franchising is a well-known means of expanding your business while transferring operational responsibilities to franchisees. The originating company, known as the franchisor, builds its brand under one or more trademarks or designs, documents a proprietary delivery system for its product or service, and develops a training program for its prospective franchisees. The franchisor generates income by the payment of franchise fees and an ongoing royalty.

Alert!

Most companies should not undertake a franchise strategy until the business system is fully established and successfully operating in at least one location.

The *Federal Trade Commission* (FTC) defines a franchise using three components: (1) the franchisee's goods and services are offered and sold under the franchisor's trademarks; (2) the franchisee is required to make a minimum payment of $500 to the franchisor; and, (3) the franchisor exercises significant control over or provides significant assistance to the franchisee's method of operation. The states have variations on the definition of a franchise, and you must comply with the laws of each state where you are selling franchises.

From a legal standpoint, the franchisor, through counsel, prepares a *franchise disclosure document* and *franchise agreement*. The franchise disclosure document, known as the *Uniform Franchise Offering Circular* (UFOC), is similar to a PPM. You can obtain a copy of the UFOC and other information pertaining to franchise registration from the *North American Securities Administrators Association* website at **www.nasaa.org**. From the main menu pull down chart, navigate to the corporation finance page and click the UFOC link on the left. The UFOC requires audited financial statements of the franchisor, so it is best to organize your accounting systems from the start to be ready for the eventual audit.

Unlike licensing, franchises are regulated by the states to varying degrees and by the FTC at the federal level. The FTC prescribes certain minimum disclosure standards and the states may require differing amounts of additional disclosures. At present, fifteen states regulate the offer and sale of franchises. In those states, the franchise must be cleared by the state before offers or sales can be made. Once your franchise is launched, there are ongoing state compliance issues that must be addressed and monitored very carefully.

Many franchisors choose to grant area franchise arrangements where, for example, multiple territories or whole states are granted to certain franchisee's subject to certain performance standards, such as opening a certain number of units per year. International franchise operations are another way to expand a domestic franchise network.

Franchisors may charge an up-front franchise fee in addition to a royalty payment, and perhaps a cooperative advertising fee as well. The entire process of designing and marketing a viable franchise and properly documenting its legal requirements is a substantial undertaking. There are companies, such as **www.ifranchise.com**, that provide consulting services for franchises, and resource websites, such as **www.franchise.com,** that provide information on franchising requirements. You should also visit the website of the *International Franchise Association* at **www.franchise.org**.

 **SBA Opportunities:** The SBA is a financing source for prospective franchise owners if the franchise system meets the SBA Eligibility Guidelines.

Business Opportunities

Business opportunities are a close cousin to franchising and *multilevel marketing* (MLM) opportunities. A business opportunity typically involves the sale or lease of products or services to a purchaser to enable that person to start a business. Picture a vending machine business. The seller may provide assistance in identifying locations or customer leads and providing supplies to the purchaser. Business opportunity sellers typically make some guarantee that the purchaser will derive more income from the business than was paid for it, and require the payment of a sum of money by the purchaser, usually under $500.

Nineteen states have business opportunity laws that generally require the seller to file a registration statement and a disclosure document similar to UFOC for franchises. Some states require a bond be posted.

Chapter 7

Friends, Angels, and Venture Capital Sources

- ▶ **Friends and Family**
- ▶ **Angels**
- ▶ **Venture Capital**
- ▶ **What They Look For**
- ▶ **Valuation**
- ▶ **Angel Networks and Entrepreneurial Forums**

Investors in your small business can take many forms. Generally, investors want a return on their investment, and seek to help guarantee that return by having some say in how the company is managed. This may be informal with some friendly advice, or a complicated agreement and ownership structure with a venture capitalist. Regardless of the arrangement, these sources can provide the financial backing you need to be a success.

Friends and Family

Friends and family are the most common source for early seed financing. At the outset of your business, they are making an investment in you as much as in your company.

You may need funds prior to actually incorporating your business, in which case the investment may take the form of borrowing from friends or family. In that case, you will need a simple *promissory note* to evidence the borrowing. You may want to include a provision in the note that the principal (and possibly the interest) can be converted into equity in your company at the option of the lender. You will probably not know the terms of investment yet, so you may wish to state that the conversion rate would be some percentage—for example, 80%—of the price the company will offer to new investors once it is organized and ready to legally raise capital.

Friends and family investors can be a mixed blessing. If you think it would be best to take out family and friends as early as possible to eliminate future problems, then you can merely pay back the promissory note when you have raised sufficient capital in your company. It is far cleaner for tax purposes if you organize the entity you are going to use and then have the new entity be the borrower rather than you personally. A variation on this theme would be to pay the notes back and give the lender a small *equity kicker* (shares of stock or membership units) in appreciation for their early support.

Angels

Angel investors are high net worth individuals who invest in emerging companies. Like celestial angels, they can be tricky to find. Typically, they tend to invest in companies in their own geographic area and will conduct varying degrees of due diligence on the company.

There are numerous angel clubs or gatherings around the country. These groups meet monthly, sometimes weekly, to hear presentations of emerging companies. In the meetings, the companies make their pitch in a twenty- to thirty-minute presentation with a few minutes for questions and answers afterwards. If any of the angel investors are interested, they follow up with the companies individually. In the height of the tech boom, some of the angel groups formed investment clubs that would review emerging companies and then invest as a group, usually through an investment partnership.

There are different kinds of angel investors. Target those that fit your current needs.

Figure 7.1: ANGEL INVESTORS

A sampling of the types of angel investors follows.

- *Retirement Investor.* This type of investor comes from senior management of a larger company and may be looking to contribute to the new company at the same level. They may be using their early retirement or pension funds to invest.

- *Value Added Investor.* These are seed investors who generally remain in the background but are very active when problems arise. They tend to invest in the $250,000 range.

- *Professional Angels.* These investors come from the traditional professions—lawyers, doctors, and accountants. Normally, they rely on the due diligence (investigation) of other parties for their investments, and tend to invest in companies that have a product or service in their professional arena. They generally do not get very involved with the business.

- *Manager Investors.* These investors may be available because of corporate downsizing. They are interested in contributing to the active management of the company with their skills. In effect, their investment is like buying back their last job. If you are short on the management side, these investors are valuable.

continued

- *Entrepreneurial Investors.* This category is the *classic* angel investor who are successful entrepreneurs and want to reinvest those profits in a variety of companies. They tend to be the largest and most active of the groups of angels.

- *Socially Responsible Investors.* The socially conscious investor tends to be a nurturing investor whose values align with those of the company to create a melding of values. This type of investor may use screens to evaluate his or her investment. For example, they may have a screen for environmentally friendly products and services.

- *Family Investors.* This type of investor represents a family unit that makes selective investments. Usually, there is one person representing the family who negotiates the investment on behalf of the group. (Family-type investors are common in the Asian community.)

- *Barter-Based Investor.* Many start-up companies need equipment and services that they will have to purchase in the marketplace from the capital they raise. You may be able to barter for the necessary equipment by exchanging equity for the goods or services. This arrangement works particularly well where you are designing an application to run on a device like a Nokia cell phone or a PalmPilot. An investment by the manufacturer of the target device could be a natural fit as barter investor.

Venture Capital

Venture capital sources are easier to identify than angels, but harder to close. Many firms and individuals call themselves venture capitalists, but they are in fact brokers who present deals to individuals or companies who invest. True venture capitalists are individuals who manage a fund that invests in particular types of businesses.

Typically, a venture fund will raise money from high net worth investors, usually in the form of a private equity fund, and then invest that fund in promising businesses. The fund has its own money, and in order to receive funding, you and your company must go through an extensive due diligence process. If you pass muster, the fund will offer you a term sheet, which can be negotiated up to a point, and then you will proceed to the signing of a stock purchase agreement in order to complete funding. Venture capital firms tend to specialize in industry sectors and some may only fund companies beyond the start-up stage.

Venture capital money is expensive and relatively hard to get. A venture fund expects a return, of five to ten times its invested money. It needs this type of return, because 70%–90% of the businesses it funds will fail or only be marginally successful. The advantage of dealing with venture capital is that is tends to attach other venture capital and provide funds for subsequent stages of growth. It also can provide interim management talent and quickly ramp up a company for the public offering—if the market is available.

A listing of venture capital funds is available in *Pratt's Guide to Venture Capital Sources*, Thompson Financial Services at 800-455-5844, or the *Dictionary of Venture Capital*, by Catherine Lister and John Harnish, John Wiley & Sons, 1996. Your company will have a distinct advantage in obtaining venture funds if you have a contact with the fund you are approaching. Always check to see what kind of companies the venture fund invests in before you submit your business plan.

Investor Funding Range: The funding ranges for various categories of investors look something like this:

Friends/Family	$100–$200,000
Business Angels	$200–$500,000
Venture Capitalists	$500,000–$2M
Private Equity Fund Managers	$5M+
IPO/Investment Bankers	$20M+

What They Look For

Here are some of the factors that angels and venture capital firms may use in evaluating your business. Even if you are not seeking venture capital funding, you should consider these factors.

- *Feasibility.* Do you have a sound product, a defined market, and a means to bring the product to market? Some companies define their market too broadly or cite volumes of meaningless industry market size and growth data.

- *Scalability.* Is the business scalable? What is the company's potential for growth? Can the business be ramped up to a larger market or is the market small by definition? Is it a lifestyle business like a small restaurant? (You can still raise capital but not from a venture capitalist.) What is the size of the market and will it accept your product?

- *Experienced Management.* Does the management have sufficient experience to implement its business plan? Is this a situation of running vs. learning? Is the inexperience of management partially offset by the depth of the board of directors or advisory board?

- *Market Risk.* Is the market risk of the business acceptable? What are the risk reducers that come into play here?

- *Viable Exit Strategy.* Does the company have a viable exit strategy? How are the investors going to realize a substantial return and how long is their investment going to be *illiquid*? For example, is the company's exit strategy to have a public offering or merger within five to ten years?

- *Value Engine.* What are the basic economics of the business? How conversant is the management with the industry and its economics? What is the channel of distribution? Is the distribution channel already established or is *missionary selling* necessary to establish the channel?

- *Intellectual or Human Capital.* What is the raw intellectual capability of the company? There has been a recent trend to assess the human capital in an organization. Remember that, notwithstanding your beautiful business plan, smart investors invest in people, not plans.

- *Commitment.* What is your commitment to the project? Do you have the ability and the motivation to give the intense focus necessary to make this company happen? If not, all the other factors are irrelevant. How are you sharing in the risk? Do you have your own money in the company?

Figure 7.2: FUNDRAISING: A REAL WORLD EXAMPLE

Eric Delisle is the former CEO of Digibelly, Inc., an innovative software firm that provided websites and e-commerce solutions to small businesses. In raising capital for his company, this is what he learned.

One of the most important things I learned in fundraising was to focus on a few primary things.

The early stage investors buy YOU. Focus on integrity and knowledge. Tell the TRUTH always. ESPECIALLY when you don't know something. Be proud of the fact that you, at least, know it is something you don't know but are willing to learn.

Know what you are talking about. Do your study and research so you are confident. It will show through in your presentation. If you are not good with numbers, have a business accountant hold YOUR hand through building your projections and use as much detail as you can muster.

Be sure to understand your risks. I recommend writing your own risk analysis document. This is a big list of **What if...** *questions that you answer to the best of your ability. When you begin making presentations to investors, they will typically ask the same questions repeatedly from one investor to the next. If you already have their questions written down BEFORE they ask them, and you can show them your best guess of how you will handle the challenge, they will not need to ask many more questions.*

Know what your exit is. One of the most important things is to have a planned exit. Whatever your planned exit is, be sure you begin with the end in mind. All investors have one thing in common—they invest expecting a positive return on their investment that they can use for something else. They don't invest because they want to tie their money up in something where they can't get it back out!

Be committed, not desperate. Don't EVER put yourself in a position where you only have one investor that you are counting on to come through without having other prospects. Investors want the best deal that others want too. The best way to accomplish this is to have at least five solid investor leads being juggled at the same time and try not to fall below that number. When one falls out, even if you still have four active, go out and start two new prospects.

Don't give presentations to anyone who can't write a check. There is no free lunch or easy way to get someone else to raise the money for you. So, if you are constantly looking to present your offer to people who would like to hear

continued

about it, or think they know someone they can talk to, or haven't told you they could invest personally if the deal was right, DON'T waste your time presenting to them or handing out business plans. Generally, business plans don't sell your investment. YOU sell your investment.

And finally...

ASK for the money. If you give a presentation, ask for the investment. I can't count the number of investor presentations I have seen where the business owner gets to the end and says, Well, that's our company. Thank you for coming. And everyone in the room gets up and walks out. Try this phrase..."Mr. Investor, I don't know if you will invest in my company, but IF YOU DID, how much would you be interested in investing?"

If you follow all of these points, you are head and shoulders above the average person asking someone to invest in their business and you will most likely earn those investors because of it. Good luck.[5]

Valuation

The subject of valuation has elements of science and art. There are formulistic models for valuation that are quantitative and other models that are qualitative. The qualitative general factors include (roughly in order of importance):

- quality of management;
- size of the market;
- strength of the product;
- possible market growth;
- competition;
- stage of development; and,
- relevant industry.

In an early stage company, a quantitative valuation has less relevance since there is little hard financial information. If your company is on the fast track for launch, the longer you wait, the more you increase the valuation. You should at least have a passing familiarity with a quantitative model for valuation.

Figure 7.3: ENTREPRENEURIAL VALUATIONS

Tarby Bryant, Chairman and CEO of Anasazi Capital Corporation (**www.gatheringofangels.com**), provides the following guidelines on entrepreneurial valuations.

Proper valuation of the entrepreneurial business is the seminal event in the corporate maturation process, and it becomes an absolute requisite when the entrepreneur wants to raise private or public capital. Once the company is properly valued, then the entrepreneur can determine how much of the company can be sold for the capital injection provided by the investor or venture capitalist. Valuation is highly subjective and is art and not science. The return that an investor requires is commensurate with the perceived risk and his investment objectives.

Let's imagine that Terabyte Technologies, Inc., a New Mexico high tech start-up, is projecting that by its fifth year, it will earn $1,000,000 after taxes on sales of $10,000,000. Suppose that the initial funding request in their business plan is estimated by Terabyte management at $800,000 and that the interested private investor requires a 50% annual compounded return on investment (ROI).

Anasazi Capital's suggested methodology of valuation is as follows:

The private investor will estimate the value of the company in the fifth year based on a multiple of earnings for companies similar to Terabyte's. We will assume that similar companies are selling at approximately 15 times earnings. This would give Terabyte a value in year five of $15,000,000. (15 x $1,000,000).

Employing this earnings multiple and the required 50% rate of return, one can calculate the present value of the company using the following formula:

$$\text{Present value} = \frac{\text{future valuation}}{(1 + i)^n}$$

Where future valuation = total estimated value of company in five years
i = required rate of return for Private Investor
n = number of years

continued

The present value of Terabyte Technologies would be calculated as follows:

$$\text{Present valuation} = \frac{\$15,000,000}{(1 + i)^n} = \frac{\$15,000,000}{(1 + .50)^5} = \$1,975,000$$

Based on the initial required funding of $800,000, the private investors' share of the Terabyte Technologies' equity would be 41% which is calculated as follows:

$$\frac{\text{Initial funding}}{\text{Present value}} = \frac{\$800,000}{\$1,975,000} = 41\%$$

Valuation of the entrepreneurial company has as many variables as noted above. The more accurate the revenue and income projections, the higher the valuation of the company, and the lower the private investors' share of Terabyte. The early private investor should require dilution protection on his stake as a first round early stage investor.[6]

At the premoney stage of your company, do not spend endless amounts of time on valuation. It is more important for you to demonstrate to investors your strategy to bring your product to market, rather than showing them an arbitrary assignment of value for your company.

Angel Networks and Entrepreneurial Forums

A source for angel networks exists at the Access to Capital Electronic Network (ACE-Net) which is a nationwide secure database accessible via the Internet at **http://acenet.csusb.edu**. In addition, MIT Enterprise Forum has eighteen chapters worldwide and offers networking opportunities for both investors and entrepreneurs. Visit their website at **http://web.mit.edu/entforum**.

Another outstanding resource for entrepreneurs is IBI Global. IBI Global seeks to promote resources and networking among entrepreneurs and help develop capital and customer markets.

IBI Global is the only known course designed to teach you what you need to know to get your business idea off the ground. It will teach you to protect and promote business ideas, formulate strategy, define markets, build a team, raise money, and meet contacts who can help you.

IBI Global hosts a seven day accelerated management training program and CEO retreat and provides free ongoing graduate support through weekly meetings across the nation to network and develop contacts.

You can learn more about IBI Global on their website at **www.IBIGlobal.com**. In addition, examples of IBI Global training are available at **www.IBISuccessChannel.com** radio and television network.

Chapter 8

Presentations and the Language of Capital

Your success in raising capital may rise or fall on the quality of your presentation to potential investors. To make a compelling presentation, you need to be highly organized, conversant with your topics, prepared for questions, and at ease speaking in public. There are three distinct elements to a successful presentation: content, design and presentation, and the presenter.

Content

When talking about the content, provide an adequate snapshot of the company, its management, the market, and the return on investment. It is useful for the presenter to tell about the product or service of the company up front. Many presenters verbally wander around for much of their presentation without giving the audience any clear idea of the business and product being discussed.

Another area of concern, in terms of content, is the management discussion. Oftentimes, companies that had some depth and experience in management gloss over it instead of emphasizing it, while at other times, a company weak in management does not tell the audience how it proposes to solve that problem and beef up the team.

The presentation of financial information presents difficulties to most speakers. Financial data in a short presentation needs to concentrate on highlights and not minute details—provide enough detail to impress upon the audience that you know what you are talking about, but not so much that you put them to sleep. A presentation is like a business plan—one of its principal purposes is to get a meeting where you will have an opportunity to elaborate upon the details.

The Presenter

The third area to focus on is the actual presenter—his or her communication skills and appearance. If you have not spoken in public quite a bit, seek out opportunities to speak and become comfortable with oral presentations. The quickest way to learn is—you guessed it—speak in public at every opportunity. Join *Toastmasters*. Attend lead share groups and networking events in your area where everyone makes a short presentation. Professional speaking coaches are everywhere, and in some of the larger cities there are coaches just for business presentations. The first skill is learning to be comfortable with public speaking, and the next is learning to present your materials in a compelling and persuasive manner. Like learning to sing or playing a musical instrument, the well-known secret is practice, practice, practice. Always rehearse your presentation with your colleagues and include a practice question and answer session.

QUICK Tip

Design and Presentation: How a presentation looks can be as important as what you say in it. Consider hiring a graphic design firm or branding firm to help put the look of your presentation together. Some of the tips they give include the following.

- Avoid putting video clips in a short presentation or embedding them in PowerPoint. A video, no matter how short, tends to eat into valuable presentation time.
- Keep a color scheme that is easy on the eye and perfectly readable. Slides cluttered with cute graphic images distract from your message.

Your personal appearance for presentations seems obvious enough. If you are asking for capital, you need to make a professional appearance relative to the business to whom you are presenting. A coat and tie or a business dress or suit is always a safe bet.

However, there can be some variation to this rule. If you are a country and western entertainer or your business is branded around a particular image, then you may wish to dress a little different. Murray Burk and Mary Spata operate a family-run business located in the village of Post Mills, Vermont, making homemade-style marinara pasta sauces, ketchups, mustards, and condiments (**www.vermontfinest.com**). Murray has developed the persona of *Uncle Dave*, a colorful Vermont farmer in a red plaid shirt and overalls. His products are branded with the character of Uncle Dave and he appears at events in full costume. In his case, the overalls are a powerful sales tool.

Figure 8.1: ADVICE TO PRESENTERS

Ike Gadsden, Managing Director of Diamond State Ventures (**www.dsventures.net**), a Delaware technology cultivator, gives the following advice to presenters.

First things first. The primary objective of your Diamond State Ventures presentation is to get a meeting with a potential investor. This ten to twelve minute presentation is not a forum to defend your intellectual property position, prove your technology or science, or give a demonstration. For now, the audience will give you the benefit of the doubt on these issues. The objective of this presentation is to persuade the audience that your business opportunity is worthy of a more detailed look.

Your presentation should be clear, concise, and to the point. A one-page executive summary about your company (written by you) will be provided to the venture forum attendees. That is where most of your details should reside. Your presentation should cull out the most salient and profound points and emphasize those. Some suggested topics for slides include:

Introduction. What is your company name, what does your company do (high-level)? Provide a real-world setting/example the audience can relate to.

Market Need. What is the pain (cost) associated with this problem? How is the market solving the problem currently?

Company Overview. How do you solve the problem better than anyone else? What is your unique niche and value proposition?

Product/Service. What do you sell?

Competition. Who else is providing solutions to this problem? Where do you rank against/amongst them? (Don't say you have no competition. There is always competition.) How are you different/better?

Intellectual Property. What is your IP? Do you have proprietary processes? (Don't go into the nuts and bolts, but instead present that it exists and the basic premise surrounding it from a business value perspective.)

Sales and Marketing. What is your go-to-market strategy? How will you drive revenues? How will you reach your customers and convince them to buy?

Management team. Who is committed to your company and what is their relevant experience/expertise?

Financial Projections. Assuming you receive the funding you need, what do you anticipate revenues to be Year 1 through Year 5? If you asked for more money, could you scale faster and become profitable sooner?

Sources and Uses. How much money have you raised so far? How much money are you asking for now? How will you use the new funding?

Summary. Review the problem that your solution solves and the importance of it in the marketplace. Review your unique value proposition. Emphasize the dedication of your team. Ask for the money.

An effective presentation:

- *focuses on a single objective (get a meeting!);*
- *is clear, concise, to the point, and readable;*
- *does not include jargon, scientific terms, or acronyms;*
- *uses color and graphics appropriately; and,*
- *does not use hard-to-read graphics or small text.*

An effective presenter:

- *does not read the slides to the audience;*
- *is confident and enthusiastic about his or her business;*
- *establishes eye contact and speaks to the audience;*
- *respects the time allotted; and,*
- *brings plenty of business cards and aggressively networks the room.*

Remember, the audience knows if you are less than prepared. The audience knows if you are less than convinced.[7]

Speaker Tips

The best speaker tip is to be prepared for anything—things will go wrong with varying frequency. The following are some very practical things to consider.

- If possible, check out the room in which the presentation will take place in advance.
- Stand at the podium, if there is a podium, and visualize the audience and your ease and confidence in presenting to them.
- If there is not a podium, which is rare, you will not be able to rely on note cards. The PowerPoint outline may be your savior.
- Check out the sound system—it is rare for most presentations to have a professional sound person running the show. Will there be a microphone? Is it stationary or portable? Is there a lavaliere-type microphone available (the one pinned to your clothes)?
- In the event that the presentation is being filmed, find out the range of the camera and stay within its visual boundaries. Also, do not turn your back to the camera, if possible.
- Rehearse your presentation several times before the big day. Watch the clock and time your conclusion accordingly—nothing is more irritating to the sponsors and audience than a speaker intentionally squeezing more time from the presentation than allotted. Arrange for your colleagues to comment on the presentation and ask you some tough questions.
- If you are going to use PowerPoint, make certain that the updated version is installed on your laptop and double-check that a projector and screen are available. You may need to buy your own projector to be certain one is always available.
- If you suffer from stage fright, you are not alone. However, that is a small consolation when you are expected to get up front and speak. The best way to overcome stage fright is to speak in public often. If you are distressed about this presentation, pick a person or two in the audience, make eye contact and give your presentation to that person or people, as if it were a conversation in your office or living room.
- Be careful about using humor—particularly the planned joke variety—in your presentation. Apart from the fact you are at a business presentation, humor, unless you are an after-dinner speaker or a comedian, can be tricky to deliver and a disaster if it does not work. If you are a naturally funny person, use your sense of irony and timing to charm your audience, let them see the natural humor in your personality.

- The final and most important tip—enjoy yourself. The presentation is your time to shine for your company. You will feel a real high when you have nailed it, even if money does not flow the first time.

Figure 8.2: THE RULES OF POWERPOINT

The use of PowerPoint can be a powerful presentation tool or a crutch that distracts the audience and derails your presentation. Aided by the ease of creation, data-driven presentations to the investor audience can be deadly.

When preparing your presentation, be cognizant of the way your slides look and the information they convey. In a ten- to twelve-minute presentation you may want to restrict the number of slides to five–seven, using the slides as you would an outline for a speech, evoking the concept and then filling in verbally. In any event, avoid chart junk. As Professor Tufte stated in his seminal essay on PowerPoint:

At a minimum, a presentation format should do no harm. Yet the PowerPoint style routinely disrupts, dominates, and trivializes content. Thus PowerPoint presentations too often resemble a school play—very loud, very slow, and very simple.[8]

A guideline for presentations is no more than four bullet points per slide and never more than one line per bullet point. Reading the words from the slide has the same effect as reading a speech—you lose contact with the audience and your credibility fades.

Print your presentation and do not look at the screen incessantly. Also, it helps for you to hand out a copy of your slides at the presentation so the audience can review them at their leisure. Make certain all of your contact information is included somewhere in the presentation.

Learning to Close and When

If you grew up in an average middle-class family, you probably had little occasion to seriously ask for money. When you did, it was probably awkward and unpleasant. Most of us started out asking for our weekly allowance.

Unless you have spent the last several years in sales—actually calling on customers and getting sales—you need to reprogram your approach and learn to ask for the money. If you cannot give an investor or a banker a level of confidence that you are comfortable asking for the necessary capital and that you have the ability and sense of mission to spend the money wisely, you will not fund your company.

It is all about closing the deal. If you are presenting to angels or venture capitalists, the closing will be a process of additional meetings and diligence before it is time to close. If you are presenting your private placement memorandum to a selected audience, it is appropriate to identify those persons who have an active interest, answer their questions, and ask them to invest.

Declining Money

Believe it or not, there are times when you should decline the money. In the case of larger investors, you should perform your own due diligence on the potential funder. What has been the experience of other companies they have funded? How active a role did they play in the management? If the funding was incremental, did it come on time and when promised? Did they add value to the company and its mission? If the funder refuses to give references, run—do not walk—away.

The reverse of the big funder is the couple on a fixed income who love you and want to put their last savings in your company. Do not take that money—it is unethical, ill-advised, and always more trouble than it is worth. Some investors just are not right for your company. Learn to recognize them, be respectful, and let them go.

Chapter 9

Corporate Governance

The decision to raise capital, how much, what type, and so on, is made by the directors, managers, or partners of a business. Recent high-profile scandals involving a few public corporations highlight the need for responsible corporate governance at all levels. Clear-cut corporate procedures and responsibilities will not only keep your new company out of trouble, but will also prove to be an attractive asset to investors when you are looking for capital.

Most corporate governance statutes are directed to corporations, but that does not mean that limited liability companies (LLCs) and partnerships should discount the importance of creating policies and procedures for running their companies. Sound corporate governance applies to all forms of business. Much of the law regarding corporate governance is decided in the courts, and in particular, the courts of the state of Delaware.

There are a number of issues that are common to all business entities. There are also those that specifically relate to corporations and LLCs. For corporate governance purposes, partnerships are a close cousin to LLCs, and they can generally adopt policies and procedures similar to that of an LLC.

Corporate governance, at its essence, is the establishment and practice of rules and procedures that regulate the affairs of the body corporate. The corporation's bylaws contain the basic rules of corporate governance for a corporation. In the case of an LLC, those rules are contained in the operating agreement, and in the case of a limited partnership, in the limited partnership agreement. The legal standard applied to directors' actions to determine whether they discharged their duty of care and loyalty is the business judgment rule. The standard applicable to LLCs and LPs may be a higher standard, rising to that of the special care required of a fiduciary because of the substantial control exercised by the managing member and general partners over their members.

Registered Agents

All companies are required to have a registered agent. A *registered agent* is authorized to accept service of process for the business, and is the designated point of contact with the state for service of process and correspondence from the state. The registered agent could be an individual or a company, but they must reside in the state where the business is registered and have a valid street address (not a post office box). In new companies, the registered agent is usually a principal of the company, but there are also companies that will serve as your registered agent for a fee.

QUICK Tip

Use a Corporate Service Company: Eventually, you should use a corporate service company as your registered agent to avoid any slip-up in receiving written communications.

The company must notify the state if they change registered agents or if their registered agent changes addresses. After all, the state needs to know how to contact your company. The state sends correspondence to the registered agent, such as the annual report, that must be completed and returned. The requirement to file is not waived because the mail was mislaid, forwarded to the wrong address, or not mailed by the state. Therefore, it is in the best interest of the company that the registered agent's information is correct and up to date, and that the company stays informed as to when filings are due. Not filing required paperwork with the state is the most common reason young companies find themselves in hot water.

Initial Reports

Many states require an initial report to be filed with the state within thirty to ninety days of the formation of a company. These reports are mailed to the registered agent and generally require a listing of the officers and directors of a corporation or the manager(s) of an LLC. Failure to file this report can result in termination of the corporate charter.

Annual Reports

A large majority of states require corporations (and about half of the states require LLCs) to make an annual filing with an agency in their state of formation and any other state in which they are qualified to do business. These reports are mailed to the registered agent, and generally require a representative of the company to provide an updated list of officers, directors (managers for an LLC), and resident agents. Failure to file these annual reports can result in termination of the corporate charter.

Money and Accounting

As part of their duty of care, the officers and directors of a corporation and the managers of an LLC are responsible for making sure that the company has sound accounting practices. This includes accounting for all assets that were transferred by the founders into the company and properly recording the income and expenses attributed to the company. The company's accountant should, at a minimum, produce annual financial statements for the company, and these statements should be made available to the shareholders and members.

Never combine or commingle personal funds or expenditures with those of the company. This problem tends to come up with start-up businesses when funds get low. Separating the company's bank account from your personal bank account allows for ease in record keeping and bookkeeping. In addition, it is advisable to put explanations on company checks, along with cash tickets and receipts for each transaction.

Do not use the company bank account for any personal expenses.

Establish separate credit card accounts for the company. If you have to, on occasion, use your personal credit card for a company expense, make a careful record of the expense and seek reimbursement from the company. Document all expenses and require employees to submit detailed expense accounts before receiving reimbursement. Manage any petty cash accounts by requiring written receipts for all withdrawals of cash.

With the help of your accountant, establish a system of checks and balances to ensure the integrity of your accounting practices. For example, in some companies, the person who records expenses and the person who writes the checks for the expenses are separate individuals. In addition, you may want to require two signatures on checks over a certain amount.

Signing Documents

When signing invoices, receipts, contracts, or other documents on behalf of the company, always put the corporate name, followed by the individual's name and title. Note the following examples.

ABC, Inc.   ABC, LLC

By: _____   By: _____

Jane Doe, President   Jane Doe, Manager

By this practice, public notice is given that the named individual is signing on behalf of the company and not in their individual capacity. If the person simply signed their name, the signor may be held personally liable for a company debt.

Bank Accounts

In order to open a bank account for your new company, you will minimally need to obtain a federal tax ID number for your company (a single member LLC without employees may use the owner's Social Security number). This number is obtained by filing a Form SS-4, which can be done online at **www.irs.gov** or by completing and mailing the form to the IRS. The bank will also require a corporate resolution, which is a standardized form normally provided by your bank. If you are an LLC, the bank may want to see a copy of your operating agreement, and if you are incorporated in another state, the bank will want to see evidence that you have qualified your foreign corporation or LLC in the state.

When establishing the company bank account, it is also a good idea to restrict who can sign checks for the company, and to require two signatures for checks above a certain amount. This way, you can control who has access to the bank account and maintain accountability for company funds.

Corporate Governance for Corporations

Corporations are entities that are created under state law. There are no federal corporations. As such, state laws control most aspects of how a corporation is governed, including provisions for the bylaws, requirements for directors and management, share certificates, required meetings, voting procedures, and so on.

Corporate Records

State corporate statutes allow shareholders access to corporate records unless there is a justifiable reason not to do so. Therefore, it is advisable to keep adequate books and records, including your bylaws, minutes, shareholder ledger, licenses, permits, and copies of significant contracts, in a centralized location.

QUICK Tip

Obtain a Corporate Book to Organize Your Records: This is a three-ring binder with tabs for organizing your articles of incorporation and any amendments, your bylaws and any amendments, your shareholder and director meeting minutes, your share certificates and shareholder ledger, and a tab for forms, licenses, and permits.

An accurate record of the shareholders of the corporation should include the name and address of each shareholder and number of shares held. You should also keep track of the date he or she became a shareholder and the certificate number he or she was issued.

Keep your corporate seal in your corporate book. This is the seal that you will use to emboss all corporate records. The seal should state the name of the company, as well as the state and year of incorporation. Keep your corporate book in a safe place, usually under the care of the secretary of the company.

Bylaws

The *bylaws* are the governing document of a corporation that set forth the duties and responsibilities of the officers and directors. They also establish orderly procedures for conducting business. The bylaws are considered to be a contract among the shareholders, directors, and officers, and typically contain the provisions regarding shareholders' rights, directors' duties, and the affairs of the corporation. (A sample set of bylaws is included in Appendix B.)

The bylaws should specify the necessity of holding annual meetings of the shareholders and directors, and detail the procedures for notifying these individuals of these meetings. The bylaws will also define what constitutes a voting majority and a quorum for the purposes of the corporation. The procedures for calling special meetings are usually described, as well as the standard order of business of any meeting. The bylaws are also the place where the specific duties of the officers of the corporation are described.

While many of these terms could be otherwise stated in the articles of incorporation, it is usually easier to adopt them as bylaws. Since bylaws are initially adopted by the directors as their internal operating procedure, the directors may generally propose changes to the bylaws at any time. Most bylaws provide that the directors can amend the bylaws but the shareholders can override the directors' amendments. Neither the bylaws nor any amendments to them are filed with the secretary of state.

If a corporation functions without bylaws, the articles of incorporation and state corporation statutes will regulate the affairs of the corporation. Since amendments to the articles of incorporation are a more cumbersome and costly way to add governance provisions, it is advisable for a corporation to adopt bylaws as a way of maintaining some flexibility in the functions of the corporation.

Officers and Directors

Policy decisions are made in a corporation by the board of directors and carried out by the officers. Directors create the policies of the corporation and officers implement those policies. Operational decisions are usually made by the officers. Directors generally delegate certain duties to the officers who are, in turn, answerable to the board of directors for their actions.

Directors are elected by the shareholders of the corporation, and officers are appointed by the directors. Therefore, the shareholders may remove a director and the directors may remove an officer.

Typically, an initial director is appointed in the articles of incorporation or appointed by the incorporator and then an initial board of directors is appointed at the initial meeting of the directors. It is prudent to designate an uneven number of directors so that the board is not ever stymied by a tied vote. Also, it is wise to stagger the terms of service of the directors so that elections of directors never result in a new, inexperienced board. This also helps maintain continuity.

The directors, in turn, appoint the officers of the corporation, who serve at the pleasure of the board unless they are given employment contracts that specify the terms under which they can be terminated. It may be unwise to place officers of the company on the board of directors, as this can thwart frank discussions and can alter the true, independent nature of the board.

Figure 9.1: BOARD OF DIRECTOR'S POWERS

The board of directors is usually granted powers by state statute and through the bylaws of the company. Those powers will typically include the power to:

- select and remove all the officers, agents, and employees of the corporation. This will include the power to:

  - prescribe such powers and duties for the officers, agents, and employees not inconsistent with the law, the articles of incorporation, or the bylaws;

  - fix compensation for the officers, agents, and employees; and,

  - require security for faithful service from the officers, agents, and employees;

- conduct, manage, and control the affairs and business of the corporation;

- make sure that rules and regulations are not inconsistent with the law, the articles of incorporation, or the bylaws;

- change the principal office of the corporation from one location to another;

- designate any place for the holding of any shareholders' meeting or meetings;

- adopt, make, and use a corporate seal;

- prescribe the forms of certificates of stock;

- alter the form of the corporate seal and of certificates of stock from time to time, as in their judgment they may deem best, provided such seal and such certificates shall at all times comply with the provisions of law;

- authorize the issue of shares of stock of the corporation from time to time, upon such terms and for such consideration as may be lawful;

- borrow money and incur indebtedness for the purposes of the corporation; and,

- cause to be executed and delivered therefore, in the corporate name, promissory notes, bonds, debentures, deeds of trust, mortgages, pledges, hypothecations, or other evidences of debt and securities.

Duties of the President. The *president* shall have general supervision, direction, and control of the business and officers of the corporation. The president shall preside at all meetings of the shareholders, and in the absence of the chairman of the board (or if there is none), at all meetings of the board of directors. The president shall be ex officio a member of all the standing committees, including the executive committee (if any), and shall have the general powers and duties of management usually vested in the office of president of a corporation. The president shall have such other powers and duties as may be prescribed by the board of directors or the bylaws.

Bifurcation of President and Chief Executive Officer. If the board of directors creates the office of chief executive officer as a separate office from president, the chief executive officer shall have the power and duty to act as the chief executive officer of the corporation. Subject to the control of the board of directors, the chief executive officer may also have general supervision, direction, and control of the corporation and its business, affairs, property, officers, agents, and employees. If there is a chief executive officer, the president shall be the chief operating officer of the corporation with responsibility for the operation of the business of the corporation in the ordinary course and shall be subject to the general supervision, direction, and control of the chief executive officer unless the board of directors provides otherwise. In case of the absence, disability, or death of the chief executive officer, if there is one, the president shall exercise all the powers and perform all the duties of the chief executive officer.

Duties of Vice President. In the absence or disability of the president, the *vice presidents*, if any, in order of their rank as fixed by the board of directors, or if not ranked, the vice president designated by the board of directors, shall perform all the duties of the president. When so acting, the vice president shall have all the powers of, and be subject to all the restrictions upon, the president. The vice presidents shall have such other powers and perform such other duties as from time to time may be prescribed for them respectively by the board of directors or the bylaws.

Duties of the Chief Financial Officer. The *chief financial officer* (who also may be called the treasurer) shall keep and maintain adequate and correct accounts of the properties and business transactions of the corporation, including accounts of its assets, liabilities, receipts, disbursements, gains, losses, capital, surplus, and shares. The books of account shall at all reasonable times be open to inspection by any director. The chief financial officer shall deposit all moneys and other valuables in the name of the corporation with such depositories as may be designated by the board of directors. He or she shall disburse the funds of the corporation as may be ordered by the board of directors. The chief financial officer shall render to the president and directors, whenever they request it, an account of all of his or her transactions as chief financial officer and of the financial condition of the corporation.

Duties of Secretary. The *secretary* shall keep the minutes of the board of directors. The secretary shall also keep the minutes of the meetings of stockholders. He or she shall attend to the giving and serving of all notices of the company, shall have charge of the books and papers of the corporation, and shall make such reports and perform such other duties as are incidental to their office and as the board of directors may direct. The secretary shall be responsible for supplying to the resident agent or principal office any and all amendments to the corporation's articles of incorporation and any and all amendments or changes to the bylaws of the corporation. The secretary will also maintain and supply to the resident agent or principal office a current statement setting forth the name of the custodian of the stock ledger, or duplicate stock ledger and the present and complete post office address, including street number, if any, where such stock ledger or duplicate stock ledger specified in the section is kept.

Required Meetings

Shareholders and directors are required to conduct annual meetings. The minutes of the meetings must be included within the corporate records. Most states allow the annual meetings to be held at a designated time and place, either within or without of the state's boundaries.

Minutes of Meetings

The minutes of a corporation's meetings should provide the complete record of corporate actions by the board of directors and document the legitimate exercise of responsible corporate governance by the directors. In small corporations, it is too easy to make important decisions during the day over the telephone, during coffee breaks, or on the golf course. All major decisions should be made by the board of directors and included in written minutes.

QUICK Tip

Rule No. 1: *Put it in writing* should be the adage for a corporation to live by.

Even if you feel that you are too busy managing the corporation to attend to the detail of the corporate minutes, you need to realize that accurate, written reports of your corporate proceedings may be your only defense if the corporation runs into trouble. Without accurate minutes, a judge or the IRS may disavow many of the corporation's actions, including executive compensation and bonuses, retirement plans, and dividend disbursements.

The minutes of any meeting should show that the meeting was properly called and that everyone there received adequate notice as required by the corporate bylaws. If a written notice of the meeting was sent out, a copy should be included. If no notice was given, the appropriate waiver of notice should accompany the minutes. The minutes should be signed by all attending, indicating agreement that the minutes accurately reflect what took place in the meeting.

For every action that is taken during a meeting, the minutes should show that the matter was properly introduced, seconded, discussed, and agreed to by a voting majority as defined in the bylaws. The complete text of any resolution, contract, report, or other document adopted or ratified in a meeting should also appear in the minutes.

There is no standard format for minutes, but items such as the time, date, and place of the meeting, along with a list of all attending, should be included. All actions by the board of directors should be recorded. Although minutes should be specific, they need not record every word of debate on every subject. They should concentrate on final decisions rather than discussion.

Shareholder Meetings

State corporation statutes require that a corporation hold at least one shareholder meeting per year. This is called an annual meeting. Meetings that are held between annual meetings are called special meetings. Special meetings may be required to vote on an impending merger or amendment to the articles that cannot wait for the annual meeting and the like. Any business requiring shareholder approval may be addressed at any shareholders' meeting.

The main topic of business at an annual meeting of shareholders is the election of directors to serve for the upcoming year. In addition, shareholders should adopt a resolution endorsing actions taken by the board of directors during the past year. All resolutions adopted by the shareholders should be recorded in the minutes, along with other documents that relate to the resolution.

Most state corporation statutes also allow shareholders to adopt resolutions without a meeting. Actions taken by shareholders without a meeting must be authorized in writing by shareholders holding a majority of the voting power and filed in the corporate minute book.

Shareholders may attend the meeting in person or vote by proxy. In most corporations, shareholders vote based on one vote per one share of common stock. Generally, common stock is voting stock and preferred stock does not vote. Certain classes of preferred stock may have voting rights for designated purposes. A proxy is an authorization to another person, usually the president or chairman of the board, to vote your stock in a particular manner. Proxies are normally given in those cases in which a shareholder cannot attend an annual or special meeting. Proxies can be revoked at any time by a shareholder. For example, a shareholder could appear at a meeting, revoke his or her proxy, and vote his or her own shares.

The bylaws may prescribe the time for the annual meeting or allow the board to set it. A written notice of the meeting should be sent to all eligible shareholders within the period required by the bylaws. The notice of the meeting should be accompanied by a proxy statement explaining the matters to be voted on and provide sufficient information to allow a shareholder to make an informed choice. Private companies are not required to file their proxy statements with federal or state regulators.

Make the Most of Meetings: In addition to conducting the business of the meeting, an annual meeting of shareholders is an ideal opportunity to highlight the accomplishments for the company for the year and to outline the plans for the forthcoming year.

Steps to Take Before an Annual Shareholder Meeting

To ensure all of the legal requirements are met for the annual shareholder meeting, several things must be done prior to the meeting date.

Send the Annual Report to the Shareholders. In a small company, this may simply be financial statements that detail the profits and losses (income statement), and assets and liabilities (balance sheet) of the corporation. The accuracy of all financial documents should be attested to by either the treasurer or company accountant. This step may not be required for a small company that has no shareholders outside of the family, but it is always a good idea to provide this information annually to the shareholders anyway. (It also keeps the family happy and lets them know that you are not squandering the family inheritance.)

Update the List of Shareholders. If there have been any changes or transfers of stock, make sure the corporate books reflect the current shareholders. When there are many shareholders, this list is required to verify voting eligibility of those attending the meetings. The secretary usually greets the shareholders at the meeting and confirms they are eligible to vote and attend the meeting.

Notify Shareholders. Shareholders must be *notified in writing* of any meetings—typically no less than ten days or more than sixty days before the meeting is held. This notification must include the purpose for the meeting, as well as the time and place where it is to be held.

Issue a Proxy Statement. When the notifications are sent out, it is a good idea to include proxy statements that will allow shareholders who cannot attend the meeting to participate by designating someone else to cast their votes for them. The proxy statement should explain the matters to be voted upon and provide sufficient information to allow a shareholder to make an informed choice.

Have an Agenda. Regardless of the number of items to be discussed and the number of shareholders or directors of the corporation, it is a good idea to put an agenda together. An agenda informs everyone involved of the topics of discussion for the meeting and keeps the meeting on purpose.

Appoint a Chairperson for the Meeting. The president usually acts as the chairperson at all meetings of the shareholders, and in the absence of the chairman of the board (or if there is none), at all meetings of the board of directors. You should also appoint a parliamentarian at all meetings. Someone who is familiar with parliamentary procedure and can be called upon if a question arises about how the meeting is being conducted or the proper requirements for ratifying a corporate decision. The secretary of the company sometimes fills this role.

Prepare Yourself to Answer Questions. Small corporations will usually be able to anticipate controversial topics, but larger corporations can be blindsided by shareholders who may be unknown to any of the officers and directors. When a large number of shareholders are anticipated to be present at the meeting, it is a good idea to arrange for your attorneys and accountants to be at the meeting with any documentation they may need to consult for reference. This material is likely to include all corporate records, contracts, leases, and tax data.

**Figure 9.2: SAMPLE SCRIPT
FOR THE ANNUAL MEETING OF SHAREHOLDERS**

A sample script for the annual meeting of shareholders is shown below. After this formal business agenda is completed, the company should make its informational presentation.

ABC, INC.

AGENDA FOR ANNUAL MEETING OF SHAREHOLDERS

February 14, 2007

10:00 A.M.

Chairperson	Will the meeting please come to order. I am Bob Anderson, Chairperson of the Board of ABC, Inc. On behalf of the Corporation, I welcome you to this annual meeting of Shareholders. We appreciate your continued interest in the Corporation, as shown by your attendance here today. Before proceeding with the business of the meeting, I will introduce the other members of your board of directors and the officers who are here today:
	Bob Anderson, the CEO of the Company, Chairperson of the Board of Directors,

---

continued

Brad Anderson, the Secretary of the Company, member of the Board of Directors,

John Jones, the Vice President of the Company, member of the Board of Directors, and

Jim Smith, the Treasurer or CFO of the Company and member of the Board of Directors.

The Secretary has a complete list of the issued and outstanding common shares as of the close of business on December 31, 2006, the record date of this meeting. Will the Secretary please report the number of shares outstanding and entitled to vote at this meeting?

Secretary

As of the close of business of December 31, 2006, the Corporation had 5,300,000 shares of common stock issued and outstanding and entitled to vote.

Chairperson

The Secretary has in his possession, and there will be filed with the records of the Corporation relating to this meeting, an affidavit of mailing certifying to the mailing on January 14, 2007 to the Shareholders of record at the close of business on December 31, 2006 of the annual report for the fiscal year ended December 31, 2006, the notice of annual meeting and the form of proxy. It appears from this affidavit and the attached exhibits that notice of this meeting has been duly given as required by law and the Corporation's bylaws.

Brad Anderson and Jim Smith are appointed as Election Judges. If there are any persons present who have not indicated their appearance with the Election Judges, will they please do so now. All persons acting as proxies should present those proxies to the Election Judges. Mr. Secretary, will you please state whether a quorum is present at this meeting and, at a later point, please report the total number of shares so represented.

Secretary

The Election Judges have reported that a quorum is present in person or by proxy.

Chairperson	Before opening the meeting to questions, I would like to proceed with the necessary business of the meeting.
	Mr. Secretary, will you please report the total number of shares represented at this meeting.
Secretary	The total number of shares represented at this meeting is 5,140,000 shares of common stock.
Chairperson	As the next order of business, I ask that the Secretary present and read the notice of annual meeting and the proof of mailing thereof.
Secretary	(Reads the Notice of Annual Meeting and the Affidavit of Mailing.)
Chairperson	Mr. Secretary, will you please file the documents with the minutes of the meeting?
Secretary	Yes.
Chairperson	The next order of business is the approval of the Annual Report for the fiscal year ended December 31, 2006. Are there any questions regarding the annual report? (Pause) May I now have a motion to approve the fiscal year 2006 annual report?
1st Shareholder	I move that the Annual Report of this Corporation as of December 31, 2006, as mailed to all Shareholders of ABC, Inc., be and the same is hereby approved.
2nd Shareholder	I second the motion.
Chairperson	I call for vote on the motion. Mr. Secretary, how do the Shareholders vote?
Secretary	(Reads the Summary of Votes approving the Annual Report.)
Chairperson	The motion is carried and the Annual Report is hereby approved.
	The next order of business is the election of five Directors of the Corporation to serve until their respective successors are duly elected and qualified. I recognize Mr. Hoffman [1st Shareholder].

continued

1ˢᵗ Shareholder	I nominate for election as Director the following persons:
	Bob Anderson
	Brad Anderson
	John Jones
	Jim Smith
	Janice Doe
2ⁿᵈ Shareholder	I second the nomination.
Chairperson	Are there any further nominations for Directors? (Pause)
	If there are no further nominations, the nominations are closed. Is there any discussion? (Pause)
	We are now ready to proceed with the vote on the nominations made at this meeting. Will the Election Judges please distribute the ballots, collect them after the vote and report the results to the Secretary?
	(To any Shareholders present) If you have already given your proxy to management, you need not vote, since the persons designated as proxies will vote for you as indicated in the proxy. Please fill in the number of shares being voted in the space provided for that purpose.

[Note for the Chairperson]: If anyone other than the management's nominees are nominated, the Chairperson should state the following:

The ballot for the election of Directors has room for the insertion of the names of those persons other than the Directors who have been nominated by the management of the Corporation. You may insert the name of any one of the other nominees and cross out the name of any nominee for whom you do not want to vote.

Secretary	The Election Judges have reported that the Shareholders have voted as follows:
	On the election of Directors, each of the five nominees has received 5,140,000 votes.

(If anyone else has been nominated, it will be necessary to name each nominee and give the number of votes for that nominee.)

[Note for the Chairperson]: A majority of common stock greater than 2,650,000 (half of the 5,300,000 outstanding shares of common stock) shares are needed for any motions taken up at the meeting. Directors are elected by plurality.

Chairperson	In view of this vote, I declare that Bob Anderson, Brad Anderson, John Jones, Jim Smith and Janice Doe have been duly elected as Directors of the Corporation for the next year.
	Is there any further business to be discussed or conducted at this meeting?
	There being no further business to be discussed or conducted, I request a motion to declare the meeting at an end.
Shareholder	I move that the meeting be closed.
Shareholder	I second the motion.
Chairperson	All those in favor, signify by saying yes. Those opposed, *no.*
	I declare this meeting is adjourned.

Steps to Take After an Annual Shareholder Meeting

Once the meeting has been properly conducted, there are still a few follow up items that must be done.

Write and Distribute the Meeting's Minutes. File the minutes of the meeting with your corporate records. The minutes should contain accurate and specific records about all decisions made during the meeting, and should be attested to by those attending.

Follow Up on All Approved Actions. Some actions taken in a meeting, such as the adoption of an amendment to the articles of incorporation, may not take effect until the documents are filed with the secretary of state.

Board of Director's Meetings

State corporation statutes require that a corporation hold at least one board of director's meeting per year. This is called an annual meeting. Meetings that are held between annual meetings are called special meetings. Any business requiring board of director approval may be addressed at any board meeting. The primary purpose of a board of directors meeting is to make the decisions that have been delegated to the directors by the shareholders, such as the election of officers to run the day-to-day operations of the company.

It is not always convenient for the directors to get together for meetings. Most state corporate statutes allow for directors to meet by telephone, in which case, written minutes should accompany the decisions of the meeting and be signed at a later date or by fax. This provision should be added into the bylaws.

Most state corporate statues also allow corporations to adopt resolutions without a meeting by *unanimous written consent* signed by all directors. Unanimous written consent is a term used for a process that allows directors or shareholders to act without a meeting if they each give their consent to specific corporate actions in writing. The consent must be unanimous for the resolutions to be properly adopted.

Resolutions

A resolution is a formal action of the directors (or in some cases, shareholders) authorizing a particular act, transaction, or officer appointment. Resolutions should be included as part of the minutes of the directors or shareholders meetings.

It is also wise to keep a catalog of resolutions that have been adopted by the board of directors and shareholders so that they can be retrieved quickly in the future. Keeping a cross-reference by the type of resolution and the date that it was made will help to maintain consistency in decision-making and enable the board to review prior actions quickly. It can become an arduous task to have to sort through all of the past minutes to determine a prior action by the board.

QUICK Tip

A Typical Form for Resolutions:

RESOLVED, that the Bylaws attached hereto as Exhibit A be, and they hereby are, adopted as the Bylaws of and for the Company; and

FURTHER RESOLVED, that the Secretary of the Company be, and he/she hereby is, authorized and directed to execute a Certificate of Secretary regarding the adoption of the Bylaws, to insert the Bylaws in the Company's Minute Book and to see that a copy of the Bylaws is kept at the Company's principal office, as required by law.

Initial Issuance of Stock

Founders' common stock should be issued by the corporation to the founders as soon after incorporation as possible and should be so stated in the minutes. If the founders of the company wait to issue their initial stock, you could incur unfavorable tax consequences. For example, if you failed to issue stock to yourself as founder and the company sells shares at a $1.00 per share, the stock you subsequently receive should be valued at $1.00 per share. You could have taxable income upon receipt unless you paid cash for the shares or transferred property of equal value to the company in return for the shares.

Corporate Governance for Limited Liability Companies

Like corporations, limited liability companies (LLCs) are creations of the state. In contrast to a corporation, an LLC has a great amount of flexibility in how it is governed and operates. That said, if you hope to attract capital, it would be wise to follow a few suggested guidelines. Some LLCs are run very informally and some are operated like a corporation.

Operating Agreement

The governing document of an LLC is called an *operating agreement*. Many states require an LLC to have an operating agreement, and in any event, an operating agreement is highly recommended if there are two or more members of an LLC. It can eliminate misunderstandings among the owners.

The operating agreement will define the following:

- the different classes of ownership, if any, and the capital contributions of each member;
- how the profits and losses of the company will be allocated among the members;
- how the company will be managed and how decisions will be made;
- the indemnification and limitation of liability for members and managers;
- how new members are admitted to the company;
- the rights and duties of members;
- whether meetings are required and how voting is to take place;
- how membership units may be transferred and how a member may withdraw from the company;
- under what conditions the company may be dissolved and the procedures for winding up the operations of the company;
- how the operating agreement may be amended; and,
- rules regarding partnership taxation.

The operating agreement is a private document among the members of the LLC. It is not filed with the state. Each member of the LLC should sign the operating agreement since it represents, in essence, a contract among the members.

Members of an LLC are normally entitled to vote on enumerated matters in the operating agreement, and the operating agreement may be amended as provided in its provisions. (A sample operating agreement is included in Appendix C.)

Managers

Decisions in an LLC can be made by the members, one or more managers, or a board of managers, which can operate much like the board of directors of a corporation. If an LLC is run by the members, they typically vote according to each member's percentage interest in the company. Meetings are held regularly and everyone participates in the decision-making process. At some point, this system can become cumbersome, especially if there are a lot of members.

If the decisions are left to a manager or board of managers, members of the LLC typically do not participate in all of the decision-making processes. Managers operate the company and the members take on a more passive role. This system is typically used when the members are investors and do not wish to take an active role in the operation of the company.

A manager does not have to be a member of the company, but often will hold some percentage of the membership. A manager of an LLC does not have unlimited personal liability like the general partner of a limited partnership, and a manager, or for that matter any member, can be another entity, like another LLC or corporation.

Officers

An LLC can have officers much like a corporation. If there are officers, they would typically be appointed by the managers or designated in the operating agreement and they would be responsible for the day-to-day operations of the company. The managers would then take on a role similar to the board of directors of a corporation overseeing the activities of the officers and answering to the members.

Meetings

While most states do not require LLCs to hold meetings of their members, an LLC should hold a meeting of the members at least once a year. Just like a shareholders' meeting of a corporation, an annual meeting of the members is a great opportunity to discuss the past years' events of the company and ratify the decisions of the managers. In addition, the operating agreement can provide that a percentage of the members can call a meeting at any time.

Sale or Issuance of Membership Units

Unlike the articles of incorporation of a corporation, the articles of organization of an LLC do not define its total authorized capital structure, and many times, neither does the operating agreement. If an LLC is looking to raise capital, however, it is advantageous to come up with a capital structure and define it in the operating agreement.

Here is a suggestion. Define three classes of membership units: A, B, and C. Class A membership units are reserved for issuance to the founding members of the company. Class B membership units are reserved for issuance to managers, officers, and consultants as performance incentives, just like stock options are used in a corporation. Class C membership units are reserved for sale to investors.

Later on, the LLC can create and define more classes of membership units, if needed to raise additional capital. The advantage in defining different classes of membership is that an LLC has the ability to allocate the net profits of the company among the classes differently. For example, unequal portions of the net profits for a period of time could be allotted to investors and founders.

Chapter 10

How to Choose Professionals

- Attorneys and Accountants
- Other Consultants
- Sequence

At some point in your entrepreneurial career, you are going to choose professionals to represent your company. Choosing these individuals is an important step in your company's development, and the good news is that you are not necessarily making a choice that cannot be changed.

Attorneys and Accountants

Most likely, your first two professionals will be an attorney and an accountant. Attorneys and accountants serve at the pleasure of their clients and you can replace them at anytime. You will probably find that you will be spending more time with your attorneys at the beginning of your business and through the funding stage, and more time with your accountants once the business stabilizes.

Figure 10.1: EVALUATING PROFESSIONALS

In evaluating your choice of professionals, particularly attorneys, the following questions might be helpful.

❑ Does your firm specialize in small and emerging businesses?

❑ Do you have experience in structuring corporations? LLCs?

❑ Do you provide advice on the choice of entities?

❑ Do you have tax expertise in the firm?

❑ Do you have securities expertise in the firm?

❑ Do you have experience in preparing securities offerings?

❑ Do you carry professional liability insurance with securities coverage?

❑ Do you handle IP work in the firm?

❑ Do you have expertise in dealing with angel investors and venture capitalists?

❑ What type of support can I expect on an ongoing basis?

❑ Who will I be working with in the firm?

❑ Can I obtain bios on the firm and its members?

❏ What is your normal turnaround time for this type of work?

❏ What is your pricing structure for fees?

❏ Do you have payment options for your fees?

❏ If you quote a fixed fee, what is included?

❏ Are you willing to take a portion of your fee in equity?

❏ Will you serve on the advisory board of the company?

The questions in Figure 10.1 are a few of the diligence questions you should ask when making your decision. Most attorneys and accountants will present you with a written engagement agreement that describes the fee structure and the scope of work. Many law firms prohibit their attorneys from serving on the board of directors of their clients because of possible conflicts between being a director and an attorney advocate.

Many law firms conduct a large portion of their business via email and the Internet. You should make it clear how you prefer communications to flow between you and the firm. Firms that are more progressive may even have extranets associated with their website where documents can be posted and reviewed confidentially by clients.

Most attorney and accountant relationships are the result of referrals by clients or colleagues. You can browse on the Internet at **www.Martindale.com** for attorneys and their biographies. Martindale-Hubbell is the leading reference source for locating attorneys in the United States. Martindale also has a rating system that rates outstanding attorneys based upon peer review. The highest rating assigned is AV followed by BV. Ratings appear with the attorney's name on the website and in the published version of their books. Martindale sponsors another lawyer locator site called **www.lawyers.com**.

Business lawyers can be a bit less visible than divorce or personal injury lawyers and do not tend to advertise as frequently. You can often meet them at venture capital conferences and entrepreneurial seminars in your area of the country. Many of the websites of business law firms contain a wealth of free information on entrepreneurial topics, as well as the biographies of the attorneys and their area of specialty.

Build from Your Resources: Accountants are a good source for attorney referrals and attorneys are a good referral source for accountants.

The decision to retain a professional should be based on a variety of factors, of which price is only one—and not the most important one. Other more important factors are competence in the area of specialty, team resources available, accessibility to the team, timely delivery of services, and amiable but professional relationship to the client. The choice of your professionals is a primarily value-based decision. New businesses need a legal counselor as much as they need a legal technician.

There are a number of excellent attorneys and accountants in this country. If you are satisfied with the experience and competence of the professional, then choose the ones that you resonate with personally. You have plenty to occupy your time with a new company—harmony among the team members will make your life much calmer and productive.

Other Consultants

Your company may have the occasion to employ other consultants in its lifetime. You should perform some measure of diligence on the consultants. Legitimate consultants will gladly provide you with a list of client references and share examples of their prior work. If anyone is doing creative work for your company, it is advisable to have a provision in the contract that their product is *work for hire*, so there is no question of ownership upon completion.

Most consultants will ask you to enter into a written agreement for their services. It is important to you that the agreement contains specific deliverables and a time period in which the deliverables are to be accomplished. Too many consulting agreements have extremely vague or general deliverables that bring no real substance or true value to the company. There are exceptions. Some well-known consultants are available to counsel with your company but do not provide reports or other deliverables—their advice alone is what they are selling. The agreement with the consultant is a contract that needs a legal review by company counsel.

Sequence

One of the more difficult tasks for the entrepreneur is to prioritize the company's interface with its professionals. New companies must normally conserve their cash resources as they build the company to go to market.

The sequence of tasks should be roughly as follows.

❑ Conduct a feasibility analysis of the product or service to determine whether you have a business.

❑ Engage an attorney to form the entity and provide preliminary documents for a *friends and family* round of raising capital.

❑ Engage an IP attorney to file trademarks and patents if applicable.

❑ Draft a business plan and hire an accountant or CFO to help with the numbers.

❑ Engage a business plan consultant if required.

❑ Engage a marketing expert to formulate a strategy.

❑ Bring in a branding/graphic specialist to begin a corporate identity package.

❑ Use a videographer to create a promotional video.

There is no set rule on sequence. Some things appear more important at different stages of the company's growth. Just make certain that the underlying business and legal structure is in place before proceeding very far.

Conclusion

Some small businesses never stop raising capital. In financing emerging businesses, it always takes longer and requires more money than you think. Start-up businesses fail for as many reasons as they succeed. Undercapitalization is near the top of the list for why they fail. Raise more capital than you think you need and begin planning your next round of financing while you are still working on the first round. It has been said that capital does not come until everything is ready.

It is a daunting challenge for the small business entrepreneur to balance the time between raising funds and running the business. If you don't raise funds, the business cannot execute its business plan, and if you don't skillfully run the business, it will make no difference how much money you raise.

On the bright side, you are building an organization that will provide for you and your family, and may someday provide a comfortable retirement. If the business develops on a grander scale, you may become quite wealthy.

Even if you fail in your initial attempt, learn from the experience and try again.

Take the tools presented in this book and make them your own. The more knowledgeable you become, the more effective you will be in dealing with your team, the business community, your investors, and your professionals.

There is no business like business.

May you live in your grandest passion!

JEB & RPL

Endnotes

[1] Used with permission, *How to Start a Business in Florida, 7th Edition*, Mark Warda, 2003, Sphinx Publishing.

[2] Used with permission, *How to Start a Business in Florida, 7th Edition*, Mark Warda, 2003, Sphinx Publishing.

[3] From an article by Burke Franklin, President of JIAN (**www.jian.com**), used by permission.

[4] Special thanks to Jay Winokur (**www.jaywinokur.com**) for his contributions to Chapter 2.

[5] Eric Delisle, CEO, Digibelly, Inc. (**www.digibelly.net**) used by permission.

[6] Tarby Bryant, Chairman and CEO, Anasazi Capital Corporation, used by permission.

[7] Courtesy of Diamond State Ventures (**www.dsventures.net**) and Gates and Company (**www.gatesandcompany.com**), used by permission.

[8] From *The Cognitive Style of PowerPoint*, an essay by Edward Tufte (**www.edwardtufte.com**).

For Further Reference

The following printed materials will provide valuable information to those who are starting and financing their small business.

For Hints on What it Takes to be Successful

Dohrmann, Bernhard, *Super Achiever Mindsets*. LSA Publishing, 2003, 247 pages.

Dyer, Wayne W., *The Power of Intention: Learning to Co-Create Your World Your Way*. Hay House, 2004, 300 pages.

Gladwell, Malcolm, *The Tipping Point: How Little Things Can Make a Big Difference*. Back Bay Books, 2002, 304 pages.

Gustafson, Joan, *A Woman Can Do That! 10 Strategies for Creating Success in Your Life*. Leader Dynamics, 2001, 208 pages.

Jaffe, Azriela, *Starting From No: Ten Strategies to Overcome Your Fear of Rejection and Succeed in Business*. Upstart Pub Co, 1999, 288 pages.

Kawasaki, Guy and Moreno, Michele, *Rules for Revolutionaries; the Capitalist Manifesto*. HarperCollins, 1999, 179 pages.

Pestrak, Debra, *Playing with the Big Boys; Success Secrets of the Most Powerful Women in Business*. Sun Publishing, 2002, 240 pages.

Wilhelm, John, *Dare to Fail While Preparing for Success*. AJ Foster Publishing, 2004, 88 pages.

For Advice on Business

American Bar Association, *The American Bar Association Legal Guide for Small Business*. Random House Information Group, 2000, 523 pages.

Collins, James, *Built to Last: Successful Habits of Visionary Companies*. HarperBusiness, 2002, 368 pages.

Collins, James, *Good to Great: Why Some Companies Make the Leap…and Others Don't*. HarperCollins, 2001, 320 pages.

Gerber, Michael E., *The E-Myth Revisited: Why Most Small Businesses Don't Work and What to Do About It*. HarperBusiness, 1995, 288 pages.

Gumpert, David E., *How to Really Start Your Own Business (3rd Edition)*. Goldhirsh Group, 1996, 268 pages.

Harroch, Richard D., *Small Business Kit for Dummies*. IDG Books Worldwide, 1998, 369 pages.

Hupalo, Peter I., *Thinking Like an Entrepreneur: How to Make Intelligent Business Decisions That Will Lead to Success in Building & Growing Your Own Company*. HCM Publishing, 1999, 272 pages.

Nesheim, John, *High Tech Start Up, Revised and Updated: The Complete Handbook for Creating Successful New High Tech Companies*. Simon & Schuster, 2000, 342 pages.

Rogers, Steve and Makonnen, Roza, *The Entrepreneur's Guide to Finance & Business: Wealth Creation Techniques for Growing a Business*. McGraw-Hill Trade, 2002, 340 pages.

Rubenstein, Herbert, *Breakthrough, Inc.—High Growth Strategies for Entrepreneurial Organizations*. Prentice Hall/Financial Times, 1999, 256 pages.

Tyson, Eric and Schell, Jim, *Small Business for Dummies*. IDG Books Worldwide, 2000, 408 pages.

For Advice on Business Plans

Franklin, Burke, *Business Black Belt*. Jian, 1998, 358 pages.

Gladstone, David J., *Venture Capital Handbook*. Prentice Hall, 1987, 368 pages.

For Advice on Valuation

Linton, Heather Smith, *Streetwise Business Valuation: Proven Methods to Easily Determine the True Value of Your Business*. Adams Media Corporation, 2004, 384 pages.

For Advice on Loans

Green, Charles, *The SBA Loan Book*. Adams Media Corporation, 1999, 218 pages.

For Advice on Financing

Benjamin, Gerald and Margulis, Joel, *Angel Financing: How to Find and Invest in Private Equity*. John Wiley & Sons, 1999, 307 pages.

Blechman, Bruce and Levinson, Jay, *Guerrilla Financing*. Mariner Books, 1992, 335 pages.

Blum, Laurie, *Free Money for Small Businesses and Entrepreneurs*. John Wiley & Sons, 1995, 304 pages.

For Advice on Getting Government Contracts

DiGiacomo, John and Kleckner, James, *Win Government Contracts for Your Small Business, 2ⁿᵈ edition* CCH, 2003, 506 pages.

For Advice on Angel Investors

Amis, David and Stevenson, Howard H., *Winning Angels: The 7 Fundamentals of Early Stage Investing*. Financial Times Prentice Hall, 2001, 304 pages.

Arkebauer, James B., *Going Public*. Dearborn Trade Publishing, 1998, 360 pages.

Benjamin, Gerald and Margulis, Joel, *The Angel Investor's Handbook: How to Profit from Early-Stage Investing*. Bloomberg Press, 2001, 368 pages.

Hill, Brian, & Power, Dee, *Attracting Capital from Angels: How their Money—and Their Experience—Can Help you Build a Successful Company*. John Wiley & Sons, 2002, 324 pages.

May, John and Simons, Cal, *Every Business Needs An Angel: Getting The Money You Need To Make Your Business Grow*. Crown Business, Random House, 2001, 256 pages.

Van Osnabrugge, Mark and Robinson, Robert, *Angel Investing: Matching Startup Funds with Startup Companies—A Guide for Entrepreneurs, Individual Investors, and Venture Capitalists*. Jossey-Bass, 2000, 320 pages.

For Advice on Venture Capitalists

Hill, Brian, & Power, Dee, *Inside Secrets to Venture Capital*. John Wiley & Sons, 2001, 304 pages.

Lister, Kate and Harnish, Tom, *Directory of Venture Capital*. John Wiley & Sons, 2000, 385 pages.

Pratt, Stanley, *Pratt's Guide to Venture Capital Sources*. Thomson Financial, 2004, 700 pages.

Wilmerding, Alex and Aspatore Books Staff, *Deal Terms—The Finer Points of Venture Capital Deal Structures, Valuations, Term Sheets, Stock Options and Getting Deals Done*. Aspatore Books, 2003, 340 pages.

Wilmerding, Alex and Aspatore Books Staff, *Term Sheets & Valuations—A Line by Line Look at the Intricacies of Venture Capital Term Sheets & Valuations*. Aspatore Books, 2002, 124 pages.

For Advice on Franchising

Dugan, Ann (editor), *The Association of Small Business Development Centers, Franchising 101*. Upstart Pub Co, 1998, 267 pages.

Seid, Michael and Thomas, Dave, *Franchising for Dummies*. For Dummies, 2000, 378 pages.

Sherman, Andrew J., *Franchising & Licensing: Two Powerful Ways to Grow Your Business*. AMACOM, 2004, 428 pages.

For Advice on Corporate Governance

American Bar Association, *Corporate Director's Guidebook*. ABA Publishing, 2004, 112 pages.

Robert, Henry M, III, et al., *Robert's Rules of Order. 10th edition*, Perseus Publishing, 2000, 704 pages.

Tortorice, Donald A., *The Modern Rules of Order: A Guide for Conducting Business Meetings*. ABA Publishing, 1999, 80 pages.

Varallo, Gregory and Dreisbach, Daniel A., *Fundamentals of Corporate Governance: A Guide for Directors and Corporate Counsel*. ABA Publishing, 1996, 171 pages.

For Advice on Bookkeeping and Organization

Caplan, Suzanne, *Streetwise Finance and Accounting*. Adams Media Corporation, 2000, 337 pages.

Kamoroff, Bernard, *Small Time Operator (27th Edition)*. Bell Springs Publishing, 2000, 200 pages.

Kravitz, Wallace, *Bookkeeping the Easy Way*. Barrons Educational Series, 1999, 328 pages.

Pinson, Linda, *Keeping the Books: Basic Recordkeeping and Accounting for the Successful Small Business*. Dearborn Trade Publishing, 2001, 210 pages.

For Advice on Marketing

Brown, Paul B. and Sewell, Carl, *Customers For Life: How to Turn That One-time Buyer into a Lifetime Customer*. Currency, 2002, 208 pages.

Fowler, David, *Newspaper Ads That Make Sales Jump: A How-to Guide*. Marketing Clarity, 1998, 74 pages.

Ogilvy, David, *Ogilvy on Advertising*. Vintage, 1985, 224 pages.

Ries, Al and Trout, Jack, *Positioning: The Battle for Your Mind*. McGraw-Hill Trade, 2001, 213 pages.

Spoelstra, John and Cuban, Mark, *Marketing Outrageously*. Bard Press, 2001, 256 pages.

Trout, Jack, *Differentiate or Die*. John Wiley & Sons, 2000, 230 pages.

Underhill, Paco, *Why We Buy*. Simon & Schuster, 200, 256 pages.

For Advice on Public Speaking and Presentations

Kusher, Malcolm, *Public Speaking for Dummies*. IDG Books, 2004, 288 pages.

For Advice on Publicity

Lupash, Joyce and Grimes, Pate, *How to Create High Impact Business Presentations*. NTC Business Books, 1993, 256 pages.

Levinson, Jay, Frishman, Rick and Lublin, Jill, *Guerrilla Publicity*. Adams Media Corporation, 2002, 304 pages.

• • • • •

The following are books published by Sourcebooks, Inc. that may be helpful to your business.

Covello, Joseph A. and Hazelgren, Brian J., *The Complete Book of Business Plans*. 1995.

Covello, Joseph A. and Hazelgren, Brian J., *Your First Business Plan*. 2005.

DuBoff, Leonard D., *The Law (In Plain English)® for Small Business*. 2004.

Fleischer, Charles H., *HR for Small Business*. 2005.

King, Ruth, *The Ugly Truth about Small Business*. 2005.

McGuckin, Francis, *Business for Beginners*. 2005.

McGuckin, Francis, *Taking Your Business to the Next Level*. 2005.

Parker, James O., *Tax Smarts for Small Business*. 2004.

Ray, James C., *The Complete Book of Corporate Forms, Second Edition*. 2005.

Root, Hal and Koening, Steve, *The Small Business Start-up Guide*. 2006.

●　●　●　●　●

The following government websites provide information that may be useful to you in starting and operating your business.

Federal Trade Commission
www.ftc.gov

Immigration & Naturalization Service
www.ins.gov

Export-Import Bank
www.exim.gov

Internal Revenue Service
www.irs.gov

Patent and Trademark Office
www.uspto.gov

Securities and Exchange Commission
www.sec.gov

Small Business Administration
www.sba.gov

Social Security Administration
www.ssa.gov

U.S. Business Advisor
www.business.gov

• • • • •

The following commercial websites provide information that may be useful to you in starting and operating your business.

www.abanet.org/abapubs
   American Bar Association Publishing.

http://acenet.csusb.edu
   Access to Capital Electronic Network. Listing service that allows investors to find small companies through a secure database.

www.americanexpress.com
   OPEN: the Small Business Network.

www.avce.com
   American Venture Capital Exchange. Website for American Venture Magazine.

www.dsventures.net
   Diamond State Ventures. A Delaware technology cultivator.

www.edwardsresearch.com
   Edwards Directory of American Factors.

www.garage.com
Garage.com. Helping entrepreneurs and investors build high-technology companies by providing advice, information and research.

www.gatheringofangels.com
Anasazi Capital Corporation. Angel network.

www.growth-strategies.com
Growth Strategies, Inc. Consulting firm for high growth businesses.

www.humwin.com
Hummer Winblad. Venture capitalist specializing in software.

www.ibiglobal.com
IBI Global. Premier entrepreneurial training.

www.icrnet.com
Angel financing introduction service.

www.inc.com
Information resource for growing companies.

www.investopedia.com
Online encyclopedia of terms and phrases used by the investment community.

www.investorlinks.com
The Web Investor. IPOs, lists of venture capitalists.

www.investorwords.com
Online dictionary of words used by the investment community.

www.jian.com
Home of BizPlan Builder software.

www.lawyers.com
Lawyer locator site sponsored by Martindale-Hubbell.

www.martindale.com
Martindale-Hubbell lawyer locator site.

www.nvst.com
Connections to private capital and to mergers and acquisitions.

www.pwcmoneytree.com
PricewaterhouseCoopers Money Tree Survey. A quarterly study of equity investments made by the venture capital community in private companies.

www.redherring.com
Red Herring. A comprehensive view of the private company and private equity landscapes for investors, entrepreneurs, and innovators.

www.siliconvalley.com
Research companies that have received venture funding and learn where venture capitalists are making investments.

www.ibisuccesschannel.com
IBI Global Success Channel. Online audio and video broadcasts of entrepreneurial training lessons.

www.tcnmit.org
Matching of start-ups and early-stage investors.

www.tdosolutions.com
Central New York Technology Development Organization (CNYTDO). Works directly with technology and manufacturing companies to smooth the transition from start-ups to mature organizations.

www.toolkit.cch.com

CCH Business Owners Toolkit. Online resource for anyone who is starting, running and growing a business.

http://web.mit.edu/entforum

MIT Enterprise Forum. Programs and networking opportunities for entrepreneurs and investors.

www.vcapital.com

Venture Capital Online. Matches start-ups with appropriate venture capitalist firms.

www.vfinance.com

Listings of venture capitalists, investment banks, business resources.

Glossary

A

accounts payable. Amount owed to creditors for goods and services.

accounts receivable. Amount due from customers for merchandise or services.

accredited investor. A person with a net worth exceeding $1 million or income over $200,000 annually in the past two years, or an institution deemed capable of understanding and able to afford the financial risks associated with purchasing unregistered securities.

angels. Friends, family, or wealthy individuals who invest their money, usually in start-up or early-stage companies.

asset. Anything owned by a business or individual that has commercial or exchange value.

B

balance sheet. Financial statement that presents a snapshot of what the business owns (assets), what it owes (liabilities), and what equity it has on a given date.

board of directors. These are the individuals who control a corporation for the benefit of the stockholders. They listen to management's recommendations and set policy for the corporation.

C

capital. Money invested in a business by the owner(s). Also called *equity*.

capital expenditures. Purchases of long-term assets, such as equipment.

cash flow. The money coming in and the money going out is the flow of cash that determines whether a business will survive. The most important aspect of any small business is the cash flow.

closing. The event that occurs when you sign legal documents binding your company and transferring cash from the venture capitalist to your company.

common stock. Units representing ownership of a corporation. The owners (shareholders) are typically entitled to vote on the selection of directors and other company matters, as well as receive dividends on their holdings. If the company is liquidated, the claims of its creditors and owners of bonds or preferred stock take precedence over the common stockholders.

convertible. Usually refers to debt or preferred stock, each of which is convertible into common stock of the company. Obviously, it is possible to have debt convertible into preferred stock and it is even possible to have preferred stock convertible into debt, although the latter is unusual.

covenant. Paragraphs in the legal documents stating the things you agree you will do and paragraphs stating what you will not do.

corporation. Form of business ownership with unlimited life and limited liability for its owners (shareholders).

D

debt service. The amount of money you have to pay on a debt in order to keep it from being in default. If you make the payments that are called for under a note or loan, then you are servicing the debt.

dilution. A term used to describe an increase or decrease in the amount of shareholders equity (net worth/book value) whenever new shares are issued by a company.

dividends. A taxable distribution made to shareholders disbursed from a portion of the company's earnings; usually paid in cash, but may be paid in additional, newly issued shares.

double taxation. In a corporation, income is taxed at the corporate level and again as part of the personal income of shareholders to whom it is distributed as dividends.

due diligence. The process of gathering and confirming information about a company and its business, management, and financial affairs to determine its feasibility and level of risk for an investment.

E

equity. Normally, it describes the preferred and common stock of a business. Also, it is frequently used to describe the amount of ownership of one person or a venture capitalist in a business.

F

factoring. Occurs when a financial institution buys a firm's accounts receivable (at a discount) and then collects the full value of the accounts from customers. Banks, through their *Visa* and *Mastercard* programs, do a form of *factoring* for merchants who accept their credit cards.

ficticious name. The name a person or business uses to conduct business with the public, but is not its actual, legal name.

G

general partner. A partner who shares ownership and has full liability for the debts of the business.

gross income. Sales less cost of goods sold.

H

hidden franchise. A term used when a licensing agreement resembles a franchise agreement too closely, resulting in additional legal hurdles associated with franchises.

I

issuer. An entity, usually a corporation, that has the ability to issue and distribute securities.

J

junior lien. A lien that is subordinate to another lien. A junior lien will be paid only after any liens above it are satisfied.

L

limited liability company (LLC). A form of business organization that combines characteristics of a corporation and a partnership. Owners have limited liability like a corporation, but the LLC is taxed as a partnership.

M

memorandum. A document similar to a prospectus, sometimes also referred to as an offering circular, that is the official document by which private placements are offered and sold.

N

net income. The profit remaining after all expenses have been deducted from income.

net worth. Excess of assets over liabilities.

O

offering circular. A disclosure and information document used to furnish information about a company and its stock offering to prospective investors; commonly used for exempt offerings and patterned after a prospectus.

options. The right given to someone to buy stock in your company.

P

partnership. An unincorporated business with more than one owner. The tax burden is shared by all the partners at their personal rate. General partners have unlimited liability. Limited partners have limited liability.

preferred shares. A separate class of a company's stock with certain preferential features over common stock that often include a right of its owners to be repaid before shareholders of common stock in the event of liquidation, rights to dividends before owners of common stock, and sometimes certain voting rights superior to those of common stock.

private placement. An offering of securities exempt from full SEC registration requirements that is usually made directly by the issuing company but may also be made by an underwriter.

***pro forma* financial statements.** Estimated income statement showing anticipated revenues, costs, and expenses over a period of time, and a balance sheet showing assets, liabilities, and equity at a fixed point in time.

profit and loss statement. Summary of the revenues, costs, and expenses over a period of time. Also called an *income statement*.

R

raising capital. Raising capital refers to obtaining capital from investors or venture capital sources.

registered agent. The person or entity listed with a state governmental agency to receive legal notices for a business organization.

Regulation A. An exemption made by the SEC from filing a full registration statement under the *Securities Act of 1933*.

Regulation D. An exemption made by the SEC from filing a full registration statement under the *Securities Act of 1933*.

S

Small Business Administration (SBA). A federal agency created in 1953 to provide assistance to small businesses by guaranteeing loans through financial institutions and assisting the management of qualified businesses.

Small Corporate Offering Registration (SCOR). An SEC-exempt offering for the sale of securities up to the amount of $1 million that must be qualified under state *blue sky laws*. Also known as ULOR.

SEC. The U.S. Securities and Exchange Commission, which is charged with the administration and enforcement of federal securities laws.

Securities Act of 1933. The federal law, including amendments, pertaining to the offering of securities administrated by the SEC.

Securities Exchange Act of 1934. The federal law, including amendments, pertaining to the trading of securities, stock exchanges, firms, and brokers administrated by the SEC.

senior lien. A lien that is superior to another lien. A senior lien will be paid before liens subordinate to it.

shareholders. Individuals or entities who own the securities (shares/stocks) of a company.

shares outstanding. The total number of shares of stock held by all shareholders.

sole proprietorship. A business form with a single owner in which the owner has total control, total liability, and the proceeds of the business are taxed at the proprietor's individual rate.

S corporation. A tax option for corporations formed under subchapter S of the federal Tax Code, in which shareholders can unanimously consent to be taxed like a partnership, permitting income and expense to *flow through* to their personal tax returns. Originally designed to avoid double taxation yet preserve limited liability, the S corporation form is now giving way in some states to the limited liability company (LLC).

V

venture capitalists. Individuals or institutions that fund early stage, high-risk businesses. They generally want some ownership in the business and expect a 20% to 50% return on investment.

W

warrants. A certificate giving its holder the right to purchase securities at a defined price within a specified time.

working capital. The excess of current assets over current liabilities.

Appendix A

Business Plan

As part of your business strategy, planning, and feasibility analysis, you will commit your plan to paper. The document produced is typically called a *business plan*. The purpose of a business plan is to articulate the vision of your business and then set out the steps for implementing that vision. Chapter 2 gives you the suggested elements of a business plan.

Initially, start-up companies will write a business plan with the ultimate goal of raising capital. You may also wish to have an *internal* business plan to chart the actual course of the business. The latter will be constantly revised as circumstances change.

The business plan provided focuses on capital raising. It is an actual business plan from a company actively trying to raise capital to fund their business idea.

NOTE: *The following business plan is used with permission from What's In Your Neighborhood.*

WHAT'S IN YOUR NEIGHBORHOOD™

Business Plan

CONFIDENTIALITY & DISCLOSURE AGREEMENT

THE INFORMATION PRESENTED IN THIS BUSINESS PLAN IS PROPRI-ETARY AND CONFIDENTIAL. IT MAY NOT BE REPRODUCED OR COM-MUNICATED IN ANY MANNER, VERBALLY, ELECTRONICALLY, OR OTH-ERWISE, WITHOUT THE WRITTEN CONSENT OF WHAT'S IN YOUR NEIGHBORHOOD, INC. IF YOU HAVE AGREED TO RECEIVE THIS PLAN, YOU SHALL BE DEEMED TO BE IN AGREEMENT THAT THIS INFORMA-TION IS PROPRIETARY AND CONFIDENTIAL, AND FULLY UNDERSTAND AND AGREE TO REFRAIN FROM TRANSFERENCE OF SAME TO ANY OTHER INDIVIDUALS OR BUSINESS ENTITIES.

IF YOU DO NOT WISH TO BE BOUND BY THIS AGREEMENT, PLEASE RETURN THIS DOCUMENT TO WHAT'S IN YOUR NEIGHBORHOOD, INC. ADDITIONALLY, THE BUSINESS PLAN IS COVERED BY U.S. COPYRIGHT LAWS. THEREFORE, REPRODUCTION OR DISSEMINATION OF CON-TENTS MAY BE IN VIOLATION OF FEDERAL LAW.

THIS DOCUMENT HAS BEEN PREPARED BY WHAT'S IN YOUR NEIGHBORHOOD, INC., SOLELY FOR INFORMATIONAL AND PROJEC-TION PURPOSES ONLY. THIS IS NOT AN OFFER TO SELL STOCK OR SECURITIES. THIS BUSINESS PLAN WAS WRITTEN FOR INDIVIDUALS TO MAKE AN EVALUATION OF THE SUBJECT MATTER CONTAINED HEREIN AND TO ASSIST THEM IN DETERMINING THEIR DESIRE TO PROCEED IN PROVIDING SUPPORT TO THE PROJECT. WHILE THE INFORMATION CONTAINED HEREIN IS FROM SOURCES DEEMED RELIABLE, WHAT'S IN YOUR NEIGHBORHOOD, INC., HAS NOT INDE-PENDENTLY VERIFIED IT. WHAT'S IN YOUR NEIGHBORHOOD, INC., MAKES NO WARRANTIES, EXPRESSED OR IMPLIED, THAT ACTUAL RESULTS OF THE PRODUCT(S) OR COMPANY WILL CONFORM TO RESULTS PROJECTED HEREIN. THIS DOCUMENT IS SUBJECT TO REVI-SION, WITHDRAWAL, OR MODIFICATION.

Executive Summary

What's In Your Neighborhood, Inc. (WIYN, Inc.) is a start-up company, whose flag-ship software product, What's In Your Neighborhood, (WIYN), will change the way neighborhood consumers and local businesses connect. The product is free to con-sumers and revenue is generated from business advertisers.

WIYN is a powerful, grass-roots desktop application that increases neighbor-hood awareness, stimulates the local economy, and provides valuable time & cost savings to residents regardless of computer ownership. WIYN addresses the prob-lem that neighborhood residents and local businesses have in using the Internet, the Yellow Pages, or other types of directories to link up with one another.

WIYN incorporates the best of proven business, delivery, and revenue models to present a convenient, easy-to-use electronic business directory that goes one step farther; it integrates pertinent neighborhood information, such as schools, parks, and recreation centers, to make WIYN the ideal neighborhood resource.

The computer and the Internet have become more prevalent and relevant in everyday life and as a result, Internet penetration in United States homes has reached nearly 75%[1]. Because of this trend, the potential market for WIYN is in excess of 125 million users. This technologically savvy market, when segmented by areas of defined shopping patterns, offers local businesses a targeted group of con-sumers, who by using WIYN have become qualified consumers searching for the business where they want to spend their money.

Businesses will spend $230 billion on advertising in general in the United States this year[2]. Yet, none of the common forms of advertising offers businesses the abil-ity to manage their advertising investment and modify their product and service mix based on quantified data pinpointing what the consumer in their community is looking for. The ability to gather its product's usage at a local level makes WIYN extremely attractive to advertising businesses, because it allows the business to manage its advertising investment.

Businesses can choose among three different monthly packages that alter their level of prominence within the product. This allows businesses to select a package that suits their advertising and data collecting needs. Through the use of proven Internet technologies, WIYN permits local businesses to leverage the power of the Internet, without competing with every business on the Internet, to reach their local consumer and bring the competition for the local consumer's dollar back to a truly local playing field.

The What's In Your Neighborhood, Inc., team has over 30 years combined expe-rience in creating high-end, user-friendly, multimedia software applications with clients ranging from the United States Navy to the United States Hispanic Chamber of Commerce. Their skills and expertise combined with their growing team of experienced business executives, creates a company poised for success.

The Company has completed its pre-development phase of growth, and is well positioned to begin its remaining three phases:

- Development—Begins immediately upon funding
- Initial Area Launch—Begins immediately after development
- Expansion—Begins 12 months after initial area launch

Each area launched will be created as a separate Limited Liability Company (LLC), with the Company acting as its managing partner. The goal is to open ten areas within six years; this includes the twelve months required for development. Therefore, the potential for WIYN, Inc. and its underlying LLCs is substantial, with conservative projections showing over $105 million in gross revenues for ten areas in 72 months and a positive annual corporate cash flow of $23 million.

This opportunity requires an investment total of $900K, in exchange for an equity ownership position in the corporation. The investment reflects all monies needed to fully develop the product.

The Company

What's In Your Neighborhood, Inc., the "Company", is a California C corporation registered in January of 2004, by the co-founders, Edward Cox, Ralph "Bud" Hartel, and Joseph Rios.

The Company is presently headquartered at 1345 Corte Bagalso, San Marcos, CA 92069, with a mailing address of P.O. Box 2679, San Marcos, CA 92079-2679.

The flagship product of the Company is called What's In Your Neighborhood, (WIYN).

The Product

What's In Your Neighborhood, Inc., is an information servicing company that brings neighborhood consumers together by finally providing them a comprehensive understanding of what their neighborhood businesses and community services has to offer, and thereby allowing them to maximize the local resources available.

The primary vehicle of this easy-to-use computer desktop application is an electronic directory that connects neighborhood consumers to their local businesses.

WIYN provides users several familiar ways to find the businesses they are ready to spend money with either by category, keyword, or business name. Innovative and helpful ways to find businesses are also provided to allow searching for businesses that are offering coupons, offering neighborhood discounts, or simply have a mapped location to display.

Users can easily find all the business' information they need from the basics: street address, phone numbers, and email addresses, to having one-click access to more in-depth information at the business' website. Businesses can even enhance their information by providing quick-glance company descriptions or an engaging audio or video commercial. All of this information is kept up-to-date and fresh through automated Internet updates, similar to common virus protection software.

What sets WIYN apart from any other directory is the additional neighborhood and civic information incorporated into its system. Users can effortlessly find neighborhood information on schools, parks, recreation centers, golf courses, and important community numbers, etc.; making WIYN the 21ˢᵗ century neighborhood resource directory, and so much more.

The user's experience is heightened through several visual innovations. WIYN is immersed in a well-designed, user-friendly multimedia interface to engage the senses through proven color schemes, animations, and sound effects.

Users are then provided a comprehensive view of their neighborhood through WIYN's Map-Centric™ methodology that displays information overlaid and tied to a prominent on-screen map.

Through the integration of proven programs WIYN becomes an even more valuable resource for neighborhood consumers and businesses. For example:

- Coupon system—This allows advertising businesses to tap into the 242 million electronic coupons downloaded last year[3] by providing users coupons they can print and redeem
- Discount card—This allows participating businesses to build brand awareness by offering neighborhood discounts to WIYN cardholders
- CouPoints™—This exclusive system mimics proven loyalty programs, such as frequent flyer miles, by rewarding users for regular and consistent use of the product with points that can be redeemed for special coupons from participating local businesses

The combination of the software, the continuous local marketing, and these programs makes WIYN a powerful, grass-roots product that increases neighborhood awareness, stimulates the local economy, and provides valuable time & cost savings to residents regardless of computer ownership.

In addition, advertising businesses profit from the ability to track the usage of the product by reporting on keyword and category search trends, coupon usage, web linking traffic, and number of times found in a search. This allows businesses to manage their advertising investment, and serve their neighborhood consumers better by quickly adapting to their quantified wants and needs, thus creating a stronger and more rewarding relationship. This is what the Company likes to call a WIYN-WIYN relationship.

The Market

Every Metropolitan Statistical Area (MSA) in the United States with a population over 500,000 is a potential market for the product. Approximately 250 of the current 321 MSAs are potential target areas translating into over 125 million potential users in the United States. In the next six years, the goal is to expand into ten of these 250 areas, or 2.5% of the market potential.

An area is defined by a zip code grouping of communities tied together by shopping patterns, similar to Yellow Page directory boundaries. These are densely populated areas with 500,000 to 1.5 million residents, where there is at least a 75% rate of computer penetration, meaning at least one computer in the home, and 15,000 or more potential advertisers. This grouping allows for three to eight neighborhoods to be serviced by one area office.

These neighborhoods are comprised of two to three communities that are defined by a shopping pattern, have 100,000 to 300,000 residents, and have 5,000 or more potential advertisers.

Internet connectivity is not a requirement to use the software. However, Internet users have now become accustomed to using their computer as a tool in everyday life. Therefore, the target residents within these neighborhoods are computer users and broadband Internet subscribers.

The Company's advertising niche is the ten million small-to-medium sized enterprises (SMEs), the bulk of which have fewer than nine employees and conduct the majority of their business within 50 miles of their locations. This indicates their understanding of the importance of reaching their local customers.

According to eMarketer, The Kelsey Group (the leading provider of strategic research and analysis, data and competitive metrics on Yellow Pages, electronic directories and local media since 1986) estimates that SMEs will spend $22 billion on advertising this year, with 46% going to Yellow Pages advertising ($10 billion)[4]. Their research also estimates that advertising dollars will be divided amongst other lead-generating tools, of which WIYN incorporates many of these same features:

Yellow Pages 46% ($10.12 billion)	**Search engine keywords 3% ($660 million)**
Newspaper 13% ($2.86 billion)	**Print coupons 2% ($440 million)**
Website 11% ($2.42 billion)	Outdoor advertising 2% ($440 million)
Direct mail 6% ($1.32 billion)	Web banners 1% ($220 million)
Magazines 6% ($1.32 billion)	Email marketing 1% ($220 million)
Radio 4% ($880 million)	Other 5% ($1.1 billion)

While large, these numbers only address the advertising dollars spent by SMEs. The advertising estimates across all businesses are significantly higher. The Kelsey Group reports that $230 billion will be spent on advertising in general in the United States this year, with advertising being split as follows[5]:

TV 28% ($64.4 billion)	**Yellow pages 6% ($13.8 billion)**
Direct Mail 21% ($48.3 billion)	Magazine 5% ($11.5 billion)
Newspaper 20% ($46 billion)	Internet 2% ($4.6 billion)
Misc. 16% ($36.8 billion)	Out of home 2% ($4.6 billion)

The Company is competing for these advertising dollars spent by local businesses and has identified several direct competitors to the product. The most prominent of these are:

- Yellow Page directories, both print and Internet based
- Local business directories, both print and Internet based
- Coupon books and mailers

These industries have long competed for the advertising dollar of local businesses, yet have built profitable and growing industries. For example, last year, the North American print Yellow Pages topped $15 billion in revenues[6], and ValPak, the most recognized direct mail coupon company in the country, estimates that it will generate $400 million in revenue this year[7].

These industries are succeeding, because businesses are compelled to advertise through any medium that could possibly work to get the local consumer into their business.

The lack of accountability from these advertising mediums, especially print, forces businesses to employ a "shotgun approach" to reach their customer. One example is a business placing ads in every directory in their area, because they do not know which directory is used by their customer. Businesses often do not know which medium is truly working for them, unless they spend their own money to survey their customers, which still does not give them accurate results. This is evident in the recent discrepancies found in the A/C Nielsen ratings between written journal documentation and verified digital tracking. There was a 50%–100% margin of error found in the journal surveys[8].

These discrepancies need not exist as consumers continue to adopt digital technology. Consumers are now using the Internet more and more to find what they want. According to the Nielsen//Net Ratings Enumeration Study released in March 2004, Internet penetration in the United States has reached nearly 75% [9].

Nielsen/Net Ratings Internet Access Penetration (United States, Home)			
	Persons (2+) with Web Access	Total Persons (2+) in U.S.	Internet Penetration
Population	204,307,000	272,810,000	74.9%

The Kelsey Group's editorial director, Greg Sterling wrote in a March 17, 2004 article[10]:

- C&R Research found 84% of United States mothers who use the Web would miss it more than any other single type of media if compelled to give up one
- Among consumers more and more people are using the Internet as a basic daily utility – and search is a key part of that experience
- Nielsen//NetRatings reported roughly 39% of Americans—114 million people—used at least one search engine during the month of January 2004, representing 76% of the active United States Internet users

Local search queries make up seven percent of all Internet searches in the United States, according to comScore, which found that in a single month nearly 36 million Internet users conducted more than 200 million searches that included local modifiers[11].

Businesses are pouring money into this new medium for several reasons:
- They want to be where their customers can find them
- They know that customers actively searching for them are in essence qualified leads; they're ready to spend money
- They want to be able to manage their advertising investment

According to the April 2004 PricewaterhouseCoopers, LLP "IAB Internet Advertising Revenue Report", online advertising has increased dramatically.

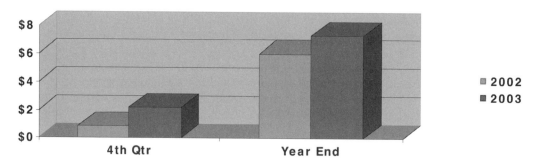

United States Internet Advertising Revenues (Billions)

Internet advertising revenue in the United States totaled nearly $2.2 billion in the fourth quarter of 2003, up more than 38% from the same time period in 2002. Internet advertising for all of 2003 totaled just under $7.3 billion, up nearly 21 percent from the 2002 total of $6.0 billion, and marked the first year-over-year annual increase since 2000. Revenues for the fourth-quarter of 2003 also experienced a healthy sequential increase of nearly 22% over the third quarter[12].

The Kelsey Group projects that by 2008, as much as $5 billion in the North American market will be going to digital forms of local advertising—IYP (Internet Yellow Pages), search, and wireless[13].

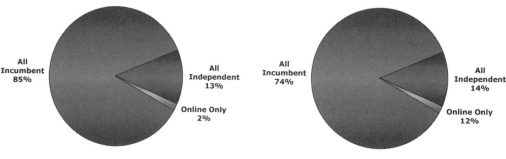

U.S. Yellowpages Share by Publisher Segment - 2003
U.S. Yellowpages Share by Publisher Segment - 2008

Source: The Kelsey Group (2004)   Source: The Kelsey Group (2004)

All the interest in local search is in direct response to a very real demand for local information online. People like to find and buy things in their neighborhood, and more consumers are turning to the Net rather than lift the 20-pound Yellow Pages. According to The Kelsey Group, the local search-based advertising market is expected to be worth $2.5 billion by 2008[14].

This phenomenon demonstrates that consumers are not only using the Internet to find what's wrong with their toilet, but to find the local plumber to fix it.

"When it comes to geo-targeted online search, more consumers clearly are using search to find local business information. A recent survey of 5500 online buyers showed that 25.1% of commercial searches (looking for a business, shopping, or doing research before buying) were local. The data also showed that 44% of respondents were performing more local commercial searches than one year ago. Furthermore, 64% of these respondents rated search engines as better than traditional offline sources of information, such as Yellow Pages, newspapers, magazines, and direct mail.[15]"

Greg Sterling, The Kelsey Group, Show Search the Money, March 17, 2004

According to Nate Elliott, an associate analyst at Jupiter Research, the two big growth drivers in Internet advertising are search (keywords) and rich media[16].

Another occurrence on the rise is non-browser Internet use. Three out of four home and work Web users go online through non-browser-based Internet applications, such as media players, instant messengers and file-sharing tools, according to Nielsen//NetRatings[17]. "Functionality has grown beyond the browser to become a fundamental piece of the overall desktop," said Abha Bahagat, senior analyst at Nielsen//NetRatings, a part of Adweek parent VNU[18]. This shows that users will quickly embrace WIYN as a desktop gateway to their neighborhood.

All of these trends positively impact WIYN's advertising revenues and product adoption. Where usage goes, so does the advertising dollar, and businesses have already started spending more on electronic mediums to reach their customers. WIYN is well poised to play a dominant role in this emerging local market.

The Team

The Company recognizes that its future success will be based on building an agile, experienced team of professionals that can manage the expected rapid growth of the Company. The Company's management philosophy will support and encourage a smooth flow of ideas, and results-oriented implementation through development, customer service, sales and marketing. The initial team players are:

Edward Cox—Chief Executive Officer, Founder

Mr. Cox has four years of experience working as a project manager and software developer. Most recently he was the technical manager for Batiz.com, Vista, CA, where he managed a team of programmers and designers in the completion of several websites and CD-ROM projects. In addition, he created and developed new products and follow-on enhancements for the United States Hispanic Chamber of

Commerce's official online career center website, Jobcentro.com. He also designed and developed back-end functionality for the award winning San Diego County Hispanic Chamber of Commerce website.

Mr. Cox is also credited with developing and maintaining an online chat module for the United States Navy used in conjunction with a multimedia CD-ROM that allowed potential recruits to connect with recruiters. Mr. Cox also developed user functionality for the first bilingual website of any branch of the United States armed services, ELNAVY.com. Prior to Batiz.com, he was with Mass Mutual, La Jolla, CA, where he was responsible for researching investments for client portfolios and managing agency investment materials. Mr. Cox holds a BS degree in Business Administration, with an emphasis in Information & Decision Systems, from San Diego State University.

Ralph "Bud" Hartel—Chief Operating Officer, Founder

Mr. Hartel has over 25 years of technical experience and proven team leadership. He was Chief Electronics Technician managing a technical team of eight on a Navy nuclear submarine electronics upgrade. Additionally he was the Chief Instructor supervising and scheduling seven instructors and maintaining the capital budget for the Spokane ITT Technical Institute electronics department. Mr. Hartel was also the operations manager for a cabinet manufacturing company responsible for revenue generation, sales force management and factory production. He also served as the CTO and Operations Officer for a software development company managing multiple Navy recruiting projects valued at over $2 million. Mr. Hartel has also managed his own consulting company utilizing his strong programming background to develop web-based data management tools. He holds multiple Microsoft certifications.

Joseph Rios—Chief Creative Officer, Founder

Mr. Rios' creative background includes multimedia design at Batiz.com, Vista, CA, where he met and worked with the founders of What's In Your Neighborhood, Inc. At Batiz.com, he was the lead interactive developer for all multimedia engagements. He also trained other interactive developers on the use of various software applications used in the building of these projects. While there, he spearheaded all of the concepts and designs, in addition to managing the creation of multimedia military recruitment marketing materials for the United States Navy, which demanded the highest level of cross-platform compatibility, system performance, and presentation techniques. He is also skilled at using all the leading website creation tools. Prior to Batiz.com, Joseph was the Webmaster and Graphic Designer for LSI Sports, Vista, CA, where he was the website designer creating all artwork and navigation used on the site. He also designed all of the company's marketing materials.

Board of Directors
Bob Mangum

Prior to establishing his own consultancy in strategic planning, infrastructure for management, financial control, corporate finance, and other senior management and board level issues more than 20 years ago, Mr. Mangum worked with and managed numerous publicly listed companies. In addition to his consultancy practice, Bob has served as a director on numerous Boards including Arizona Small Business Association, Inc., Arizona Internet and E-Commerce Association, as well as, numerous other technology, service, manufacturing and product related corporations. Mr. Mangum brings years of fiduciary, corporate governance, and cost-control experience to enhance the Company's functionality, performance and efficiency.

Marie "Mimi" Zeller

Marie has over 15 years experience in franchising including eight years with Domino's Pizza, Inc. and over three years with Mail Boxes Etc., where she recently served as senior vice president-operations, overseeing the franchise operations of 3,400 domestic locations.   She also played a vital role in new product development and negotiated over 60 national agreements with companies such as Xerox, Konica and Pitney Bowes. Her assistance with small business owners has encompassed areas of finance, marketing, training and operations. Marie has a bachelor's degree in business administration, with a concentration in marketing, from the University of Kentucky. She completed a Harvard executive mini-MBA management course and has experience as a corporate keynote speaker at several large conventions.

Advisors & Professional Service Providers

The Company understands the importance of building a strong executive team. The founders are currently looking for an individual to add to the executive team with a history of directory experience and other individuals (including that of a Chief Financial Officer, and VP of Sales and Marketing) to meet the short-term and long-term goals of the company. The founders have also identified the following advisors and professional service providers to work with them on an as-needed basis.

Ken "Jake" Jakubowski—Emerald First LLC

Ken Jakubowski is currently Chief Financial Officer of Emerald First LLC, a startup financial services company headquartered in San Diego. He has over 20 years of progressive financial management experience with an emphasis on planning, budgeting, financial analysis, treasury, M&A, international finance, and accounting. He is a strong corporate finance generalist and strategic thinker with excellent leadership, analytical and communications skills. Prior to joining Emerald First LLC, he was Vice President, Finance at GMAC Insurance, a $1.3 billion personal lines insurance company based in Winston-Salem, NC. He has served as an adjunct professor in the evening MBA program at The Johns Hopkins University lecturing in International Capital Markets and Corporate Finance, and has frequently presented at the Babcock Graduate School of Management, Wake Forest University. He holds an MBA from The University of Michigan and an undergraduate degree in Economics from Kalamazoo College.

Greg Writer—The Writer Group

Greg Writer currently serves as President and CEO of his firm, and is an executive with more than 18 years of experience in corporate finance, capital formation, executive level management, mergers, acquisitions, and sales/marketing. He is an aggressive, venture-minded multi-tasker who has consistently converted risks to rewards and facilitated the formation and funding of many start-up companies. He consults in the areas of capital engineering, capital acquisition, creation of business plans, and development of business strategy. He speaks and trains on topics about growing your businesses through better marketing.

Tim Ristine—The Writer Group

Tim Ristine is currently serving as the COO of The Writer Group. He is an accomplished executive with over 20 years of marketing, business planning, product management, and sales experience with products and services sold to the retail, financial, telecommunications, healthcare, energy, computer, aerospace, and automotive industries through direct and reseller channels. He is experienced in turnaround and re-start companies as well as large enterprises. He holds an MBA from Northeastern University, a MSEE with a major in computer science and software from the University of New Mexico, and a BS degree in mathematics. He speaks regularly and trains on topics about growing your businesses through better marketing.

Vincent Molina—Vincent G. Molina & Associates

Vincent Molina provides consultation in business development, corporate structure, and capital acquisition for product and service-driven companies from the start-up stage through seed capital, and also works closely with the client's service providers. Mr. Molina has more than 20 years of experience in the corporate arena in the areas of training and management and currently participates on the U.S.A. Today's Small Business Panel, which serves 20 million entrepreneurs. In addition, Mr. Molina is the president of the publishing company, Creative Alternatives, Inc., and creator of the Communicating With...™ book series.

Burk & Reedy Law—Corporate Legal Counsel

Jim Burk provides corporate legal counsel and has been in the private practice of law for over 30 years. He specializes in emerging companies in the initial stages of organization and growth. He has also been a senior partner in law firms located in New York and Washington, D.C. Mr. Burk's law practice includes general business matters that pertain to corporations, contracts, venture capital finance, tax, asset protection, and securities law. Alan Reedy is a corporate and tax attorney and has been in the private practice of law for over 30 years. He is a Certified Public Accountant and Certified Financial Planner. Mr. Reedy assists companies in business contract and tax matters that include securities, intellectual property, and tax and asset protection.

Maria Crimi Speth—Jaburg & Wilk, P.C.

Maria Crimi Speth practices in the areas of intellectual property and commercial litigation, representing clients throughout the United States. She focuses her practice on assisting businesses in protecting their trademarks, copyrights, trade secrets, and other intellectual property through preventative measures to avoid disputes, and through aggressive measures when disputes arise. Ms. Speth has authored articles on the topics of litigation and intellectual property published in The Business Journal, the Arizona Journal of Real Estate & Business, and the Arizona Attorney.

Mike Starkweather—Kunzler & Associates

Mike Starkweather exclusively focuses his practice in the intellectual property law area. He started his practice as a Patent Examiner in Washington, D.C. After working in the Patent Office, he spent several years working as in-house counsel for several major corporations, including IBM, Xerox, and AT&T. In addition to prosecuting hundreds of software, electrical, and mechanical inventions, Mr. Starkweather has been involved in performing major intellectual property audits, including audits for a 30-million and a 100-million dollar acquisition. Mr. Starkweather has recently been teaching at the University of Utah on IP Valuation and Strategies. He also teaches a seminar in Los Angeles to Emerging Enterprises about intellectual property. His philosophy is that "patents are a tool for the businessman to achieve his objectives within a given budget."

Howard Lim—How Studios Inc ®

Howard Lim supports his clients to realize the rewards of growth and earnings through Image Marketing™—his uniquely integrated system of multiple graphic design disciplines, branding, and visualization. An award-winning creative director and graphic designer, he pioneered solutions that enabled ABC to broadcast on the first computerized off-line motion graphics on TV, allowed Zylan to launch one of the first graphically integrated effective websites, and reformatted an extended length interface design, MGM's classic movie The Great Escape, onto DVD—a first for the studio. Today, Howard leads a team of professionals who successfully communicate the powerful visions of America's emerging and leading companies, including a select group on the Fortune 500. He continuously exceeds the expectations of clients like Apple Computers, UCLA, ABC networks, Disney, DreamWorks, Honda, Mitsubishi, Philips Media and Toshiba.

The Plan

The Company has completed its pre-development phase. The appropriate steps have been taken to now enter the development phase. They are:

- Filed and received provisional patent protection for the software's interface functionality
- Filed for trademark protection of the product name, "What's In Your Neighborhood"
- Completed a 56 page secondary market research study on the industry, probable users, competitors, and potential market gaps
- Developed a professionally narrated automated walkthrough demo of the product for investors
- Begun the team building process
- The next phases are development, launch, and expansion.

The development phase is budgeted for 12 months. Here the groundwork will be established to launch the first area by achieving the following milestones:

- Prototype development—Create the functional specifications of the software, and then outsource the programming of these modules to trusted technology companies in California and India. This strategy allows for rapid development of the product, while keeping overhead expenditures low in this development phase.
- Brand identity development—Create a strong, consistent image of the product and company through all mediums that lets everyone know that WIYN is a top-notch grassroots product whose company cares about its neighbors.
- Perform additional market research—The information that is gathered from consumers and businesses will supplement the Company's current research in evaluating market acceptance and price points, this will allow it to sharpen its sales and marketing strategies to best serve these stakeholders.
- Develop sales tools and advertising materials—Based on the Company's refined strategies, sales tools and advertising materials will be developed to support these strategies, such as a website, brochures, business sign-up web forms, sales videos, etc.
- Complete alpha, beta, and QA testing—WIYN will be tested and ready to go prior to the initial launch.

The next phase is where the proverbial "rubber meets the road"; the Company gears up for the launch of the initial sales area, and begins implementation of the revenue model.

The Company will create separate Limited Liability Companies (LLCs) for each sales area that it enters into. The purpose for this is the flexibility and benefits this structure offers to both investors and the Company. WIYN, Inc. will license out its technology, as well as provide all administrative, technical, accounting and ancillary support to each Area LLC. This enables each Area LLC to solely focus on sales within its predetermined geographic boundary. The Company will act as the managing partner for the Area LLC and will be paid a monthly management fee as well as additional fees for all services provided. These fees, in addition to yearly membership distributions, are where the Company's revenue is generated. The Area LLC will derive its revenue through the implementation of the revenue model.

The revenue model is simple. Advertising space on the product is sold to businesses within the product's geographic boundary. Businesses are differentiated by the number of different ways a user can find them within the product. This distinction is accomplished by offering businesses three monthly packages from $49.95, $89.95, and $149.95 per month. These prices are competitive in comparison to print and internet-based Yellow Page and business directories, and reflective of the targeted consumers' perceived value to the advertisers. Each package represents differing features and levels of prominence available to the advertiser. This monthly subscription model alleviates the cost associated with actively seeking renewals, and allows more energy to be placed in constantly acquiring new advertisers.

In addition to these advertisers, up to nine local advertisers will have maximum exposure on the product, by being designated as a 'Featured Business'. Featured businesses enjoy company logo placement on all WIYN advertising and product packaging for the year, including Cable TV commercials, Print Ads, and the CD-ROM package front or back cover. Featured businesses are highlighted within the product in the 'Featured Business' section, they are listed first in all applicable search results, their logo depicting their location is found on the map in all user searches, and these advertisers have access to more product usage reports, such as reporting across all business categories in the directory. This premium placement is similar to purchasing the back-cover in a Yellow pages directory, and is available for $15,000 per year per advertiser.

The milestones to achieve this phase are:

Corporate:

- Establish the corporate office—Establish the corporate office in San Diego County.
- Hire key personnel—Hire the Vice President of Sales & Marketing, as well as an Administrative Assistant, and begin working with outsourced professionals, such as a part-time Chief Financial Officer.
- Refine the Sales and Marketing strategies—The new VP of Sales & Marketing will be instrumental in refining the sales and marketing strategies developed by the board of directors.
- Hire Area Director and Administrative Assistant—The Area Director will be responsible for establishing the Area office, and the hiring and training of inside and outside Sales Representatives. (In Area One, the Vice President of Sales & Marketing will serve as the Area Director to reduce costs.)
- Begin PR campaign—Through the use of newspapers, magazines, and research company reports, the Company will begin to establish third party credibility for the product.

- Begin marketing campaign to potential advertisers—This campaign will have one clear message: businesses will see more customers, make more sales, and realize bigger dollars, as a result of participating in WIYN.
- Begin marketing campaign to Area consumers—The campaign will create product awareness in the neighborhood through the use of direct mail inserts and 30-second radio spots telling consumers of the benefits of WIYN and 30-second cable television commercials visually introducing the product to consumers. By associating the product with local and national neighborhood businesses, and reinforcing this through product packaging, product credibility and familiarity are established, thereby decreasing the possibility that the product will be discarded as junk mail.
- Distribute software—All homes and businesses within the neighborhood will be direct mailed the product on CD-ROM. By using the United States Post Office, verification of actual distribution can be provided to advertisers. Because the product is transported on CD-ROM, it makes it very easy to distribute through other channels. A limited number of CD-ROMs will be provided to local realtors to hand out to clients new to the area; home developers to insert in their welcome packages; and, Chambers of Commerce to insert in their relocation packages and to hand out to walk-in visitors. Once the software is installed, the CD-ROM is no longer needed, so users can even pass the CD-ROM on to friends and family. The primary distribution will occur on an annual basis, just like the Yellow Pages, to maintain product awareness.

Area LLC
- Establish Area office—The Area office will serve as office space for all Sales Representatives in the area. (In Area One, the Corporate office will serve as the Area LLC office to reduce costs.)
- Lease sales equipment—Sales equipment, such as laptops and cell phones will be leased to minimize the outlay of capital to purchase and to easily keep up with technology.
- Hire Sales Representatives—Area Director will be tasked to hire Sales Representatives. Sales Representatives will have two to three years sales experience.
- Train Sales Representatives—Sales Representatives will be trained to be consultants and help businesses find the best value for their marketing dollar. Automated sales tools will make this process more efficient. A wireless internet-connected laptop to access the web-based sales system will allow Sales Representatives to sign-up new businesses on the spot, track their individual sales, and maintain their appointment schedule. The laptop also allows them to show businesses the compelling selling video to further highlight the benefits WIYN will provide them.
- Begin Sales—The Area LLC will initially target businesses that fall within the most referenced and fastest growing headings in the Yellow Pages. They are restaurants, physicians & surgeons, automobile parts and repair, pizza, attor-

neys, cable television, carpet & rug cleaners, cellular telephone equipment & supplies, child care/day care centers, contractors, electric contractors, employment agencies, hearing aids, motels, and mortgages[19]. When a sale is made a setup fee is collected and a simple credit card or bank authorization draft is setup to begin the business' monthly payments.

As this area is refined, the next step is to replicate this cookie-cutter model in ten areas over the next five years. This ultimately generates a substantial positive cash flow that provides for self-funded continued growth.

The Potential

The potential of WIYN can be viewed from two different perspectives: the Corporation and the Area LLC. Since the initial launch area is the basis for future growth and does not begin until after the initial 12 months of development is complete, the Company is showing a five year forecast for the Area LLC and then a six year forecast for WIYN, Inc., which shows expansion into ten areas.

The Area LLC model shows at year five $12.0 million in revenues against $1.3 million in direct expenses. These revenues represent 12,019 advertising businesses across eight neighborhoods spending on average of $81.95 per month, in addition to 24 featured advertisers each spending $15K per year. The direct expenses include the cost for the replication and delivery of the CD-ROMs for each neighborhood, the mileage reimbursement for each Outside Sales Representative, Management and Inside Sales Representative bonuses, and Outside Sales Representative commissions. This translates into an 89% gross profit margin. The net profit margin at year five is 71%.

Area LLC—Five-Year Forecast

	Year 1	Year 2	Year 3	Year 4	Year 5
Revenue	1,299,065	8,232,316	10,892,540	11,491,201	12,021,845
Direct Expenses	1,240,520	2,097,923	1,300,587	1,312,560	1,323,173
Gross Profit	58,545	6,134,393	9,591,953	10,178,641	10,698,672
GPM%	5%	75%	88%	89%	89%
Operating Expenses	2,527,472	2,841,835	2,081,792	2,124,516	2,166,880
Total Expenses	3,767,993	4,939,757	3,382,379	3,437,076	3,490,053
Net Income Before CA LLC Fees	(2,468,927)	3,292,559	7,510,161	8,054,125	8,531,793
Provision for CA LLC Fees	6,800	12,590	12,590	12,590	12,590
Net Income(Loss)	(2,475,727)	3,279,969	7,497,571	8,041,535	8,519,203
Net Profit Margin%	-191%	40%	69%	70%	71%

Detailed financial projections are available on request.

The Corporate model shows at year six $46.3 million in revenues against $3.7 million in direct expenses. These revenues represent the contributions made by ten Area LLCs to corporate that include member distributions, management fees, and servicing fees, based on $105,109,339 in gross revenues. The direct expenses include the cost of providing each Area LLC with administrative, technical, accounting, and ancillary support. This translates into a 92% gross profit margin. The net profit margin at year six is 50%.

Corporate—Six-Year Forecast (Ten Areas)

	Year 1	Year 2	Year 3	Year 4	Year 5	Year 6
Revenue	0	595,938	2,589,275	9,408,922	23,710,602	46,322,361
Direct Expenses	0	485,938	1,522,600	3,386,493	4,248,589	3,695,627
Gross Profit	0	110,000	1,066,675	6,022,429	19,462,013	42,626,734
GPM %	n/a	18%	41%	64%	82%	92%
Operating Expenses	422,083	983,352	1,463,648	1,494,455	1,525,261	1,556,067
Net Income Before Income Tax	(422,083)	(873,352)	(396,973)	4,527,974	17,936,752	41,070,667
Provision for Income Taxes	0	0	0	1,216,458	7,862,337	18,030,023
Net Income (Loss)	(422,083)	(873,352)	(396,973)	3,311,516	10,074,415	23,040,644
Cumulative Net Income (Loss)	(422,083)	(1,295,435)	(1,692,408)	1,619,108	11,693,524	34,734,168
Net Profit Margin %	n/a	-147%	-15%	35%	42%	50%

The Liquid Strategy

The Company's philosophy is to reward investors as soon as economically and legally possible. Therefore, in year four, pending the existence of retained earnings, the Company may begin declaring dividends. At the six year mark, the Company will explore two possible liquidity strategies for investors:

- Optional company stock buy-back at a graduated rate
- Begin actively looking for a possible acquisition or merger

Either strategy will reward investors handsomely.

Funding

We have broken up our stages of funding into two logical raises. Our first and current raise will consist of seeking capital solely for the development of our software application and to position us for the initial area launch. Equity shares will be sold in WIYN, Inc. in order to raise the $900,000 needed for this development phase. This phase is budgeted for 12 months.

The second raise will be seeking $1.6M for the establishment of a solid scalable corporate framework and $3.0M for the launch of our first sales area. This round will be unique in that investors will be investing in WIYN, Inc., and WIYN—San Diego, LLC.

To provide investors the quickest cash return on their investment, we have decided to structure each sales area as a Limited Liability Company (LLC). This allows investors to receive the benefits of pass-through losses in the area's first year of operation, and then receive membership distributions as the area becomes profitable. These distributions may continue for the life of the area.

The investors in WIYN, Inc., not only benefit from the revenue the first Area LLC generates for the corporation, they also reap the rewards of each and every area that is open from then on.

Equity in WIYN, Inc. will be sold to raise the $1.6M. Membership units will simultaneously be sold in WIYN—San Diego, LLC to raise the $3.0M.

No further investment is anticipated for either entity.

Expansion will initially occur through the creation and funding of LLCs in each additional sales area.

The Company sees each Area LLC as a profitable investment vehicle that provides investors an ongoing stream of revenue.

To get additional financial information, please contact Edward Cox at 760-443-3869.

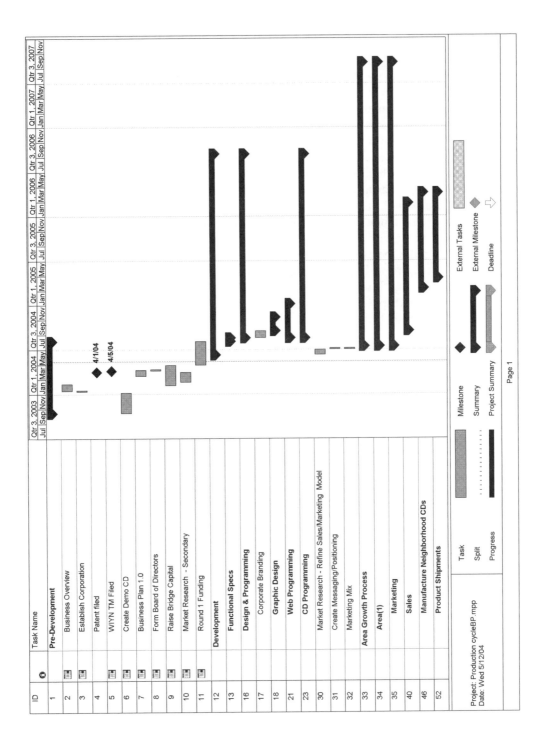

Supporting Sources

[1] *Wall Street Journal,* March 18, 2004.
[2] Small Business Depends on Yellow Pages and Newspapers. www.centerformediaresearch.com/cfmr_brief.cfm?fnl=031117
[3] More consumers are using online coupons as companies begin to offer them for a wider array of products. *New York Times,* March 17, 2003.
[4] SMEs Tap Into Premium Search. www.emarketer.com/news/article.php?1002698
[5] Small Business Depends on Yellow Pages and Newspapers. www.centerformediaresearch.com/cfmr_brief.cfm?fnl=031117
[6] Local Search: The Hybrid Future http://searchenginewatch.com/searchday/article.php/3296721
[7] ValPak website. www.valpak.com/info/franchise/franchise_opps_content.jsp
[8] Nielsen Reports More Diverse Television Viewing Patterns Among African American and Latino Audiences. www.nielsenmedia.com
[9] NetRatings: Internet Is 75% Full; comScore: They're Full Of It. www.mediapost.com/dtls_dsp_news.cfm?newsId=242865
[10] Show Search the Money. http://www.imediaconnection.com/content/3043.asp
[11] comScore Bows qSearch Local. www.mediapost.com/dtls_dsp_news.cfm?newsID=240422&newsDate=03/03/2004
[12] Online Ad Spending Grows over 20% in 2003. http://www.emarketer.com/news/article.php?1002760
[13] The Kelsey Group. www.kelseygroup.com
[14] Search Engines Going Loco for Local...But When Will Small Business Get Real? www.searchenginejournal.com/index.php?p=484
[15] Show Search the Money. www.imediaconnection.com/content/3043.asp
[16] Online advertising roars back. http://money.cnn.com/2004/02/18/technology/techinvestor/hellweg/index.htm
[17] Non-browser Internet Use on the Rise. www.mediainfo.com/eandp/news/article_display.jsp?vnu_content_id=2060808
[18] Ibid.
[19] Study Finds Internet Yellow Pages References Hit 1.6 Billion in 2003. www.mediapost.com/dtls_dsp_news.cfm?newsId=247028

Appendix B

Corporation Formation Documents

After consulting with your professionals, you will most likely need to form an entity to raise capital. Most entrepreneurs will form either a corporation or a limited liability company. This appendix contains a number of documents that you will find helpful as references for forming a corporation. (Appendix C contains documents for forming and operating a limited liability company.)

The documents in this appendix follow the formation and growth of a fictitious company, Anderson Industries, Inc, that was founded by Bob Anderson in October 2000.

Articles of Incorporation

The *Articles of Incorporation* describe, in abbreviated form, certain basic organizational attributes of your corporation—name, authorized capital (shares), registered agent, etc. The articles are filed with the appropriate state agency (in most cases the secretary of state or state corporation commission) along with a state-required fee. The information is public knowledge. The information presented in the Articles of Incorporation is fairly standardized and many states have even created a fill-in-the-blank form for filing.

Bob Anderson has founded this corporation by himself and will serve as the incorporator (person responsible for the accuracy of the information in the Articles of Incorporation) and the registered agent (the official point of contact for the corporation). The name Anderson Industries, Inc. could probably be a bit more imaginative depending on the type of products or services the corporation intends to offer, but it will suffice for these purposes.

Of particular importance to a corporation planning to raise capital is the FIFTH Article in this example. It is recommended that a corporation create two classes of shares if it intends to raise capital—common shares to be held by the founders and preferred shares to be sold to investors. (See Chapter 5 for an explanation of this structure.)

Bylaws

The *bylaws* are the internal governing document of a corporation. They should be drafted shortly after a corporation is formed and adopted by the board of directors at their first meeting. The bylaws should spell out the rights of the shareholders, the rights, duties, and responsibilities of the board of directors and officers, and other matters such as the requirement to keep accurate books and records.

In this example, the board of directors of the corporation has adopted a set of bylaws that grants much of the decision making power to the board of directors. The board of directors or the shareholders may amend the bylaws in accordance with Article VII of the bylaws.

Minutes of Initial Directors' Meeting

The first act of a newly formed corporation should be to hold an initial meeting of the board of directors. A number of decisions regarding the governance and operation of the company will be made at this initial meeting. If initial directors were not designated in the Articles of Incorporation, then they should be designated in these initial minutes. The officers should then be appointed by the board of directors.

The bylaws and corporate seal should be adopted. The decision to be taxed under Subchapter S should be made and Form 8832 filed with the IRS. Your corporation is a C corporation by default and no filing is necessary if you wish to remain a C corporation.

The minutes should designate where the corporate banking will be done and adopt dates for a fiscal year. Stock should also be issued to the founders of the company and the officers of the company should be authorized to file all paperwork necessary to register the corporation with the IRS and state authorities.

Take note that Bob Anderson is filling all of the officer roles. This is not uncommon with a newly formed corporation and may continue for the first phases of the corporation. One of the many duties that Mr. Anderson should undertake in this development phase of the corporation is to find other qualified candidates to fill some of the officer and director roles— often a difficult task before the corporation has even raised capital.

Some new companies, especially those with only one or a few shareholders, who also serve as the initial board of directors, will take action through unanimous consent instead of meeting and taking votes. Included here is an Action by Unanimous Written consent in lieu of the Organizational Meeting of the Board of Directors of Anderson Industries, Inc., that addresses the matter that would have been resolved at an initial meeting.

How These Documents Help With the Financing of Your Business

Money is attracted to a sound, dynamic organization. Having a well-drafted set of bylaws that establishes how a company will conduct its business and make decisions is attractive to investors. Providing adequate notice, holding required meetings, and making prudent decisions in accordance with the bylaws and prevailing laws is indicative that a corporation is organized in other aspects of its business.

Talent is also attracted to organization. Persons who you wish to serve on your board of directors will want to know that decisions are being made according to a set of established rules as they join in and become responsible for the decision-making process of the corporation.

ARTICLES OF INCORPORATION
OF
ANDERSON INDUSTRIES, INC.

The undersigned, being a natural person of full age and acting as the incorporator for the purpose of forming the business corporation hereinafter named pursuant to the provisions of the Corporations Code of the State of California, does hereby adopt the following articles of incorporation.

FIRST: The name of the corporation (hereinafter referred to as the "corporation") is Anderson Industries, Inc.

SECOND: The existence of the corporation is perpetual.

THIRD: The purpose of the corporation is to engage in any lawful act or activity for which a corporation may be organized under the General Corporation Law of California, other than the banking business, the trust company business or the practice of a profession permitted to be incorporated by the California Corporations Code.

FOURTH: The name and the complete business or residence address within the State of California of the corporation's initial agent for service of process within the State of California in accordance with the provisions of subdivision (b) of Section 1502 of the Corporations Code of the State of California are as follows:

Name	Address
BOB ANDERSON	3499 Malcolm Avenue
	Los Angeles, California 90010

FIFTH: The corporation shall have two classes of Shares. The corporation is authorized to issue 15,000,000 shares, 10,000,000 of which are Shares of Common Stock at $0.001 par value each, and 5,000,000 Shares of which are Preferred Stock at $0.001 par value each.

The rights, preferences, privileges and restrictions of the Preferred Stock shall be determined at a later date by a vote of the Board of Directors, in accordance with the provisions of Section 202(e)(3) of the Corporations Code, as the same may be amended or supplemented.

The Board of Directors of the corporation may issue any or all of the aforesaid authorized shares of the corporation from time to time for such consideration as it shall determine and may determine from time to time the amount of such consideration, if any, to be credited to paid-in surplus.

SIXTH: In the interim between meetings of shareholders held for the election of directors or for the removal of one or more directors and the election of the replacement or replacements thereat, any vacancy which results by reason of the removal of a director or directors by the shareholders entitled to vote in an election of directors, and which has not been filled by said shareholders, may be filled by a majority of the directors then in office, whether or not less than a quorum, or by the sole remaining director, as the case may be.

SEVENTH: The liability of the directors of the corporation for monetary damages shall be eliminated to the fullest extent permissible under California law.

EIGHTH: The corporation is authorized to provide indemnification of agents (as defined in Section 317 of the Corporations Code) for breach of duty to the corporation and its shareholders through bylaw provisions or through agreements with the agents, or both, in excess of the indemnification otherwise permitted by Section 317 of the Corporations Code, subject to the limits on such excess indemnification set forth in Section 204 of the Corporations Code.

IN WITNESS WHEREOF, the undersigned incorporator has executed these Articles of Incorporation on this 14th day of October 2000.

_____

BOB ANDERSON, Incorporator

BYLAWS
OF
ANDERSON INDUSTRIES, INC.
(a California corporation)

ARTICLE I
SHAREHOLDERS

1. CERTIFICATES FOR SHARES. Each certificate for shares of the corporation shall set forth thereon the name of the record holder of the shares represented thereby, the number of shares and the class or series of shares owned by said holder, the par value, if any, of the shares represented thereby, and such other statements, as applicable, prescribed by Sections 416–419, inclusive, and other relevant Sections of the General Corporation Law of the State of California (the "General Corporation Law") and such other statements, as applicable, which may be prescribed by the Corporate Securities Law of 1968 of the State of California and any other applicable provision of law. Each such certificate issued shall be signed in the name of the corporation by the Chair of the Board of Directors, if any, the President, if any, or a Vice President, if any, and by the Chief Financial Officer or an Assistant Treasurer or the Secretary or an Assistant Secretary. Any or all of the signatures on a certificate for shares may be facsimile. In case any officer, transfer agent, or registrar who has signed or whose facsimile signature has been placed on a certificate for shares shall have ceased to be such officer, transfer agent, or registrar before such certificate is issued, it may be issued by the corporation with the same effect as if such person were an officer, transfer agent, or registrar at the date of issue.

In the event that the corporation shall issue the whole or any part of its shares as partly paid and subject to call for the remainder of the consideration to be paid therefor, any such certificate for shares shall set forth thereon the statements prescribed by Section 409 of the General Corporation Law.

The corporation may issue a new certificate for shares or for any other security in the place of any other certificate theretofore issued by it, which is alleged to have been lost, stolen, or destroyed. As a condition to such issuance, the corporation may require any such owner of the allegedly lost, stolen, or destroyed certificate or any such owner's legal representative to give the corporation bond, or other adequate security, sufficient to indemnify it against any claim that may be made against it, including any expense or liability, on account of the alleged loss, theft, or destruction of any such certificate or the issuance of such new certificate.

2. FRACTIONAL SHARES. Subject to, and in compliance with, the provisions of Section 407 and any other provisions of the General Corporation Law, the corporation may, but need not, issue fractions of a share originally or upon transfer. If the corporation does not issue fractions of a share, it shall in connection with any original issuance of shares arrange for the disposition of fractional interest by those entitled thereto, or pay in cash the fair value of fractions of a share as of the time when those entitled to receive such fractions are determined, or issue scrip or warrants in registered or bearer form which shall entitle the holder to receive a certificate for a full share upon the surrender of such scrip or warrants aggregating a full share. A certificate for a fractional share shall, but scrip or warrants shall not unless otherwise provided therein, entitle the holder to exercise voting rights, to receive dividends thereon and to participate in any of the assets of the corporation in the event of liquidation. The Board of Directors may cause scrip or warrants to be issued subject to the condition that they shall become void if not exchanged for a certificate or certificates representing a full share or full shares, as the case may be, before a specified date or that any of the shares for which scrip or warrants are exchangeable may be sold by the corporation, and any proceeds thereof distributed to the holder of any such scrip or warrants or any other condition which the Board of Directors may impose.

3. SHARE TRANSFERS. Upon compliance with any provisions of the General Corporation Law and/or the Corporate Securities Law of 1968 which may restrict the transferability of shares, transfers of shares of the corporation shall be made only on the record of shareholders of the corporation by the registered holder thereof, or by his or her attorney thereunto authorized by power of attorney duly executed and filed with the Secretary of the corporation or with a transfer agent or a registrar, if any, and on surrender of the certificate or certificates for such shares properly endorsed and the payment of all taxes, if any, due thereon.

4. RECORD DATE FOR SHAREHOLDERS. In order that the corporation may determine the shareholders entitled to notice of any meeting or to vote or be entitled to receive payment of any dividend or other distribution or allotment of any rights or entitled to exercise any rights in respect of any other lawful action, the Board of Directors may fix, in advance, a record date, which shall not be more than sixty (60) days or fewer than ten (10) days prior to the date of such meeting or more than sixty (60) days prior to any other action.

If the Board of Directors shall not have fixed a record date as aforesaid, the record date for determining shareholders entitled to notice of or to vote at a meeting of shareholders shall be at the close of business on the business day next preceding the day on which notice is given or, if notice is waived, at the close of business on the business day next preceding the day on which the meeting is held; the record date for determining shareholders entitled to give consent to corporate action in writing without a meeting, when no prior action by the Board of Directors has been taken, shall be the day on which the first written consent is given; and the record date for determining shareholders for any other purpose shall be at the close of business on the day on which the Board of Directors adopts the resolution relating thereto, or the sixtieth (60th) day prior to the date of such other action, whichever is later.

A determination of shareholders of record entitled to notice of or to vote at a meeting of shareholders shall apply to any adjournment of the meeting unless the Board of Directors fixes a new record date for the adjourned meeting, but the

Board of Directors shall fix a new record date if the meeting is adjourned for more than forty-five (45) days from the date set for the original meeting.

Except as may be otherwise provided by the General Corporation Law, shareholders at the close of business on the record date shall be entitled to notice and to vote or to receive any dividend, distribution or allotment of rights or to exercise the rights, as the case may be, notwithstanding any transfer of any shares on the books of the corporation after the record date.

5. MEANING OF CERTAIN TERMS. As used in these Bylaws in respect of the right to notice of a meeting of shareholders or a waiver thereof or to participate or vote threat or to assent or consent or dissent in writing in lieu of a meeting, as the case may be, the term "share" or "shares" or "shareholder" or "shareholders" refers to an outstanding share or shares and to a holder or holders of record of outstanding shares when the corporation is authorized to issue only one class of shares, and said reference is also intended to include any outstanding share or shares and any holder or holders of record of outstanding shares of any class upon which or upon whom the Articles of Incorporation confer such rights where there are two or more classes or series of shares or upon which or upon whom the General Corporation Law confers such rights notwithstanding that the Articles of Incorporation may provide for more than one class or series of shares, one or more of which are limited or denied such rights thereunder.

6. SHAREHOLDER MEETINGS.

a. TIME. An annual meeting for the election of directors and for the transaction of any other proper business and any special meeting shall be held on the date and at the time as the Board of Directors shall from time to time fix.

b. PLACE. Annual meetings and special meetings shall be held at such place, within or without the State of California, as the directors may, from time to time, fix. Whenever the directors shall fail to fix such place, the meeting shall be held at the principal executive office of the corporation.

c. CALL. Annual meetings may be called by the directors, by the Chairman of the Board, if any, Vice Chairman of the Board, if any, the President, if any, the Secretary, or by any officer instructed by the directors to call the meeting. Special meetings may be called in like manner and by the holders of shares entitled to cast not less than ten percent of the votes at the meeting being called.

d. NOTICE. Written notice stating the place, day, and hour of each meeting, and, in the case of a special meeting, the general nature of the business to be transacted or, in the case of an Annual Meeting, those matters which the Board of Directors, at the time of mailing of the notice, intends to present for action by the shareholders, shall be given not less than ten (10) days (or not less than any such other minimum period of days as may be prescribed by the General Corporation Law) or more than sixty (60) days (or more than any such maximum period of days as may be prescribed by the General Corporation Law) before the date of the meeting, either personally or by mail or other means of written communication, charges prepaid by or at the direction of the directors, the President, if any, the Secretary or the officer or persons calling the meeting, addressed to each shareholder at his or her address appearing on the books of the corporation or given by him or her to the corporation for the purpose of notice, or, if no such address appears or is given, at the place where the principal executive office of the corporation is located or by publication at least once in a newspaper of general circulation in the county in which the said principal executive office is located. Such notice shall be deemed to be delivered when deposited in the United States mail with first class postage thereon prepaid, or sent by other means of written communication addressed to the shareholder at his or her address as it appears on the stock transfer books of the corporation. The notice of any meeting at which directors are to be elected shall include the names of nominees intended at the time of notice to be presented by the Board of Directors for election. At an annual meeting of shareholders, any matter relating to the affairs of the corporation, whether or not stated in the notice of the meeting, may be brought up for action except matters which the General Corporation Law requires to be stated in the notice of the meeting. The notice of any annual or special meeting shall also include, or be accompanied by, any additional statements, information, or documents prescribed by the General Corporation Law. When a meeting is adjourned to another time or place, notice of the adjourned meeting need not be given if the time and place thereof are announced at the meeting at which the adjournment is taken; provided that, if after the adjournment a new record date is fixed for the adjourned meeting, a notice of the adjourned meeting shall be given to each shareholder. At the adjourned meeting, the corporation may transact any business which might have been transacted at the original meeting.

The transactions of any meeting, however called and noticed, and wherever held, shall be as valid as though had at a meeting duly held after regular call and notice, if a quorum is present and if, either before or after the meeting, each of the shareholders or his or her proxy signs a written waiver of notice or a consent to the holding of the meeting or an approval of the minutes thereof. All such waivers, consents, and approvals shall be filed with the corporate records or made a part of the minutes of the meeting. Attendance of a person at a meeting constitutes a waiver of notice of and presence at such meeting, except when the person objects, at the beginning of the meeting, to the transaction of any business because the meeting is not lawfully called or convened and except that attendance at a meeting shall not constitute a waiver of any right to object to the consideration of matters required by the General Corporation Law to be included in the notice but not so included, if such objection is expressly made at the meeting. Except as otherwise provided in subdivision (f) of Section 601 of the General Corporation Law, neither the business to be transacted nor the purpose of any regular or special meeting need be specified in any written waiver of notice, consent to the holding of the meeting, or the approval of the minutes thereof.

   e. CONDUCT OF MEETING. Meetings of the shareholders shall be presided over by one of the following officers in the order of seniority and if present and acting - the Chairman of the Board, if any, the Vice Chairman of the Board, if any, the President, if any, a Vice President, or, if none of the foregoing is in office and present and acting, by a chairman to be chosen by the shareholders. The Secretary of the corporation, or in his absence, an Assistant Secretary, shall act as secretary of every meeting, but, if neither the Secretary nor an Assistant Secretary is present, the Chairman of the meeting shall appoint a secretary of the meeting.

f. PROXY REPRESENTATION. Every shareholder may authorize another person or persons to act as his or her proxy at a meeting or by written action. No proxy shall be valid after the expiration of eleven months from the date of its execution unless otherwise provided in the proxy. Every proxy shall be revocable at the pleasure of the person executing it prior to the vote or written action pursuant thereto, except as otherwise provided by the General Corporation Law. As used herein, a "proxy" shall be deemed to mean a written authorization signed or an electronic transmission authorized by a shareholder or a shareholder's attorney in fact giving another person or persons power to vote with respect to the shares of such shareholder, and "signed" as used herein shall be deemed to mean the placing of such shareholder's name or other authorization on the proxy, whether by manual signature, typewriting, telegraphic or electronic transmission or otherwise by the shareholder or the shareholder's attorney in fact. Where applicable, the form of any proxy shall comply with the provisions of Section 604 of the General Corporation Law.

g. INSPECTORS—APPOINTMENT. In advance of any meeting, the Board of Directors may appoint inspectors of election to act at the meeting and any adjournment thereof. If inspectors of election are not so appointed, or, if any persons so appointed fail to appear or refuse to act, the Chairman of any meeting of shareholders may, and on the request of any shareholder or a shareholder's proxy shall, appoint inspectors of election, or persons to replace any of those who so fail or refuse, at the meeting. The number of inspectors shall be either one or three. If appointed at a meeting on the request of one or more shareholders or proxies, the majority of shares represented shall determine whether one or three inspectors are to be appointed.

The inspectors of election shall determine the number of shares outstanding and the voting power of each, the shares represented at the meeting, the existence of a quorum, the authenticity, validity, and effect of proxies, receive votes, ballots, if any, or consents, hear and determine all challenges and questions in any way arising in connection with the right to vote, count, and tabulate all votes or consents, determine when the polls shall close, determine the result, and do such acts as may be proper to conduct the election or vote with fairness to all shareholders. If there are three inspectors of election, the decision, act, or certificate of a majority shall be effective in all respects as the decision, act, or certificate of all.

h. QUORUM; VOTE; WRITTEN CONSENT. The holders of a majority of the voting shares shall constitute a quorum at a meeting of shareholders for the transaction of any business. The shareholders present at a duly called or held meeting at which a quorum is present may continue to do business until adjournment notwithstanding the withdrawal of enough shareholders to leave less than a quorum if any action taken, other than adjournment, is approved by at least a majority of the shares required to constitute a quorum. In the absence of a quorum, any meeting of shareholders may be adjourned from time to time by the vote of a majority of the shares represented thereat, but no other business may be transacted except as hereinbefore provided.

In the election of directors, a plurality of the votes cast shall elect. No shareholder shall be entitled to exercise the right of cumulative voting at a meeting for the election of directors unless the candidate's name or the candidates' names have been placed in nomination prior to the voting and the shareholder has given notice at the meeting prior to the voting of the shareholder's intention to cumulate the shareholder's votes. If any one shareholder has given such notice, all shareholders may cumulate their votes for such candidates in nomination.

Except as otherwise provided by the General Corporation Law, the Articles of Incorporation or these Bylaws, any action required or permitted to be taken at a meeting at which a quorum is present shall be authorized by the affirmative vote of a majority of the shares represented and voting at the meeting; provided, that said shares voting affirmatively shall also constitute at least a majority of the required quorum.

Except in the election of directors by written consent in lieu of a meeting, and except as may otherwise be provided by the General Corporation Law, the Articles of Incorporation, or these Bylaws, any action which may be taken at any annual or special meeting may be taken without a meeting and without prior notice, if a consent in writing, setting forth the action so taken, shall be signed by holders of shares having not less than the minimum number of votes that would be necessary to authorize or take such action at a meeting at which all shares entitled to vote thereon were present and voted. Directors may not be elected by written consent except by unanimous written consent of all shares entitled to vote for the election of directors. Notice of any shareholder approval pursuant to Section 310, 317, 1201 or 2007 without a meeting by less than unanimous written consent shall be given at least ten (10) days before the consummation of the action authorized by such approval, and prompt notice shall be given of the taking of any other corporate action approved by shareholders without a meeting by less than unanimous written consent to those shareholders entitled to vote who have not consented in writing. Elections of directors at a meeting need not be by ballot unless a shareholder demands election by ballot at the election and before the voting begins. In all other matters, voting need not be by ballot.

7. ANNUAL REPORT. Whenever the corporation shall have fewer than one hundred shareholders as said number is determined as provided in Section 605 of the General Corporation Law, the Board of Directors shall not be required to send to the shareholders of the corporation the annual report prescribed by Section 1501 of the General Corporation Law unless it shall determine that a useful purpose would be served by causing the same to be sent or unless the Department of Corporations, pursuant to the provisions of the Corporate Securities Law of 1968, shall direct the sending of the same.

ARTICLE II
BOARD OF DIRECTORS

1. FUNCTIONS. Except as any provision of law may otherwise require, the business and affairs of the corporation shall be managed and all corporate powers shall be exercised by or under the direction of its Board of Directors. The Board of Directors may delegate the management of the day-to-day operation of the business of the corporation to a management company or other person, provided that the business and affairs of the corporation shall be managed and all corporate powers shall be exercised under the ultimate direction of the Board of Directors. The Board of Directors shall have authority to fix the compensation of directors for services in any lawful capacity.

2. QUALIFICATIONS AND NUMBER. A director need not be a shareholder of the corporation, a citizen of the United States, or a resident of the State of California. The number of directors constituting the Board of Directors shall be not less than three (3) or more than seven (7). Subject to the foregoing provisions and the provisions of Section 212 of the General Corporation Law, the number of directors may be changed from time to time by an amendment of these Bylaws. No decrease in the authorized number of directors shall have the effect of shortening the term of any incumbent director.

3. ELECTION AND TERM. The initial Board of Directors shall consist of the persons elected at the meeting of the incorporator or incorporators, all of whom shall hold office until the first annual meeting of shareholders and until their successors have been elected and qualified, or until their earlier resignation, removal from office or death. Thereafter, directors who are elected to replace any or all of the members of the initial Board of Directors or who are elected at an annual meeting of shareholders, and directors who are elected in the interim to fill vacancies, shall hold office until the next annual meeting of shareholders and until their successors have been elected and qualified, or until their earlier resignation, removal from office, or death. In the interim between annual meetings of shareholders or of special meetings of shareholders called for the election of directors, any vacancies in the Board of Directors, including vacancies resulting from an increase in the authorized number of directors which have not been filled by the shareholders, and including any other vacancies which the General Corporation Law authorizes directors to fill, except for a vacancy created by the removal of a director, may be filled by directors or by the sole remaining director, as the case may be, in the manner prescribed by Section 305 of the General Corporation Law. Vacancies occurring by reason of the removal of directors which are not filled at the meeting of shareholders at which any such removal has been effected may be filled by the directors if the Articles of Incorporation or a Bylaw adopted by the shareholders so provides. Any director may resign effective upon giving written notice to the Chairman of the Board, if any, the President, if any, the Secretary or the Board of Directors, unless the notice specifies a later time for the effectiveness of such resignation. If the resignation is effective at a future time, a successor may be elected to the office when the resignation becomes effective.

The shareholders may elect a director at any time to fill any vacancy which the directors are entitled to fill, but which they have not filled. Any such election by written consent other than to fill a vacancy created by removal shall require the consent of a majority of the shares.

The name and the address of each initial director elected by the incorporator or incorporators are set forth in the minutes of the organization of the incorporator or incorporators at which each said initial director was elected, and said name and the address are hereby made a part of these Bylaws as if fully set forth therein.

4. DIRECTOR MEETINGS.

a. TIME. Meetings shall be held at such time as the Board shall fix, except that the first meeting of a newly elected Board shall be held as soon after its election as the directors may conveniently assemble.

b. PLACE. Meetings may be held at any place, within or without the State of California, which has been designated in any notice of the meeting, or, if not stated in said notice or, if there is no notice given, at the place designated by resolution of the Board of Directors.

c. CALL. Meetings may be called by the Chair of the Board, if any, by the President, if any, by any Vice President or Secretary, or by any two directors.

d. NOTICE AND WAIVER THEREOF. No notice shall be required for regular meetings for which the time and place have been fixed by the Board of Directors. Special meetings shall be held upon at least four (4) days' notice by mail or upon at least forty-eight (48) hours' notice delivered personally or by telephone or by any other means authorized by the provisions of Section 307 of the General Corporation Law. Notice of a meeting need not be given to any director who signs a waiver of notice or a consent to holding the meeting or an approval of the minutes thereof, whether before or after the meeting, or who attends the meeting without protesting, prior thereto or at its commencement, the lack of notice to such director. A notice or waiver of notice need not specify the purpose of any regular or special meeting of the Board of Directors. All such waivers, consents and approvals shall be filed with the corporate records or made a part of the minutes of the meeting.

e. QUORUM AND ACTION. A majority of the authorized number of directors shall constitute a quorum except when a vacancy or vacancies prevents such majority, whereupon a majority of the directors in office shall constitute a quorum, provided such majority shall constitute at least either one-third of the authorized number of directors or at least two directors, whichever is larger, or unless the authorized number of directors is only one. A majority of the directors present, whether or not a quorum is present, may adjourn any meeting to another time and place. If the meeting is adjourned for more than twenty-four (24) hours, notice of any adjournment to another time or place shall be given prior to the time of the adjourned meeting to the directors, if any, who were not present at the time of the adjournment. Except as the Articles of Incorporation, these Bylaws and the General Corporation Law may otherwise provide, the act or decision done or made by a majority of the directors present at a meeting duly held at which a quorum is present shall be the act of the Board of Directors. Members of the Board of Directors may participate in a meeting through use of conference telephone or other communications equipment, and participation by such use constitutes presence in person at any such meeting, provided the conditions prescribed by the provisions of Section 307 of the General Corporation Law are met.

A meeting at which a quorum is initially present may continue to transact business notwithstanding the withdrawal of directors, provided that any action which may be taken is approved by at least a majority of the required quorum for such meeting.

f. CHAIRMAN OF THE MEETING. The Chair of the Board, if any, and if present and acting, shall preside at all meetings. Otherwise, the President, if any and present and acting, or any director chosen by the Board, shall preside.

5. REMOVAL OF DIRECTORS. The entire Board of Directors or any individual director may be removed from office without cause by approval of the holders of at least a majority of the shares provided, that unless the entire Board is removed, an individual director shall not be removed when the votes cast against such removal, or not consenting in writing to such removal, would be sufficient to elect such director if voted cumulatively at an election of directors at which the same total number of votes were cast, or, if such action is taken by written consent, in lieu of a meeting, all shares entitled to vote were voted, and the entire number of directors authorized at the time of the director's most recent election were then being elected. If any or all directors are so removed, new directors may be elected at the same meeting or by such written consent. The Board of Directors may declare vacant the office of any director who has been declared of unsound mind by an order of court or convicted of a felony.

6. COMMITTEES. The Board of Directors, by resolution adopted by a majority of the authorized number of directors, may designate one or more committees, each consisting of two or more directors to serve at the pleasure of the Board of Directors. The Board of Directors may designate one or more directors as alternate members of any such committee, who may replace any absent member at any meeting of such committee. Any such committee, to the extent provided in the resolution of the Board of Directors, shall have all the authority of the Board of Directors except such authority as may not be delegated by the provisions of the General Corporation Law.

7. WRITTEN ACTION. Any action required or permitted to be taken may be taken without a meeting if all of the members of the Board of Directors shall individually or collectively consent in writing to that action. The written consent or consents shall be filed with the minutes of the proceedings of the Board. The action by written consent shall have the same force and effect as a unanimous vote of the directors.

ARTICLE III
OFFICERS

The corporation shall have a Chair of the Board or a President or it may have both, a Secretary, a chief financial officer and such other officers with such titles and duties as may be necessary to enable it to sign instruments and share certificates. Subject to the foregoing, any number of offices may be held by the same person. The titles, powers, and duties of officers shall be set forth in the resolution or instrument choosing them. The Chairman of the Board, if any, and/or the President, if any, the Secretary, the chief financial officer, and any Vice President or other executive officer shall be chosen by the Board of Directors. Any Assistant Secretary, Assistant Treasurer, or other junior officer shall be chosen by the Board of Directors or in the manner prescribed by the Board of Directors.

The President or, if a President shall not have been chosen, the Chairman of the Board shall be the general manager and chief executive officer of the corporation unless the resolution choosing him or her shall provide otherwise. The Treasurer shall be the chief financial officer unless the resolution choosing him or her shall provide otherwise.

Unless otherwise provided in the resolution or instrument choosing the same, all officers shall be chosen for a term of office running until the meeting of the Board of Directors following the next annual meeting of shareholders and until their successors have been chosen and qualified.

Any officer, or any agent chosen by the Board of Directors, may be removed by the Board whenever in its judgment the best interests of the corporation will be served thereby.

ARTICLE IV
BOOKS AND RECORDS—STATUTORY AGENT

The corporation shall keep at its principal executive office in the State of California or, if its principal executive office is not in the State of California, at its principal business office in the State of California, the original or a copy of the Bylaws as amended to date, which shall be open to inspection by the shareholders at all reasonable times during office hours. If the principal executive office of the corporation is outside the State of California, and, if the corporation has no principal business office in the State of California, it shall, upon request of any shareholder, furnish a copy of the Bylaws as amended to date.

The corporation shall keep adequate and correct books and records of account and shall keep minutes of the proceedings of its shareholders, Board of Directors, and committees, if any, of the Board of Directors. The corporation shall keep at its principal executive office, or at the office of its transfer agent or registrar, a record of its shareholders, giving the names and addresses of all shareholders and the number and class of shares held by each. Such minutes shall be in written form. Such other books and records shall be kept either in written form or in any other form capable of being converted into written form.

The name and address of the agent for service of process within the State of California is BOB ANDERSON, 3499 Malcolm Avenue, Los Angeles, California 90010.

ARTICLE V
CORPORATE SEAL

The corporate seal shall set forth the name of the corporation and the State and date of incorporation.

ARTICLE VI
FISCAL YEAR

The fiscal year of the corporation shall be fixed, and shall be subject to change, by the Board of Directors.

ARTICLE VII
CONTROL OVER BYLAWS

After the initial Bylaws of the corporation shall have been adopted by the initial director or board of directors of the corporation, the Bylaws may be amended or repealed or new Bylaws may be adopted by the shareholders entitled to exercise a majority of the voting power or by the Board of Directors; provided, however, that the Board of Directors shall have no control over any Bylaw which fixes or changes the authorized number of directors of the corporation; provided further, that any control over the Bylaws herein vested in the Board of Directors shall be subject to the authority of the aforesaid shareholders to amend or repeal the Bylaws or to adopt new Bylaws; and provided further that any Bylaw amendment or new Bylaw which changes the minimum number of directors to fewer than five shall require authorization by the greater proportion of voting power of the shareholders as hereinbefore set forth.

I HEREBY CERTIFY that the foregoing is a full, true, and correct copy of the Bylaws of Anderson Industries, Inc., a California corporation, as in effect on the date hereof.

WITNESS my hand and the seal of the corporation.

_____

Date

_____ (SEAL)

BOB ANDERSON, Secretary of Anderson Industries, Inc.

ACTION BY UNANIMOUS WRITTEN CONSENT
in lieu of the ORGANIZATIONAL MEETING
of THE BOARD OF DIRECTORS
of
ANDERSON INDUSTRIES, INC.

The undersigned, constituting the sole member of the Board of Directors of Anderson Industries, Inc., a California corporation (the "Company"), pursuant to the provisions of the California General Corporation Law, hereby adopt the following resolutions by unanimous written consent.

ARTICLES OF INCORPORATION

RESOLVED, that the Articles of Incorporation of the Company filed with the California Secretary of State on October 14, 2000, be, and they hereby are, ratified and affirmed.

APPOINTMENT OF DIRECTOR

RESOLVED, that, effective as of this date, the following person is hereby appointed as the sole director of the Company to serve until the first annual meeting of stockholders or until his successor(s) are duly elected and qualified:

BOB ANDERSON

APPOINTMENT OF OFFICERS

RESOLVED, that the following persons be, and they hereby are, appointed as officers of the Company, to serve until the next annual meeting of Directors or until their successors are duly appointed and have qualified.

CEO	Bob Anderson
Vice President	Bob Anderson
Secretary	Bob Anderson
Treasurer or CFO	Bob Anderson

ADOPTION OF BYLAWS

RESOLVED, that the Bylaws attached hereto as Exhibit A be, and they hereby are, adopted as the Bylaws of and for the Company; and

FURTHER RESOLVED, that the Secretary of the Company be, and he/she hereby is, authorized and directed to execute a Certificate of Secretary regarding the adoption of the Bylaws, to insert the Bylaws in the Company's Minute Book and to see that a copy of the Bylaws is kept at the Company's principal office, as required by law.

ADOPTION OF CORPORATE SEAL

RESOLVED, that the seal, an impression of which is affixed in the margin hereof,

be and hereby is, adopted as the seal of the corporation.

ADOPTION OF FORM OF STOCK CERTIFICATES

RESOLVED, that the attached form(s) of stock certificate(s) be, and hereby is/are, approved and adopted as the stock certificate(s) of the corporation.

EMPLOYER TAX IDENTIFICATION NUMBER

RESOLVED, that the appropriate officers of the Company be, and each of them hereby is, authorized and directed to apply to the IRS District Director for an employer's identification number on Form SS-4.

S-CORPORATION ELECTION

RESOLVED, that the President is hereby authorized to file Form 2553 with the Internal Revenue Service, thereby electing to have the Company taxed under Subchapter S of the Internal Revenue Code.

WITHHOLDING TAXES

RESOLVED, that the Treasurer be, and he/she hereby is, authorized and directed to consult with the bookkeeper, auditors, and attorneys of the Company in order to be fully informed as to, and to collect and pay promptly when due, all withholding taxes that the Company may now be (or hereafter become) liable.

STATEMENT BY DOMESTIC STOCK CORPORATION

RESOLVED, that the appropriate officers of the Company shall file with the California Secretary of State a statement of the names of the President, Secretary, Chief Financial Officer, and incumbent directors, together with a statement of the location and address of the principal office of the Company, and designating BOB ANDERSON as agent for service of process.

DESIGNATION OF DEPOSITORY

RESOLVED, that Bank of America, be, and hereby is, designated as the Depository of this Company, and that the Officers of the Company are hereby directed to prepare, execute, and file any necessary authorizations to complete and effect the designation.

FURTHER RESOLVED, that all checks, drafts and other instruments obligating the Company to pay money shall be signed on behalf of the Company by BOB ANDERSON.

FURTHER RESOLVED, that all form resolutions required by any such depository be, and they hereby are, adopted in such form used by such depository, and that the Secretary be, and he/she hereby is, (i) authorized to certify such resolutions as having been adopted by this Unanimous Written Consent and (ii) directed to insert a copy of any such form resolutions in the Minute Book immediately following the Unanimous Written Consent; and

FURTHER RESOLVED, that any such depository to which a certified copy of these resolutions has been delivered by the Secretary of the Company be, and it hereby is, authorized and entitled to rely upon such resolutions for all purposes until it shall have received written notice of the revocation or amendment of these resolutions adopted by the Board of Directors of the Company.

FISCAL YEAR

RESOLVED, that the fiscal year of the Company shall end on the 31st day of December of each year.

PRINCIPAL OFFICE

RESOLVED, that the principal executive office of the Company shall be at 3499 Malcolm Avenue, Los Angeles, California 90010.

MANAGEMENT POWERS

RESOLVED, that the Officers of the Company be, and each of them hereby is, authorized to sign and execute in the name and on behalf of the Company all applications, contracts, leases, and other deeds and documents or instruments in writing of whatsoever nature that may be required in the ordinary course of business of the Company and that may be necessary to secure for operation of the corporate affairs, governmental permits and licenses for, and incidental to, the lawful operations of the business of the Company, and to do such acts and things as such officers deem necessary or advisable to fulfill such legal requirements as are applicable to the Company and its business.

FURTHER RESOLVED, that the proper Officers of the Company be, and each of them hereby is, authorized and directed to obtain the consent of the Company's shareholders to the foregoing election and to execute and file Forms required by the State of California.

RATIFICATION

RESOLVED, that all prior acts done on behalf of the Company by the sole incorporator or his/her agents be, and the same hereby are, ratified and approved as acts of the Company.

INCORPORATION EXPENSES

RESOLVED, that the Officers of the Company be, and each of them hereby is, authorized and directed to pay the expenses of the incorporation and organization of the Company.

DOCUMENTATION OF BUSINESS TRANSACTIONS OF THE COMPANY

RESOLVED, that the Chief Financial Officer is hereby authorized and directed to procure such books as are necessary and proper for the transaction of business of the Company.

CONSIDERATION IN EXCHANGE FOR COMPANY'S ACCEPTANCE OF BOB ANDERSON'S OFFER TO CONTRIBUTE HIS IDEAS, EXPERTISE, AND TIME TO THE COMPANY

RESOLVED, that an offer from BOB ANDERSON to contribute his original ideas, expertise, and time to the Company in consideration for the issuance of shares of Common Stock is hereby accepted. The President and the Secretary are directed to issue BOB ANDERSON certificates representing 4,000,000 fully paid and non-assessable shares of the Common Stock of the Company.

FURTHER RESOLVED, that the President and Secretary are hereby directed to execute in the name of the Company any agreement or agreements in accordance with the offer of BOB ANDERSON and to issue and deliver in accordance with such agreement or agreements the appropriate number of fully paid and non-assessable shares of the Common Stock of the Company.

ADDITIONAL FILINGS

RESOLVED, that the appropriate Officers of the Company be, and each of them hereby is, authorized and directed, for and on behalf of the Company, to make such filings and applications, to execute and deliver such documents and instruments, and to do such acts and things as such officer deems necessary or advisable in order to obtain such licenses, authorizations, and permits as are necessary or desirable for the Company's business, and to fulfill such legal requirements as are applicable to the Company and its business and to complete the organization of the Company.

This Action by Unanimous Written Consent may be signed in one or more counterparts, each of which shall be deemed an original, and all of which shall constitute one instrument. This Action by Unanimous Written Consent shall be filed with the minutes of the proceedings of the Board of Directors of the Company.

RESOLVED, that the Action by Unanimous Written Consent be filed in this Corporation's minute books.

IN WITNESS WHEREOF, the undersigned have executed this Action by Unanimous Written Consent as of the October 21, 2000.

_____   [SEAL]

BOB ANDERSON, Secretary
ATTEST:

_____

BOB ANDERSON, Director

Appendix C

Limited Liability Company Formation Documents

If, after consultation with your professional team, you decide to form a limited liability company, you will need to file Articles of Organization with the state and draft an internal governing document called an *operating agreement.*

Articles of Organization

Some states, including California, have reduced the *Articles of Organization* filing to a fill-in-the-blank form, which is fine because the articles generally contain far less information than the articles of incorporation of a corporation.

In the example provided, Bob Anderson is organizing a limited liability company called Anderson Industries, LLC. The only other information provided is the name and address of the resident agent and how the LLC will be managed—either by the member or one or more managers. Mr. Anderson has chosen to have Anderson Industries, LLC managed by a manager rather than by the members (like a general partnership), which is usually recommended if the company is planning to admit investors as members. This way the manager can retain effective control of the organization and avoid the need to round up all of the members each time a decision has to be made on behalf of the company. Later on, Mr. Anderson may expand the decision making process to include a board of managers, either in a voting or advisory capacity.

Operating Agreement

An *operating agreement* for an LLC is somewhat more comprehensive than the bylaws of a corporation. In part this is due to the more complex tax structure of an LLC and the need to delineate the profit and loss sharing arrangement among the members.

In the sample operating agreement, the members divide the profits and losses of the company according to the percentage of the company that each member owns. For example, if a member owns 5% of the outstanding membership units of the company, he or she would be entitled to 5% of the company's profits and losses after expenses.

Bob Anderson has been appointed as manager of the company and, as such, has the exclusive responsibility for managing the business and affairs of the company. Conversely, the members have no authority to transact daily business on behalf of the company and only limited decision-making power.

State of California
Secretary of State

File # _____

LIMITED LIABILITY COMPANY
ARTICLES OF ORGANIZATION

A $70.00 filing fee must accompany this form.

IMPORTANT – Read instructions before completing this form.

This Space For Filing Use Only

ENTITY NAME (End the name with the words "Limited Liability Company," "Ltd. Liability Co.," or the abbreviations "LLC" or "L.L.C.")

1. NAME OF LIMITED LIABILITY COMPANY

Anderson Industries, LLC

PURPOSE (The following statement is required by statute and may not be altered.)

2. THE PURPOSE OF THE LIMITED LIABILITY COMPANY IS TO ENGAGE IN ANY LAWFUL ACT OR ACTIVITY FOR WHICH A LIMITED LIABILITY COMPANY MAY BE ORGANIZED UNDER THE BEVERLY-KILLEA LIMITED LIABILITY COMPANY ACT.

INITIAL AGENT FOR SERVICE OF PROCESS (If the agent is an individual, the agent must reside in California and both Items 3 and 4 must be completed. If the agent is a corporation, the agent must have on file with the California Secretary of State a certificate pursuant to Corporations Code section 1505 and Item 3 must be completed (leave Item 4 blank).

3. NAME OF INITIAL AGENT FOR SERVICE OF PROCESS

Bob Anderson

4. IF AN INDIVIDUAL, ADDRESS OF INITIAL AGENT FOR SERVICE OF PROCESS IN CALIFORNIA   CITY   STATE   ZIP CODE

3499 Malcolm Avenue   Los Angeles   CA   90010

MANAGEMENT (Check only one)

5. THE LIMITED LIABILITY COMPANY WILL BE MANAGED BY:

[X] ONE MANAGER

[ ] MORE THAN ONE MANAGER

[ ] ALL LIMITED LIABILITY COMPANY MEMBER(S)

ADDITIONAL INFORMATION

6. ADDITIONAL INFORMATION SET FORTH ON THE ATTACHED PAGES, IF ANY, IS INCORPORATED HEREIN BY THIS REFERENCE AND MADE A PART OF THIS CERTIFICATE.

EXECUTION

7. I DECLARE I AM THE PERSON WHO EXECUTED THIS INSTRUMENT, WHICH EXECUTION IS MY ACT AND DEED.

Bob Anderson
SIGNATURE OF ORGANIZER

January 14, 2005
DATE

Bob Anderson
TYPE OR PRINT NAME OF ORGANIZER

RETURN TO (Enter the name and the address of the person or firm to whom a copy of the filed document should be returned.)

8. NAME

FIRM   Bob Anderson

ADDRESS   3499 Malcolm Avenue

CITY/STATE/ZIP   Los Angeles, CA 90010

LLC-1 (REV 03/2005)

APPROVED BY SECRETARY OF STATE

OPERATING AGREEMENT
OF
ANDERSON INDUSTRIES, LLC
A CALIFORNIA LIMITED LIABILITY COMPANY

SECTION 1: FORMATION, NAME, PURPOSE, TERM AND DEFINITIONS

Section 1.1 Formation. The parties to this Agreement hereby enter into a written Operating Agreement pursuant to the CALIFORNIA Limited Liability Company Act (the "Act"), to set forth the terms and conditions of their joint undertaking as Members of the Company, and to carry out the purposes of the Company as further described herein, in accordance with the provisions of this Agreement and the laws of the State of CALIFORNIA.

Section 1.2 Name. The name of the Company is ANDERSON INDUSTRIES, LLC. The Company's business shall be conducted under said name, the name "ANDERSON INDUSTRIES," and/or such other names as the Manager may from time to time deem necessary or advisable, provided that necessary filings under applicable assumed or fictitious name statutes are first obtained.

Section 1.3 Offices and Resident Agent. The name and address of the Resident Agent of the Company in the State of CALIFORNIA is BOB ANDERSON, 3499 MALCOLM AVENUE, LOS ANGELES, CALIFORNIA 85254. The principal office of the Company shall be 3499 MALCOLM AVENUE, LOS ANGELES, CALIFORNIA 85254, or such other location as the Manager may, from time to time, designate by notice to the Members.

Section 1.4 Purpose. The purpose and business of the Company shall be to advertise and market software and video games.

Section 1.5 Term. The term of the Company commenced on January 14, 2005, upon the acceptance for filing of the Articles of Organization of the Company by the CALIFORNIA Secretary of State, and shall have a perpetual existence, unless earlier dissolved in accordance with Section 9.1 hereof.

Section 1.6 Defined Terms. The defined terms used in this Agreement, unless the context otherwise requires, shall have the meanings specified herein or as set forth in Exhibit B, which is attached hereto.

SECTION 2: MEMBERS, PERCENTAGE INTERESTS,
CAPITAL CONTRIBUTIONS

Section 2.1 Members: Exhibit A. The names, addresses, Capital Contributions, and Percentage Interests of all Members shall be designated in Exhibit A, which is attached hereto. The Manager shall cause Exhibit A to be amended from time to time to reflect the withdrawal of one or more Members or the admission of one or more additional Members.

Section 2.2 Capital Contributions. On or prior to the date of this Agreement, each existing Member shall make a Capital Contribution to the Company in an amount set forth opposite such Member's name in Exhibit A.

Section 2.3 Minimum Interest of the Manager. A Manager shall not be required to own an Interest in the Company.

Section 2.4 Additional Capital Liability of Members. No Member shall have any obligation to contribute capital to the Company except to the extent of the Capital Contribution of such Member described in this Section 2. No Member of the Company shall have any obligation or duty to advance or loan funds to the Company for the purpose of satisfying liabilities of the Company or any operating or carrying costs associated with the Company's business. No Member shall be personally liable for the obligations of the Company, whether arising in contract, tort, or otherwise, solely by reason of being a Member of the Company.

Section 2.5 No Interest. No interest shall be paid or due by or from the Company on any contributions to the capital of the Company, or any advances made by a Member to the Company.

Section 2.6 Indebtedness to Members. Any indebtedness of the Company owed to a Member shall provide that the payment of principal and interest (if any) shall be made only if, and to the extent that, payment of a distribution to the Member could then be made under applicable provisions of the Act without the imposition on the Member of any liability for repayment to the Company.

Section 2.7 Withdrawal of Capital by Interest Holders. Except as otherwise specifically provided in this Agreement, prior to the liquidation of the Company no Interest Holder shall have the right to require the return of his/her/its Capital Contribution or the balance of his/her/its Capital Account. There is no agreed upon time when the Capital Contribution of an Interest Holder is to be returned. No Interest Holder shall have any right to demand and receive property, in lieu of cash, in return of his/her/its Capital Account. Provided, however, the Company shall have the option to distribute property in lieu of cash in the event the Company does not have cash resources available to it for such purpose.

SECTION 3: MEMBER INTERESTS, EXTRAORDINARY ACTIONS, DILUTION

Section 3.1 Admission of Members. Subject to the limitations set forth in Section 3.4 hereof, the Manager shall have the right, at any time and from time to time, to admit one or more Members and/or to sell additional Membership Interests (or rights to acquire additional Interests), provided that any such Person receiving Interests shall make a Capital Contribution to the Company (in cash or other property) corresponding to the fair value of such Interest, as determined in the sole discretion of the Manager.

Section 3.2 Conditions for New Members. Notwithstanding anything contained herein to the contrary, no Person at any time shall be admitted as a Member of the Company unless: The Person delivers to the Company a written instrument agreeing to be bound by the terms of this Agreement, as it may have been amended from time to time; and the admission of such Person as a Member will not result in the termination of the Company.

Section 3.3 Extraordinary Actions. Subject to the limitations set forth in Sections 3.4 and 3.5 hereof, the Manager shall have the right at any time, in their sole discretion, and upon such terms and conditions as they shall determine in their sole discretion, provided they obtain the prior written consent of a Majority in Interest of the Members, to cause the Company to: (1) Convert from a limited liability company to a corporation; and (2) Engage in a public offering of its securities; transfer a substantial portion of its other assets not in the ordinary course of business; or incur any debt in any single transaction in excess of the greater of (a) One Hundred Thousand U.S. Dollars ($100,000), or (b) the accumulated capital and reserves of the Company.

In the event of the occurrence of any of the actions described in this Section 3.3, all Members hereby covenant to cooperate fully and timely with such action and to take any and all actions and execute any and all documents necessary or appropriate to effectuate such action. In the event the Company converts to a corporation and the Manager, in their sole discretion, determines that the Company should be taxed as an S corporation for federal and applicable state income tax purposes, all Members hereby covenant to cooperate fully and timely with such election and to take any and all actions and execute any and all documents necessary or appropriate to effectuate such election.

Notwithstanding the above, nothing herein shall be construed to restrict or otherwise limit the exercise by any Member, upon the occurrence of such a transaction, of such rights as may be provided to Members under the Act or under other applicable statutes.

Section 3.4 Dilution and Percentage Interest of the Members. All Interests shall be diluted on a Pro Rata Basis to the extent Interests are added or increased in accordance with this Section 3, including without limitation a dilution resulting from a private or public offering of securities.

Section 3.5 Merger or Consolidation. A Majority in Interest of the Members shall be required to approve whether the Company should be acquired by or otherwise enter into a merger or consolidation transaction with another limited liability company, or with a limited partnership, a corporation, or a business trust having transferable units of beneficial interest, regardless of whether the Company is the surviving entity of such transaction.

SECTION 4: DISTRIBUTION OF CASH & PROCEEDS; ALLOCATIONS OF TAX ITEMS

Section 4.1 Distribution of Net Available Cash Flow. The Company shall distribute all or a portion of the Net Available Cash Flow to the Members at the sole discretion of the General Manager 75 days following the end of each calendar quarter.

Section 4.2 Net Capital Proceeds. Proceeds received form a Capital Transaction, less any amounts that the General Manager determines, in their sole discretion, are necessary for the payment of or due provision for (a) the liabilities of the Company to all creditors, including the expenses of the Capital Transaction, and/or (b) additional requirements for funds in connection with the Company's business, shall be allocated to all Members in proportion to their percentage interests. Notwithstanding the foregoing, this Section 4.3 shall not apply to any distributions made in connection with a termination of the Company, which distributions shall be governed by Section 9.3 hereof.

Section 4.3 Tax Distributions. The Company shall make distributions to Interest Holders to enable them to pay taxes on allocations to them of Net Profits and proceeds from Capital Transactions.

Section 4.4 Acknowledgment. All of the Members hereby acknowledge that no distribution of Available Cash Flow or Net Capital Proceeds pursuant to this Section 4 shall be made to the Members to the extent that the Manager determine, in their sole discretion, that all or a portion of such funds are necessary for the payment of or due provision for the (a) liabilities of the Company to all creditors, including the expenses of a Capital Transaction, and/or (b) additional requirements for funds in connection with the Company's business.

Section 4.5 Capital Accounts and Tax Allocations. A separate Capital Account shall be maintained for each Interest Holder. Each Capital Account shall be adjusted annually, unless this Agreement, the acts of the Members in accordance with this Agreement, or the applicable Regulations require a more frequent adjustment. The maintenance of Capital Accounts and allocation of the Company's tax items shall follow the provisions of Exhibit C, attached hereto; provided, however, that the Company at all times shall conform to the requirements of any Regulations issued with respect to the maintenance of Capital Accounts and the allocation of tax items. The Company shall exercise its best efforts to take all actions necessary to cause the allocation of tax items among the Interest Holders to reflect the actual and anticipated allocation of the Company's distributions, as set forth in this Section 4 and in Section 9.3 hereof, in conformity with the Capital Account maintenance requirements contained in the Regulations.

SECTION 5: MANAGEMENT OF THE COMPANY

Section 5.1 Appointment of Manager: Executive Employment. The Members hereby appoint BOB ANDERSON as the Manager of the Company. The Managers may enter into employment agreements with the Company further delineating the duties, rights, compensation and covenants of the Manager. Any employment agreements shall be read in conjunction with this Agreement.

Section 5.2 Exclusive Authority of Manager. Except as specifically provided in this Agreement and any Manager's employment agreement, the exclusive responsibility for managing the business and affairs of the Company is hereby granted to the Manager pursuant to the Act. Each of the Members appoints and authorizes the Manager to serve as the sole agent of the Company, (except to the extent that certain discretionary acts may be delegated by the Manager to certain executive employees of the Company). The Manager may exercise all powers of the Company and do all such lawful acts necessary to manage the affairs and operations of the Company as are not by statute, regulations, the Articles of Organization, or other applicable documentation required to be exercised or done by any of the other Members. Any Person dealing with the Manager shall be authorized to rely upon the authority of the Manager to bind the Company in accordance with the rights, powers, and duties described in this Agreement. The Manager shall be an "Authorized Person" of the Company, and shall be authorized to execute or file any document required or permitted to be executed or filed on behalf of the Company, or to otherwise act as an agent of the Company, as provided under the Act.

Section 5.3 Binding Authority with Respect to Documents. The Manager shall have the right, power, and authority, acting at all times for and on behalf of the Company, to enter into and execute any agreement or agreements, promissory note or notes, and any other instruments or documents, and to undertake and do all acts necessary to carry out the purposes for which the Company was formed. In no event shall a party dealing with the Company with respect to any document signed or action undertaken on behalf of the Company have the right to inquire into:

    a. The necessity or expediency of any act or action of the Manager;

    b. Personal information of a Manager if the Manager is a natural person;

    c. Any act or failure to act by the Company;

    d. The identities of Members other than the Manager; or,

    e. The existence or non-existence of any fact or facts that constitute conditions precedent to acts by the Manager (including, without limitation, conditions, provisions, and other requirements herein set forth relating to borrowing and the execution of any encumbrances to secure the borrowing) or that are in any other manner germane to the affairs of the Company.

Any and every Person relying upon any document signed or action taken by the Manager on behalf of the Company or claiming thereunder may conclusively presume that (i) at the time or times of the execution and/or delivery thereof, this Agreement was in full force and effect, (ii) any instrument or document was duly executed in accordance with the terms and provisions of this Agreement and is binding upon the Company without requiring the approval or consent of any of the Members thereof, and (iii) the Manager was duly authorized and empowered to execute and deliver any and every such instrument or document for and on behalf of the Company.

Section 5.4 Specific Authority.

In furtherance and not in limitation of the provisions of Section 5.2 hereof and of the other provisions of this Agreement, but subject to any limitations contained in this Agreement (including without limitation Section 3.7 hereof) and a Manager's employment agreement, the Manager is specifically authorized and empowered, in Manager's sole discretion, without regard to the approval thereof by the Members, to:

    a. Direct the employees of the Company to execute, acknowledge, and deliver any and all documents, agreements, notes, contracts, bank resolutions, signature cards, releases, or other instruments on the Company's behalf;

b. Make any and all decisions that the Company may be entitled and/or required to make under the terms of any and all documents, agreements (including employment agreements), or other instruments relative to the ownership, operation, management, and supervision of the Company's business;

c. Execute for and on behalf of the Company, and in accordance with the terms of this Agreement, deeds absolute, mortgages (which term "mortgages" is hereby defined for all purposes of this Agreement to include Deeds of Trust, financing statements, chattel mortgages, pledges, conditional sales contracts, and similar security instruments), leases, contracts, promissory notes, or other legal documents all of which instruments so duly executed as provided herein shall be valid and binding upon the Company;

d. Cause the Company to incur indebtedness or obtain financing (including without limitation loans from Members or Affiliates of Members at competitive rates); to issue promissory notes or other evidences of indebtedness; to prepay in whole or in part, recast, increase, modify, or extend any liabilities affecting the business of the Company and assumed in connection therewith; to provide security or collateral in connection with any Company indebtedness or to encumber or pledge any Company assets; to execute any extensions or renewals of encumbrances with respect to any assets used in the Company's business; and to confess judgment on behalf of the Company in connection with any Company borrowings;

e. Cause the Company to enter into leases of real or personal property in furtherance of any or all of the purposes of the Company;

f. Cause the Company to purchase real property or personal property and to make reasonable and necessary capital expenditures and improvements with respect to such property for use in connection with the operation and management of the Company's business; to finance such purchases or expenditures, in whole or in part, by giving the seller or any other Person a security interest in the property purchased;

g. Cause the Company to sell, exchange, or otherwise dispose of any or all of the assets of the Company, or enter into any Capital Transaction involving the assets or business of the Company, including any or all of the components of the Company's business, whether such components are real property, personal property, or intellectual property, mixed or intangible, such as goodwill, if any;

h. Cause the Company to redeem or acquire the Interest of any Interest Holder pursuant to the terms of this Agreement or pursuant to the Manager's authority hereunder, and to exercise any options or other rights with respect to the Interest of any Interest Holder, on behalf of the Company or for the Manager's own account;

i. Open accounts and deposit and maintain funds in the name of the Company in banks, savings and loan associations, money market funds, or such other financial instruments as the Manager deems necessary or appropriate;

j. Pay all costs or expenses connected with the operation or management of the Company, including all debts and other obligations of the Company, from its bank accounts by check or other customary means (without commingling with the funds of any other Person);

k. Establish reserves in such amounts as the Manager shall deem appropriate;

l. Enter into, perform, and carry out contracts with any Person, including any of the Members or Affiliates of the Members, at reasonably competitive rates of compensation for the performance of any and all services that may at any time be necessary, proper, convenient or advisable to carry on the Company's business, including entering into exclusive and nonexclusive arrangements;

m. Monitor the quality of services and products provided by vendors to the Company, and add, discharge, or replace such vendors as needed in accordance with applicable state law;

n. Appoint and discharge executive employees of the Company and delegate specific duties and authority to Persons who may or may not be employees of the Company;

o. Employ or engage Persons in the operation and management of the Company's business, on such terms and for such reasonable compensation as the Manager shall determine (at arm's length prices and in keeping with comparable salaries for comparable work), in good faith, to be appropriate and in the best interests of the Company;

p. Approve the hiring and firing of all employees and agents of the Company, subject to the terms and conditions of any employment policies and procedures of the Company, and subject to the terms of this Agreement, any other written agreements and applicable state law;

q. Evaluate the performance of all employees and agents of the Company, including its executive employees, and monitor the quality of services provided by employees and agents of the Company;

r. Establish and monitor the compensation requirements (reasonable compensation set at arm's length prices and in keeping with comparable salaries for comparable work) of all employees and agents of the Company, including its executive employees;

s. Apply for, make proffers and commitments with regard to, and obtain any and all governmental permits, approvals, and licenses necessary and appropriate in connection with or in anyway related to the Company's business;

t. Place and carry public liability, workmen's compensation, fire, extended coverage, business interruptions, errors and omissions, and such other insurance as may be necessary or appropriate for the protection of the interests and property of the Company;

u. Authorize the lending of money by the Company at prevailing interest rates, including lending to borrowers who may be Members or Affiliates of Members of the Company;

v. Initiate, settle, and defend legal actions on behalf of the Company, including any litigation, arbitration, mediation, examination, investigation, inquiry, regulatory proceeding, or other similar matter contemplated by the Company, threatened by any Person or in or with which the Company may become involved;

w. Submit a claim or liability involving the Company to arbitration;

x. Prepare, maintain, file, and disseminate returns, reports, statements, and other information for distribution to the Internal Revenue Service, the state of California Franchise Tax Board or Secretary of State, the Members, and for submission to any governmental or regulatory authority or agency;

y. Deal directly with relevant state and United States regulatory authorities on behalf of the Company and render decisions with respect to matters involving such authorities;

z. Cause the Company to create one or more wholly or partially owned domestic or foreign subsidiaries, which may be corporations, limited liability companies, or other forms of business entities;

aa. Enter into agreements with Members as appropriate; and,

bb. Generally, do all things consistent with any and all of the foregoing on behalf of the Company.

Section 5.5 Obligations of the Managers.

a. The Manager shall take all actions that may be necessary or appropriate (i) for the continuation of the Company's valid existence as a limited liability company under the applicable state laws; (ii) for the operation, management, and supervision of the Company's business in accordance with the provisions of this Agreement and applicable laws and regulations.

b. The Manager shall oversee the preparation, review, and safekeeping of the Company's records and books of accounts of all operations, receipts and expenditures of the Company, and shall institute and maintain such internal controls as may be required to comply with all laws and regulations applicable to the Company.

c. The Manager shall deliver to the Members copies of "Information Tax Returns" required under applicable Federal or state income tax laws, including the Internal Revenue Code of 1986, as amended, as soon as such return may reasonably be prepared, but not later than the due date of such return as may be extended pursuant to statutory or administrative provision. Such returns shall reflect the allocation of the profits or losses of the Company and other tax items as provided in this Agreement to each Member for the Fiscal Year then ended and shall serve as the annual accounting report to be provided to the Interest Holders. The cost of all such reports shall be paid by the Company at the Company's expense.

d. The Manager shall deliver copies of this Agreement, the Articles of Organization, or any amendments thereto to each Member.

Section 5.6 No Duty to Consult. Except as otherwise specifically provided herein, the Manager shall have no duty or obligation to consult with or seek the advice of the Members.

Section 5.7 Contracting on Behalf of the Company; Related Persons. The Manager, on behalf of the Company, may employ a Member, or a Person related to or affiliated with a Member, to render or perform a service, or may contract to buy property from, or sell property to, any such Member or other Person; provided, that (i) any such transaction shall be on terms that are fair and equitable to the Company, comparable to those charged by unrelated parties, and no less favorable to the Company than the terms, if any, known to be available from unrelated and unaffiliated Persons; and (ii) all parties with whom the Company contracts will of such qualifications to be consistent with the requirements and guidelines of applicable California law. The Manager may employ, engage, and contract with, on behalf of the Company, such Persons, firms, or corporations as the Manager, in the Manager's discretion, shall deem advisable for the operation and management of the business of the Company, including such managing agents, attorneys, accountants, insurance brokers, appraisers, experts, consultants, and lenders, on such reasonable terms and for such reasonable compensation, as the Manager, in the Manager's discretion, shall determine. Any such Person, firm, or corporation may include the Manager, or an Affiliate of the Manager, or entities otherwise employed or retained by the Manager or in which the Manager has an interest, provided the compensation paid is in accordance with normal fees charged by independent parties for similar services.

Section 5.8 Tax Elections. The Manager shall be authorized to take such actions as the Manager, in the Manager's discretion, deems necessary or desirable in order to comply with requirements of the Act as promulgated by the Internal Revenue Code of 1986, as amended, for the purposes of complying with federal, local, and state tax requirements. The Manager shall have the power on behalf of the Company, to make, or to refrain from making, or to revoke, any elections and determinations referred to in the Act and the Internal Revenue Code of 1986, as amended, including, but not limited to the method(s) of depreciation, the amortization of organizational expenses, and the method of accounting to be employed by the Company. All elections shall be made by the Manager with the Internal Revenue Service (IRS), as applicable, in his or her sole discretion, in consideration of the advice of the Company's accountants and the underlying interests of the Interest Holders as a whole. In the event that evidence shall be provided that such election was or shall become disadvantageous to any one or more of the Interest Holders, such evidence shall not be deemed to be a demonstration of the commission of an act of willful misconduct or negligence on the part of the Manager. The Manager shall not be responsible to consider the impact on specific members in making any elections.

Section 5.9 Tax Matters Partner. BOB ANDERSON shall act as the "Tax Matters Partner" under the Internal Revenue code of 1986, as amended. The Tax Matters Partner shall, within fifteen (15) business days of receipt thereof, forward to each

Member a photocopy of any correspondence relating to the Company received from the Internal Revenue Service that relates to matters that are of material importance to the Company and/or its Members. The Tax Matters Partner shall, within fifteen (15) business days thereof, advise each Member in writing of the substance of any conversation held with any representative of the Internal Revenue Service that relates to matters that are of material importance to the Company and/or such specific Members. Any reasonable costs incurred by the Tax Matters Partner for retaining accountants and/or attorneys on behalf of the Company in connection with any Internal Revenue Service inquiry or audit of the Company shall be charged as expenses of the Company. The Tax Matters Partner shall provide each Interest Holder with copies of any notices of judicial or administrative proceedings and any other information required by law. The Company expenses of such proceedings shall be paid by the Company out of its assets. With respect to any such matter, the Tax Matters Partner shall be entitled to make all decisions and enter into any agreements on behalf of the Company, which in his or her sole discretion are deemed to be reasonable under the circumstances. In any event, the Tax Matters Partner shall not be obligated to contest or otherwise challenge any adjustments made by the Internal Revenue Service. The Manager shall not be required to furnish additional funds to the Company for purposes of entering into or pursuing any proceedings on behalf of the Company. Each Member who elects to participate in any proceedings with respect to such matters shall be responsible for any expenses incurred by such Member in connection with such proceedings.

Section 5.10 Outside Activities. Subject to the provisions of any employment agreement, the Manager, on the Manager's own account or in conjunction with others, shall be authorized to engage in other business activities or possess interests in other ventures notwithstanding the Manager's duties and responsibilities as the Manager of the Company. Notwithstanding the foregoing restrictions, the Manager, and any Affiliates of the Manager, shall not be obligated to present to the Company any particular investment opportunity that may come to their attention even if such opportunity is of a character that might be suitable for investment by the Company or its Members.

Section 5.11 Resignation or Removal of Manager. At any time, BOB ANDERSON may resign as Manager upon giving at least ninety (90) days prior written notice to the other Members. Any successor Manager may resign upon giving at least ninety (90) days prior written notice to the other Members. A Manager may be removed as Manager only for cause, as defined in any employment agreement, as determined by the affirmative vote of the Members owning one hundred percent (100%) of the outstanding Membership Units of the Company as a group, including any Units owned by the Manager or the Manager's Affiliates. The withdrawal of the Manager shall be deemed to include:

a. The death of the acting Manager;

b. The dissolution of a corporate Manager (provided that, to the extent allowed under the Act and to the extent consistent with relevant Regulations, the inadvertent dissolution and loss of corporate charter by a corporate Manager shall not constitute a dissolution for purposes of this Agreement if its corporate status is reinstated with reasonable promptness after discovery of such loss of charter); or,

c. The dissolution of a Manager that is a partnership or another limited liability company. The effective date of a withdrawal under this Section 5.11 shall be the date of the event giving rise to the withdrawal.

Section 5.12 Replacement of Manager. In the event of the withdrawal of the Manager, the Members holding a majority of all the outstanding Membership Units of the Company as a group, held by the Manager, may elect one or more successor Manager(s). Any powers exercisable by the Manager under this Agreement or otherwise shall be exercisable by any successor Manager(s). If a successor Manager is not elected, any powers conferred upon the Manager under this Agreement shall be exercisable by the Members pursuant to the Act. Other than as set forth in Section 5.11, the withdrawing Manager is not required to withdraw as a Member.

SECTION 6: RIGHTS, DUTIES, AND REPRESENTATIONS OF MEMBERS

Section 6.1 No Authority to Act. In accordance with the Articles of Organization of the Company, no Member shall be an agent of the Company or have authority to act for the Company solely by virtue of being a Member. The Members shall not take part in the management of the business nor transact any business for the Company in their capacity as Members, nor shall they have power to sign for or to bind the Company; provided, however, the Members shall have the right to participate in certain decisions as provided herein. In the event that a Member is also an employee or agent of the Company, any activities of a Member in such capacity shall solely be under the supervision and direction of the Manager or other executive employees of the Company.

Section 6.2 Meetings and Voting by Members. Meetings of the Members shall be held, and voting shall be conducted, as determined by (i) the Manager or (ii) 10% of the interested members. Written notice of the meeting must be given not less than ten (10) days nor more than sixty (60) days before the date of the meeting. The only business that may be transacted at the meeting is as stated in the meeting notice.

The Members shall be authorized to vote concerning such matters as shall be specifically provided under the terms and conditions of this Agreement and such matters as shall be referred to the Members for voting by the Manager. Except as specifically provided in this Agreement, the unanimous consent of the Members shall not be required with respect to any matter concerning the Company, and the vote of a Majority in Interest of all the Members shall constitute the approval of such matter by the Members. In no event shall an Interest Holder or other transferee of an Interest be entitled to vote with respect to such matters until such time as such Interest Holder or transferee shall be admitted to the Company as a Member.

Section 6.3 Review of Books and Records. The Manager shall be authorized to establish standards for the restriction of the accessibility to the Members or to any Interest Holders of the Company documents and information relating to the Company. This authority shall include the right to restrict accessibility to such information to a particular Member or Interest Holder in the event such Person, directly or indirectly, becomes engaged in, or has otherwise acquired an interest in, or an enterprise competitive with the Company's business. The Manager may maintain the confidentiality of trade secrets or any other information the disclosure of which the Manager believes in good faith to be detrimental or potentially damaging to the Company's business, or otherwise not in the best interests of the Company. The Manager, in its sole discretion, may determine what information shall be treated as confidential in nature and not available for review, such as information relating to the compensation of executive employees. The Manager also shall be authorized to restrict accessibility with respect to matters required by law or by agreement with a third party to be kept confidential. Subject to the foregoing restrictions, any Member shall be authorized to review and inspect Company documents and information that may be required by law to be subject to the review of members. A Member who is interested in reviewing such information shall be required to notify the Manager in writing at least ten business days prior to the date requested for the review. In such written notice, the Member shall be required to state the nature of the review and the purpose reasonably related to such Member's interest in the Company. Inspection and review shall be performed during normal business hours at the principal office of the Company. Any costs associated with such inspection, including any photocopying charges, shall be the responsibility of such Member.

Section 6.4 Representations and Warranties of Members. Each Member shall immediately notify the Manager if any of the statements made herein or in any subscription documents or questionnaires submitted with such Member's counterpart signature page to this Agreement shall become adversely affected or untrue in any material respect. Each of the Members represents and warrants to the Company as follows:

a. The Member is the sole party in interest as to its participation in the Company;

b. The Member is acquiring its Interest without any present intention of selling or otherwise disposing of such Interest at any particular time or on the happening of any particular event or circumstance, and that the Member has no reason to anticipate any change in circumstances or any other occasion or event that would cause the sale or other disposition of any Interest. The Member acknowledges that the Interest acquired is subject to certain restrictions on Transfer described herein and, accordingly, is not an entirely liquid investment. The Member also represents and warrants that the Member has made an independent investigation with respect to the acquisition of such Interest and has reviewed the purchase with advisors, to the extent that it deemed such assistance advisable;

c. The Member is not engaged in, nor otherwise holds an interest in, directly or indirectly, an enterprise competitive with the Company's business; and,

d. The Member understands that the Manager and the Company are represented in matters concerning the Company and this offering by common legal counsel. Accordingly, Members should not consider the common counsel of the Manager and the Company to be their independent counsel and should consult with their own legal counsel on all matters concerning the Company or an investment therein. The common legal counsel and other experts performing services for the Manager may also perform services for affiliates of the Manager.

Section 6.5 Covenants Concerning Confidentiality. Each of the Members recognizes that its relationship with the Company may provide the Member with specialized knowledge, which, if used in competition with the Company, could cause serious harm to the Company. Each of the Members acknowledges that the knowledge and information acquired by the Member concerning the Company's technology, ideas, strategies, services, finances, systems, forms, business methods and procedures, costs, prices, credit practices, existing and prospective contracts, personnel records, methods used and preferred by the Company's business and affiliates, and all such other relevant business knowledge and information, whether written or otherwise, constitute a vital part of the Company's business and is confidential business information some of which may be trade secrets (hereinafter sometimes collectively referred to as the "Confidential Materials") except to the extent such information may be otherwise lawfully and readily available to the general public, and that such information may be acquired through its involvement and participation in the Company.

As a material inducement to the Company and the Manager to admit each of the Members to the Company, each of the Members covenants as follows:

a. The Member shall not at any time, without the written consent of the Company, directly or indirectly, use, divulge, furnish, make available, or disclose for any purpose whatsoever, any aspect concerning the Confidential Materials, which has been made available to the Member as a result of its association with the Company.

b. Upon the termination of the Member's affiliation with the Company, the Member will return all Confidential Materials, whether prepared by the Company or by the Members, that constitute records of the Company or that contain any information relating to the Company's business. Such records shall include, by way of illustration and not in limitation of such category of items, all financial statements, records, reports, books, lists, files, letters, memoranda, disks and other materials, and any information or data fixed in any tangible medium of expression from which can be perceived, reproduced, or otherwise communicated any information or data relating to the Company's business.

SECTION 7: TRANSFER OF INTERESTS

Section 7.1 General Restrictions. Except as specifically provided in this Agreement, no Interest Holder at any time shall, voluntarily or involuntarily, transfer any of its Interest to any Person. In addition to the restrictions on the Transfer of Interests set forth in this Section 7, no Interest Holder shall Transfer all or any portion of the Holder's Interest, or any rights with respect to such Interest, unless the following conditions are satisfied:

a. The Manager approves the transfer;

b. The Transfer will not require registration of the Interest under any federal or state securities laws;

c. The transferee delivers to the Company a written instrument agreeing to be bound by the terms of this Agreement;

d. The Transfer will not result in the termination of the Company pursuant to Code Section 708;

e. The Transfer will not result in the Company being subject to the Investment Company Act of 1940, as amended; and,

f. The transferee or the transferor delivers the following information to the Company: (i) the transferee's taxpayer identification number; and (ii) the transferee's initial tax basis in the transferred Interest.

Section 7.2 Dissolution of a Member or Sale or Transfer of Interests.

a. If a Member (the "Selling Member") at any time receives a bona fide offer (the "Offer") from a third party (the "Prospective Purchaser") to purchase all or a portion of the Selling Member's said Interest (the "Offered Interest"), and the Selling Member desires to sell the Offered Interest to the Prospective Purchaser, the Selling Member first must deliver to the Company, written notice containing all material terms and conditions of the Offer and offering to sell the Offered Interest upon the terms set forth in the Offer. The recipients of said notice (collectively, the "Optionors"), then shall have the option to elect to purchase all (but not less than all) of the Offered Interest in accordance with the terms contained in the Offer, in the following order of priority: The Interest Holders owning any other Interests, on a Pro Rata Basis among themselves, or, in such other proportions as they shall agree, shall have the right of refusal to purchase any remaining portion of the Offered Interest.

b. If any of the Optionors desire to purchase the Offered Interest, they must elect to exercise said option by sending written notice of such election to the Selling Member within fifteen business days after receiving notice of the Offer. If any of the Optionors exercise their option hereunder, settlement on the purchase of the Offered Interest shall occur within the later to occur of (a) thirty (30) business days following the date of such notice or (b) the latest date for closing provided in the Offer.

c. If none of the Optionors purchases the Offered Interest in accordance with this Section 7.2, then the Selling Member shall have the right to Transfer the Offered Interest to the Prospective Purchaser, provided that:

1) The Transfer is upon terms no more favorable to the Prospective Purchaser than those contained in the Offer;
2) The Transfer is consummated within sixty (60) days after the expiration of the time period during which the Company's option could have been exercised; and,
3) The conditions to Transfer set forth in Section 7.1 hereof are satisfied.

Section 7.3 Right of Refusal—Potential Interests.

a. If an Interest Holder of a potential Interest (the "Offeror") at any time receives a bona fide offer (the "Offer") from a third party (the "Prospective Purchaser") to purchase all or a portion of the Offeror's Interest (the "Offered Interest"), and the Offeror desires to sell the Offered Interest to the Prospective Purchaser, the Offeror first must deliver to the Company written notice containing all material terms and conditions of the Offer and offering to sell the Offered Interest to the Company upon the terms set forth in the Offer. The Company, in the sole discretion of the Manager, then shall have the option to elect to purchase the Offered Interest in accordance with the terms contained in the Offer, by sending written notice thereof to the Offeror within fifteen business days after receiving notice of the Offer. If the Company exercises its option hereunder, settlement on the purchase of the Offered Interest shall occur within the later to occur of (a) thirty (30) business days following the date of such notice or (b) the latest date for closing provided in the Offer.

b. If the Company does not purchase the Offered Interest in accordance with this Section 7.3, then the Offeror shall have the right to Transfer the Offered Interest to the Prospective Purchaser, provided that:
1) The Transfer is upon terms no more favorable to the Prospective Purchaser than those contained in the Offer;
2) The Transfer is consummated within 60 days after the expiration of the time period during which the option could have been exercised; and,
3) The conditions to Transfer set forth in Section 7.1 hereof are satisfied.

Section 7.4 Reasonableness of Restrictions: Void Transfers. Each Interest Holder acknowledges that the restrictions described in this Section 7 are reasonable in view of the purposes of the Company and the relationship of the Members. Any Transfer of an Interest that does not fully comply with all applicable provisions of this Agreement shall be null and void and without effect, ab initio. Any Person who claims to be the transferee of an Interest, or any Person to whom rights attributable to any such Interest are attempted to be transferred in violation of this Section, shall not be entitled to: vote on matters coming before the Members, participate in the management of the Company, act as an agent of the Company, receive distributions from the Company or have any other rights in or with respect to such Interest.

Section 7.5 Enforceability. It is recognized by the parties that the provisions of this Section 7 are of particular importance for the protection and promotion of their existing and future interests. The parties further acknowledge that the relationship of all of the Members is and will be such that, in the event of any breach of the restrictions and procedures set forth in this Agreement, a claim for monetary damages may not constitute adequate remedy and that irreparable damage would result if this Agreement were not enforced. If any dispute arises concerning the Transfer of an Interest in the Company, a preliminary restraining order and an injunction may be issued to restrain the Transfer pending determination of the controversy. Should any controversy arise concerning the right or obligation to purchase or sell any Interest in the Company, such right or obligation shall be enforceable in a court by a decree of specific performance. Such remedy shall be cumulative and not exclusive, and shall be in addition to any other remedy that the parties may have. No objection to the form of action or to the relief prayed for in any proceeding for the specific performance of this Agreement shall be raised by any party, in order that such relief may be obtained by the other party or parties not in breach hereunder.

SECTION 8: CESSATION OF MEMBERSHIP

Section 8.1 Voluntary Withdrawal. No Member or Interest Holder shall be entitled to Voluntarily Withdraw from the Company prior to the termination of the Company. No Member or Interest Holder shall be entitled to receive the fair market value of its Interest in the Company at any time prior to the termination of the Company except to the extent otherwise provided in Section 9.3 hereof upon the dissolution and winding up of the affairs of the Company.

Section 8.2 Involuntary Withdrawal. Immediately upon the occurrence of an Involuntary Withdrawal of a Member, the successor or legal representative of such Member shall not become a Member, but shall become an Interest Holder entitled to such rights (economic and otherwise) provided under the Act to the assignee of an interest in a limited liability company, except that such successor shall not be entitled to receive in liquidation of the Interest, pursuant to the Act, the fair market value of the Member's Interest as of the date of the Member's Involuntary Withdrawal from the Company.

SECTION 9: DISSOLUTION AND WINDING UP

Section 9.1 Events of Dissolution of Company. Notwithstanding any provisions of the Act to the contrary, the Company shall be dissolved only upon the happening of any of the following events:

    a. Upon the expiration of the term of the Company as stated in the Articles of Organization;

    b. Upon the determination of a Majority in Interest of Members that the Company shall be dissolved; or,

    c. Upon such time as there are fewer than two Members of the Company.

Section 9.2 Continuation of business. The cessation of membership by a Member of the Company shall not cause dissolution of the Company.

Section 9.3 Winding Up. If the Company is dissolved and the business of the Company is not continued in accordance with Section 9.1(c) hereof, the Manager shall wind up the Company's affairs. In the event of the liquidation of the Company, a reasonable time shall be allowed for the orderly liquidation of the assets of the Company and the discharge of liabilities. On winding up of the Company, the assets of the Company shall be distributed as follows:

a. To the payment of debts and liabilities of the Company (other than those owed to other Members) and the expenses of liquidation;

b. To the establishment and funding of such reserves as the Manager or the liquidating agent, if there be one, may reasonably deem necessary for contingent liabilities or obligations of the Company, provided that such reserves, or any part thereof, not required to be paid over for such contingent liabilities shall be distributed as hereinafter provided;

c. To the repayment of any loans or advances made by any Members to the Company (in proportion to their respective advances if the amount available for repayment shall be insufficient to satisfy all such advances); and,

d. To each of the Interest Holders on account of such Interest Holder's Interest in the Company in an amount equal to each such Interest Holder's positive Capital Account balance immediately preceding the liquidation of the Company, but after giving effect to any tax allocations under Section 4.5 hereof and Exhibit C, which is attached hereto and incorporated by reference herein.

It is the intention of the Members that the foregoing distributions under Sub-Paragraph (d) shall be in accordance with the distribution provisions set forth in Section 4 hereof. Each Interest Holder's Capital Account shall be adjusted for the Company's taxable year during which such liquidation occurs. Liquidating distributions shall be made by the end of such taxable year (or, if later, within ninety (90) days after the date of such liquidation).

Section 9.4 No Obligation to Restore Deficit Account Balances. No Interest Holder shall be required to contribute to the capital of the Company any amount necessary to restore a deficit balance in such Interest Holder's Capital Account to zero. No Interest Holder shall have any rights of contribution with respect to any such deficit balances in any Interest Holder's Capital Account.

Section 9.5 Liquidating Agent or Trust. In the discretion of the Manager, a pro rata portion of the distributions that would otherwise be made to the Interest Holders under Section 9.3 hereof may be:

a. distributed to a trust established for the benefit of the Interest Holders for the purposes of liquidating Company assets, collecting amounts owed to the Company, and paying any contingent or unforeseen liabilities or obligations of the Company to the Interest Holders arising out of or in connection with the Company. The assets of any such trust shall be distributed to the Interest

Holders from time to time, in the reasonable discretion of the Manager, in accordance with the same priorities and in the same proportions as the amount distributed to such trust by the Company as would otherwise have been distributed to the Interest Holders pursuant to this Agreement or

b. withheld to provide a reasonable reserve for Company liabilities (contingent or otherwise) to reflect the unrealized portion of installment obligations owed by the Company, provided that such withheld amounts shall be distributed to the Interest Holders as soon as practicable.

Section 9.6 Articles of Cancellation and Articles of Dissolution. If the Company is dissolved, the Manager promptly shall file Articles of Dissolution with the State of CALIFORNIA, and upon the mailing of proper notices, shall file Articles of Cancellation with the State of CALIFORNIA concerning the termination of the Company. If there is no Manager remaining on the Manager, then the Articles of Cancellation shall be filed by the last Person to be a Member; if there are no remaining Members, nor a Person who last was a Member, then the Articles shall be filed by the legal or personal representative of the Person who last was a Member.

SECTION 10: INDEMNIFICATION OF THE MANAGERS

Section 10.1 General. The Company shall indemnify the Manager against all claims by Persons other than the Members or the Company which arise in connection with the business of the Company, including attorney's fees, and including any claim or liability arising by reason of an error of judgment, act, or omission of such party, whether or not disclosed to the Members, provided that the actions (or failure to act) of the Manager did not constitute gross negligence, willful misconduct, or willful misrepresentation with respect to such error, act, or omission. Advances from the Company for payment of costs and attorney's fees as incurred shall be authorized only if the action was initiated by a third party who is not a Member and the indemnitee agrees to repay the advanced funds to the Company in the event they are not entitled to indemnification hereunder. Any indemnification under this Section shall be recoverable only out of the assets of the Company, and no Member shall have any personal liability with respect thereto.

Section 10.2 Limitation of Liability. The Manager shall not be liable or accountable in damages to the Company or to any of the Interest Holders with respect to any act, omission, or error in judgment, whether or not constituting negligence, taken in its capacity as the Manager on behalf of the Company, except for any act or omission constituting gross negligence, willful misconduct, or willful misrepresentation.

Section 10.3 Successful Defense of Litigation. In addition to, and not in limitation of, any rights set forth in this Agreement or provided under the Act, the Manager, if successful on the merits or otherwise in the defense of any proceeding in which it was made a party by reason of acting in the capacity of the Board of Managers, shall be indemnified against reasonable expenses (including without limitation attorney's fees, other professional fees, court costs, and travel costs) incurred by the Manager in connection with such proceeding.

SECTION 11: POWER OF ATTORNEY FOR LIMITED PURPOSES

Section 11.1 Manager as Attorney-in-Fact. Each Interest Holder hereby makes, constitutes, and appoints the Manager, his/her/its true and lawful attorney-in-fact for such Interest Holder and in his/her/its name, place, and stead and for his/her/its use and benefit, to sign, execute, certify, acknowledge, swear to, file, and record (a) this Agreement and all agreements, certificates, instruments, and other documents amending or changing this Agreement as now or hereafter amended in accordance with this Agreement that the Manager may deem necessary, desirable, or appropriate including, without limitation, amendments, or changes to reflect: (i) the exercise by the Manager of any power granted to the Manager under this Agreement; (ii) any amendments adopted by the Members in accordance with the terms of this Agreement; (iii) the admission of any Member pursuant to the terms of this Agreement; and, (iv) the disposition by any Member of an Interest in the Company and (b) any certificates, instruments, and documents as may be required by, or may be appropriate under the laws of the State of CALIFORNIA or any other state or jurisdiction in which the Company is doing or intends to do business. Each Interest Holder authorizes such attorney-in-fact to take any further action that such attorney-in-fact shall consider necessary or advisable in connection with any of the foregoing, hereby giving such attorney-in-fact full power and authority to do and perform each and every act or thing whatsoever requisite or advisable to be done and performed in connection with the foregoing as fully as such Interest Holder might or could do and perform personally, and hereby ratifying and confirming all that any such attorney-in-fact shall lawfully do and perform or cause to be done and performed by virtue thereof or hereof.

Section 11.2 Nature as Special Power. The power of attorney granted pursuant to this Section:

a. Is a special power of attorney coupled with an interest, and is irrevocable;

b. May be exercised by any such attorney-in-fact by listing the Interest Holders executing any agreement, certificate, instrument, or other document with the single signature of any such attorney-in-fact acting as attorney-in-fact for such Interest Holders; and,

Shall survive the death, disability, legal incapacity, bankruptcy, insolvency, dissolution, or cessation of existence of an Interest Holder and shall survive the delivery of an assignment by an Interest Holder of the whole or a portion of his/her/its interest in the Company, except that where the assignment is of such Interest Holder's entire interest in the Company and the assignee, with the consent of the Manager, is admitted to the Company as a Member, the power of attorney shall survive the delivery of such assignment for the sole purpose of enabling any such attorney-in-fact to effect such substitution.

SECTION 12: AMENDMENT

Section 12.1 Required Vote as to Noneconomic Matters. With respect to any matters not specifically set forth in Section 12.2 hereof, the required vote for the approval of any proposed amendment to this Agreement shall be a Majority in Interest of the Members. The Manager, in consultation with the Company's legal counsel, shall make the determination of whether a proposed amendment shall constitute a matter for approval pursuant to this Section 12.1.

Section 12.2 Unanimous Consent for Certain Amendments. Notwithstanding the provisions of Section 12.1 hereof, if the effect of any proposed amendment to this Agreement or to the Articles of Organization would be to increase the liability of the Members, or to change the contributions required of the Members, the rights and interest of any Member in distributions from the Company or any Members' rights upon liquidation of the Company, such proposed amendment shall be adopted only upon the unanimous written consent of all the Members.

SECTION 13: MISCELLANEOUS PROVISIONS

Section 13.1 Books. All of the books of account, records, and data, together with an executed copy of the Articles of Organization and any amendments thereto, shall at all times be maintained at the principal office of the Company, or at such other place as is designated by the Manager.

Section 13.2 Banking. All funds of the Company shall be deposited in its name in such checking account or in other accounts as shall be designated by the Manager. All withdrawals therefrom are to be made upon checks signed by those Persons who may from time to time be designated by the Manager.

Section 13.3 Accountants. All financial statements requiring delivery to the Members under this Agreement shall be audited by Certified Public Accountants chosen by the Manager. Such statements shall be prepared in accordance with the accounting procedures and elections as may be determined from time to time by the Manager in consultation with such accountants.

Section 13.4 Notices. All notices required under this Agreement shall be in writing and shall be deemed to have been given and effective three days following deposit of same in a receptacle of the United States Postal Service by certified or registered mail, postage prepaid, or upon personal delivery or transmittal by electronic means. Notices shall be addressed as follows, or at such other addresses designated by notice to the Company: (i) if to the Company or to the Manager, at the principal office thereof set forth in Section 1.3 hereof; (ii) if to any Interest Holder, at the address set forth in Exhibit A, as may be amended from time to time.

Section 13.5 Further Assurances. The parties hereto shall execute, acknowledge, and deliver such further instruments the Manager may deem expedient or necessary in the operation of the Company and the achievement of its purpose, and shall perform such further acts and things as may be required or appropriate to carry out the intent and purpose of this Agreement.

Section 13.6 Integration. This Agreement constitutes the entire agreement among the parties pertaining to its subject matter and supersedes all prior and contemporaneous verbal and written agreements and undertakings of the parties in connection therewith.

Section 13.7 Binding Effect. Except as otherwise provided herein and subject to the restrictions on assignment set forth herein, all provisions of this Agreement shall be binding upon, inure to the benefit of, and be enforceable by and against the parties hereto and each of their respective heirs, executors, administrators, personal representatives, successors, and assigns.

Section 13.8 Counterparts. This Agreement may be executed in one or more counterparts, each of which shall constitute one Agreement, binding on all the parties hereto, even though all the parties are not signatories to the original or the same counterpart. In addition, this Agreement may contain more than one counterpart of the signature page and this Agreement may be executed by the affixing of the signatures of each of the Members to one of such counterpart signature pages; all of such signature pages shall be read as though one, and they shall have the same force and effect as though all of the signers had signed a single signature page.

Section 13.9 Headings. The headings of the sections of this Agreement are inserted for convenience or reference only and shall not be deemed to be part of this Agreement.

Section 13.10 Agency. Except as provided herein, nothing herein contained shall be construed to constitute any Member hereof the agent of any other Member hereof or to restrict the Members from carrying on their own respective businesses or activities.

Section 13.11 Gender. Wherever appropriate, any reference herein to the singular shall include the plural, any reference to the masculine shall include the feminine gender, and any reference to "it" shall include "his" or "her" or vice versa, as the case may be.

Section 13.12 Reimbursement for Company Expenses. The Company shall reimburse any Member or an Affiliate of any Member who has, prior to or after the execution of this Agreement, made payments for or on behalf of the Company, subject, however, to the terms of any other agreements of such Members with the Company.

Section 13.13 Severability. Every provision of this Agreement is intended to be severable. If any term or provision hereof is illegal or invalid for any reason whatsoever, such illegality or invalidity shall not affect the validity or legality of the remainder of this Agreement.

Section 13.14 Incorporation by Reference. Every exhibit, schedule, or appendix attached to this Agreement and referenced herein is hereby incorporated into this Agreement by reference.

Section 13.15 Applicable Law. The laws of the State of CALIFORNIA shall govern the validity of this Agreement, the construction of its terms and the interpretation of the rights and duties of the Members.

COUNTERPART SIGNATURE PAGE TO
OPERATING AGREEMENT

This Counterpart Signature Page, when duly executed by the undersigned and attached to that certain Operating Agreement of ANDERSON INDUSTRIES, LLC, shall make the undersigned a party to said Agreement and shall bind the undersigned to the terms and conditions of said Agreement.

IN WITNESS WHEREOF, the undersigned has executed this Operating Agreement as of the day and year first above written and executed this Counterpart Signature Page as of the date written below.

ANDERSON INDUSTRIES, LLC

By: _____
BOB ANDERSON, Manager

State _____

ss.

County _____

On this _____ day of _____, _____, before me, _____, the undersigned officer, personally appeared BOB ANDERSON, known to me to be the person whose name is signed to the foregoing instrument, and acknowledged the execution thereof for the uses and purposes therein set forth.
IN WITNESS WHEREOF I have hereunto set my hand and official seal.

_____

Notary Public

_____

My Commission Expires

EXHIBIT A: CAPITAL CONTRIBUTION

Member	# of Membership Units	Capital Commitment
BOB ANDERSON	765,000	$5,000
3499 MALCOLM AVENUE		
LOS ANGELES, CALIFORNIA 85254		

TOTAL COMMITMENTS: $5,000

EXHIBIT B: DEFINITIONS

For purposes of the Operating Agreement of ANDERSON INDUSTRIES, LLC, and the Exhibits attached thereto, the following terms shall, unless the context otherwise requires, have the meanings specified in this Exhibit B.

"Act" means the CALIFORNIA Limited Liability Company Act, as amended from time to time.

"Adjusted Capital Account Deficit" means, with respect to any Interest Holder, the deficit balance, if any, in the Interest Holder's Capital Account as of the end of the relevant taxable year, after giving effect to the following adjustments: (a) the deficit shall be decreased by the amounts which the Interest Holder is obligated to restore pursuant to Section 1 of Exhibit C to the Agreement, or is deemed obligated to restore pursuant to Regulations Section 1.704-l(b)(2)(ii)(c); and (b) the deficit shall be increased by the items described in Regulations Section 1.704-l(b)(2)(ii)-(d)(4), (5) and (6).

"Affiliate" means, with respect to any Member, any Person: (a) which owns more than 50% of the voting interests of the Member; (b) in which the Member owns more than 50% of the voting interests; or (c) in which more than 50% of the voting interests are owned by a Person that has a familial or business relationship with the Member.

"Agreement" or "Operating Agreement" means the Operating Agreement of the Company, as it may be amended from time to time.

"Bankruptcy," "Bankrupt" and derivations thereof, means the occurrence of any of the following events with respect to the applicable Person: (a) the Person makes an assignment for the benefit of creditors; (b) the Person files a voluntary petition of bankruptcy; (c) the Person is adjudged bankrupt or insolvent or there is entered against the Person an order for relief in any bankruptcy or insolvency proceeding; (d) the Person files a petition or answer seeking for the Person any reorganization, arrangement, composition, readjustment, liquidation, dissolution, or similar relief under any statute, law, or regulation; (e) the Person seeks, consents to, or acquiesces in the appointment of a trustee for, receiver for or liquidation of the Person or of all or any substantial part of the Person's properties; (f)any proceeding against the Person seeking reorganization, arrangement, composition, readjustment, liquidation, dissolution, or similar relief under any statute, law or regulation, which continues for 120 days after the commencement thereof, or the appointment of a trustee, receiver, or liquidator for the Person or all or any substantial part of the Person's properties without the Person's agreement or acquiescence, which appointment is not vacated or stayed for 120 days or, if the appointment is stayed, for 120 days after the expiration of the stay the appointment is not vacated; not only to an adjudication, finding, or determination of bankruptcy under the federal Bankruptcy Code, but also to an adjudication of insolvency under any state or local insolvency procedure.

"Capital Account" means an account for each Interest Holder maintained on the books of the Company in accordance with the following provisions: (a) An Interest Holder's Capital Account shall be credited with the Interest Holder's Capital Contributions, the amount of any Company liabilities assumed by the Interest Holder (or which are secured by Company property distributed to the Interest Holder), the Interest Holder's distributive share of Net Profits, and any item in the nature of income or gain specially allocated to such Interest Holder pursuant to the provisions of Exhibit C to the Agreement (other than Section 6 thereof); (b) An Interest Holder's Capital Account shall be debited with the amount of money and the Gross Asset Value of any Company property distributed to the Interest Holder, the amount of any liabilities of the Interest Holder assumed by the Company (or which are secured by property contributed by the Interest Holder to the Company), the Interest Holder's distributive share of Net Losses and any item in the nature of expenses or losses specially allocated to such Interest Holder pursuant to the provisions of Exhibit C to the Agreement; (c) In the event of the Transfer of an Interest in accordance with the Agreement, the transferee shall succeed to the Capital Account of the transferor to the extent the Capital Account is attributable to the transferred Interest; (d) If the book value of Company property is adjusted pursuant to the provisions of Exhibit C to the Agreement, the Capital Account of each Interest Holder shall be adjusted to reflect the aggregate adjustment in the same manner as if the Company had recognized gain or loss equal to the amount of such aggregate adjustment; and (e) It is intended that the Capital Accounts of all Interest Holders shall be maintained and adjusted in accordance with the Code and the Regulations promulgated thereunder, and all provisions of the Agreement relating to the maintenance of Capital Accounts shall be interpreted and applied in a manner consistent with those Regulations. In determining the amount of liabilities for purposes of the foregoing, there shall be taken into account Code Section 752(c) and any other applicable provisions of the Code or Regulations.

"Capital Contribution" means, with respect to any Member, the total amount of cash and the fair market value of any other assets contributed (or deemed contributed under Regulations Section 1.704-l(b)(2)(iv)(d)) as capital to the Company with respect to the Interest held by such Member, net of liabilities assumed or to which the contributed assets may be subject at the time of such contribution.

"Capital Transaction" means any transaction not in the ordinary course of business which results in the Company's receipt of cash or other consideration other than Capital Contributions, including, without limitation, proceeds of sales or exchanges or other dispositions of assets not in the ordinary course of business, financings, refinancings, condemnations, recoveries of damage awards, and insurance proceeds.

"Code" means the Internal Revenue Code of 1986, as amended. Any reference to a section thereof shall be deemed to include any corresponding tax provision in statutory codes of any state or a political subdivision thereof, or CALIFOR-NIA, and shall be deemed to include any corresponding provision of any future Internal Revenue Codes of the United States.

"Company" means the limited liability company formed and continued under the Agreement.

"Depreciation" means, for each Fiscal Year, an amount equal to the depreciation, amortization, or other cost recovery deduction allowable with respect to an asset for such Fiscal Year, except that if the Gross Asset Value of an asset differs from its adjusted basis for federal income tax purposes at the beginning of such Fiscal Year, Depreciation shall be an amount which bears the same ratio to such beginning Gross Asset Value as the federal income tax depreciation, amortization, or other cost recovery deduction for such Fiscal Year bears to such beginning adjusted tax basis; provided, however, that if the adjusted basis for federal income tax purposes of an asset at the beginning of such Fiscal Year is zero, Depreciation shall be determined with reference to such beginning Gross Asset Value using any reasonable method selected by the Manager.

"Executive Employee" means an employee of the Company to whom the Manager has delegated specific duties and authority to carry out the operation and management of the Company's business.

"Fiscal Year" means any of the applicable periods ending on December 31 during the existence of the Company, or any other applicable period for which the Company shall close its books and records for accounting and tax reporting purposes.

"Gross Asset Value" means, with respect to any asset, the asset's adjusted basis for federal income tax purposes, except as follows:

    a. the initial Gross Asset Value of any asset contributed by a Member to the Company as a Capital Contribution shall be the gross fair market value of such asset, as determined by the contributing Member and the Manager;

    b. the Gross Asset Values of all Company assets shall be adjusted to equal their respective gross fair market values, as determined by the Manager, as of the following times: (i) the acquisition of an additional interest in the Company by any new or existing Interest Holder in exchange for more than a de minimis Capital Contribution, (ii) the distribution by the Company to an Interest Holder of more than a de minimis amount of Property as consideration for an Interest in the Company; and (iii) the liquidation of the Company within the meaning of Regulations Section 1.704-l(b)(2)(ii)(g), provided, however, that adjustments pursuant to clauses (i) and (ii) above shall be made only if the Manager reasonably determines that such adjustments are necessary or appropriate to reflect the relative economic interests of the Interest Holders;

c. the Gross Asset Value of any Company asset distributed to any Interest Holder shall be adjusted to equal the gross fair market value of such asset on the date of distribution as determined by the distributee and the Manager; and,

d. the Gross Asset Values of Company assets shall be increased (or decreased) to reflect any adjustments to the adjusted basis of such assets pursuant to Code Section 734(b) or Code Section 743(b), but only to the extent that such adjustments are taken into account in determining Capital Accounts pursuant to Regulations Section 1.704-l(b)(2)(iv)(m), as promulgated pursuant to the Code and Section 30(f) hereof and Section 3(g) of Exhibit C to the Agreement; provided, however, that Gross Asset Values shall not be adjusted pursuant to this Section to the extent the Manager determines that an adjustment pursuant to Section (b) hereof is necessary or appropriate in connection with a transaction that would otherwise result in an adjustment pursuant to this Section. If the Gross Asset Value of an asset has been determined or adjusted pursuant to Section (a) or (b) hereof, such Gross Asset Value shall thereafter be adjusted by the Depreciation taken into account with respect to such asset for purposes of computing Net Profits and Net Losses.

"Interest" means an Interest Holder's entire economic right, title, and ownership interest in the Company at any particular time.

"Interest Holder" means any Person who owns an Interest, whether as a Member or as an unadmitted economic transferee of or successor-in-interest to an Interest.

"Involuntary Withdrawal" means, with respect to any Member, the occurrence of any of the following events:

a. The Member becomes bankrupt;

b. If the Member is an individual, the Member's death or the adjudication by a court of competent jurisdiction that the Member is incompetent to manage the Member's person or property;

c. If the Member is acting as a Member by virtue of being a trustee of a trust, the termination of the trust;

d. If the Member is a partnership or another limited liability company, the dissolution and commencement of winding up of the partnership or limited liability company;

e. If the Member is a corporation, the dissolution of the corporation or the revocation of its charter; or,

f. If the Member is an estate, the distribution by the fiduciary of the estate's entire interest in the limited liability company.

"LLC" refers to the Company, ANDERSON INDUSTRIES, LLC.

"LLC Minimum Gain" has the same meaning as "Partnership Minimum Gain" set forth in Regulations Sections 1.704-2(b)(2) and 1.704-2(d). LLC Minimum Gain shall be computed separately for each Interest Holder in a manner consistent with the Regulations under Code Section 704(b).

"Majority in Interest" means the Members that own, in the aggregate, more than 50% of all the Percentage Interests in the Company.

"Member(s)" means, individually and collectively, each Person who executes the Agreement and is admitted to the Company as a Member in accordance with the terms and conditions set forth in the Agreement.

"Member Nonrecourse Debt" has the meaning for "Partner Nonrecourse Debt" set forth in Regulations Section 1.704-2(b)(4).

"Member Nonrecourse Debt Minimum Gain" means an amount, with respect to each Member Nonrecourse Debt, equal to the LLC Minimum Gain that would result if such Member Nonrecourse Debt were treated as a Nonrecourse Liability, determined in accordance with Regulations Section 1.704-2(i)(3).

"Member Nonrecourse Deductions" has the meaning for "Partner Nonrecourse Deductions" set forth in Regulations Sections 1.704-2(i)(1) and 1.704-2(i)(2).

"Net Available Cash Flow" means:

    a. All cash receipts as shown on the books of the Company for any Fiscal Year (excluding Capital Contributions from Members, proceeds of Company loans or borrowing, excess financing proceeds, or net proceeds to the Company from the sale or the disposition of any of the assets of the Company), reduced by cash disbursements in such Fiscal Year for Company purposes including all costs and expenses associated with the conduct of the business of the Company, all payments made on account of and with respect to Company loans and borrowings, all costs and expenses of Company financing and all costs and expenses of operating and managing the assets of the Company, all loans and advances made by the Company and all cash reserves set aside by the Manager, which shall be deemed in its sole discretion, reasonable and necessary to accomplish the purposes of the Company's business; or

    b. Any other funds other than Net Available Cash Flow, including amounts previously set aside as reserves, deemed available for distribution in the sole discretion of the Manager.

"Net Capital Proceeds" means the gross receipts received by the Company from a Capital Transaction, less any and all amounts that the Manager determines, in its sole discretion, are necessary for the payment of or due provision for (a) the liabilities of the Company to all creditors, including the expenses of the Capital Transaction, and/or (b) additional requirements for funds in connection with the Company's business. Net Capital Proceeds in any Fiscal Year will include any amounts of receipts from a Capital Transaction received in prior Fiscal Years and previously set aside as reserves by the Manager, deemed available at the sole discretion of the Manager for distribution to the Interest Holders.

"Net Profits" and "Net Losses" means, for each Fiscal Year, an amount equal to the Company's taxable income or loss for such Fiscal Year, determined in accordance with Code Section 703(a) (for this purpose, all items of income, gain, loss, or deduction required to be stated separately pursuant to Code Section 703(a)(1) shall be included in taxable income or loss), with the following adjustments:

a. Any income of the Company that is exempt from federal income tax and not otherwise taken into account in computing Net Profits or Net Losses pursuant to this Section shall be allocated separately among the Interest Holders and shall not be added to such taxable income or loss;

b. Any expenditures of the Company described in Code Section 705(a)(2)(B) or treated as Code Section 705(a)(2)(B) expenditures pursuant to Regulations Section 1.704-l(b)(2)(iv)(i), and not otherwise taken into account in computing Net Profits or Net Losses pursuant to this Section shall be subtracted from such taxable income or loss;

c. In the event the Gross Asset Value of any Company asset is adjusted pursuant to Section 15(b) or (c) hereof, the amount of such adjustment shall be taken into account as gain or loss from the disposition of such asset for purposes of computing Net Profits or Net Losses;

d. Gain or loss resulting from any disposition of Property with respect to which gain or loss is recognized for federal income tax purposes shall be computed by reference to the Gross Asset Value of the property disposed of, notwithstanding that the adjusted tax basis of such property differs from its Gross Asset Value;

e. In lieu of the depreciation, amortization, and other cost recovery deductions taken into account in computing such taxable income or loss, there shall be taken into account Depreciation for such Fiscal Year, computed in accordance with Section 15 hereof;

f. To the extent an adjustment to the adjusted tax basis of any Company asset pursuant to Code Section 734(b) or Code Section 743(b) is required pursuant to Regulations Section 1.704-l (b)(2)(iv)(m)(4), to be taken into account in determining Capital Accounts as a result of a distribution other than in complete liquidation of an Interest Holder's Interest, the amount of such adjustment shall be treated as an item of gain (if the adjustment increases the basis of the asset) or loss (if the adjustment decreases the basis of the asset) from the disposition of the asset and shall be taken into account for purposes of computing Net Profits or Net Losses; and

g. Notwithstanding any other provision of this Section, any items which are specially allocated pursuant to Section 3 or 4 of Exhibit C to the Agreement shall not be taken into account in computing Net Profits or Net Losses. The amounts of the items of Company income, gain, loss or deduction available to be specially allocated pursuant to Sections 3 and 4 of Exhibit C to the Agreement shall be determined by applying rules analogous to those set forth in Sections (a) through (g) above.

"Nonrecourse Deductions" has the meaning set forth in Regulations Section 1.704-2(b)(1).

"Nonrecourse Liability" has the meaning set forth in Regulations Section 1.752-1(a)(2).

"Percentage Interest(s)" means the percentage which the Interest(s) of the applicable Member or Interest Holder, or group of Members or Interest Holders, bears to the entire applicable group of Members or Interest Holders, as set forth in Exhibit A.

"Person" means any individual, estate, corporation, partnership, association, limited liability company, trust, or other entity.

"Pro Rata Basis" means an allocation of the referenced distributions, tax items, dilution or other item among the group of Members or Interest Holders being referred to proportionate with said Persons' relative Percentage Interests.

"Regulations" means the Regulations of the U.S. Department of Treasury promulgated under the Code.

"Transfer" means, when used as a noun, any voluntary or involuntary sale, hypothecation, pledge, assignment, attachment, gift, or other disposition, and, when used as a verb, means, voluntarily or involuntarily to sell, hypothecate, pledge, assign, permit the attachment of, or otherwise dispose of.

"Voluntary Withdrawal" means a Member's dissociation with the Company by means other than a Transfer or an Involuntary Withdrawal.

EXHIBIT C: TAX ALLOCATIONS

Section 1. Net Profits. After giving effect to the special allocations set forth in Sections 3 and 4 of this Exhibit C, Net Profits for any Fiscal Year shall be allocated among all of the Interest Holders on a Pro Rata Basis.

Section 2. Net Losses. After giving effect to the special allocations set forth in Sections 3 and 4 of this Exhibit C, Net Losses for any Fiscal Year shall be allocated as set forth in Section 2(a) hereof, subject to the limitation in Section 2(b) hereof.

    a. Net Losses for any Fiscal Year shall be allocated in the following order and priority: (i) first, to all of the Interest Holders on a Pro Rata Basis in an amount equal to the excess, if any, of (1) the cumulative Net Profits allocated pursuant to this Section for all prior Fiscal Years, over (2) The cumulative Net Losses allocated pursuant to this Section for all prior Fiscal Years; and (ii) The balance, if any, to all of the Interest Holders on a Pro Rata Basis.

    b. The Net Losses allocated pursuant to Section 2(a) of this Exhibit C shall not exceed the maximum amount of Net Losses that can be so allocated without causing any Interest Holder to have an Adjusted Capital Account Deficit at the end of any Fiscal Year. In the event some but not all of the Interest Holders would have Adjusted Capital Account Deficits as a consequence of an allocation of Net Losses pursuant to Section 2(a) of this Exhibit C, the limitation set forth in this Section 2(b) shall be applied on an Interest Holder by Interest Holder basis so as to allocate the maximum permissible Net Losses to each Interest Holder under Regulations Section 1.704-l(b)(2)(ii)(d), . All Net Losses in excess of the limitations set forth in this Section 2(b) shall be allocated to all of the Interest Holders on a Pro Rata Basis.

Section 3. Special Allocations. The following special allocations shall be made in the following order:

    a. Minimum Gain Chargeback. Except as otherwise provided in Regulations Section 1.704-2(f), and notwithstanding any other provision of this Exhibit C, if there is a net decrease in LLC Minimum Gain during any Fiscal Year, each Interest Holder shall be specially allocated items of Company income and gain for such Fiscal Year (and, if necessary, subsequent Fiscal Years) in an amount equal to such Interest Holder's share of the net decrease in LLC Minimum Gain, determined in accordance with Regulations Section 1.704-2(g). The items to be so allocated shall be determined in accordance with Regulations Sections 1.704-2(f)(6) and 1.704-2(j)(2). This Section 3(a) is intended to comply with the minimum gain chargeback requirement in Regulations Section 1.704-2(f), and shall be interpreted consistently therewith.

    b. Member Minimum Gain Chargeback. Except as otherwise provided in Regulations Section 1.704-2(i)(4), notwithstanding any other provision of this Exhibit C, if there is a net decrease in Member Nonrecourse Debt Minimum Gain attributable to a Member Nonrecourse Debt during any Company Fiscal Year, each Interest Holder who has a share of the Member Nonrecourse Debt Minimum Gain attributable to such Member Nonrecourse Debt, determined in accordance with Regulations Section 1.704-2(i)(5), shall be specially allocated items of Company income and gain for such Fiscal Year (and, if necessary, subsequent Fiscal Years) in an amount equal to such Person's share of the net decrease in Member Nonrecourse Debt Minimum Gain attributable to such Member Nonrecourse Debt, determined in accordance with Regulations Section 1.704-2(i)(4). Allocations pursuant to the previous sentence shall be made in proportion to the respective amounts required to be allocated to each Interest Holder pursuant thereto. The items to be so allocated shall be determined in accordance with Regulations Sections 1.704-2(i)(4) and 1.704-2(j)(2). This Section 3(b) is intended to comply with the minimum gain chargeback requirement in Regulations Section 1.704-2(i)(4), and shall be interpreted consistently therewith.

c. Qualified Income Offset. In the event any Interest Holder unexpectedly receives any adjustments, allocations or distributions described in Regulations Sections 1.704-1(b)(2)(ii)(d)(4), 1.704-1(b)(2)(ii)(d)(5), or 1.704-1(b)(2)(ii)(d)(6), items of Company income and gain shall be specially allocated to each such Interest in an amount and manner sufficient to eliminate, to the extent required by the Regulations, the Adjusted Capital Account Deficit of such Interest Holder as quickly as possible, provided that an allocation pursuant to this Section 3(c) shall be made only if and to the extent that such Interest Holder would have an Adjusted Capital Account Deficit after all other allocations provided for in this Exhibit C have been tentatively made as if this Section 3 were a part of the Agreement.

d. Gross Income Allocation. In the event any Interest Holder has a deficit Capital Account at the end of any Company Fiscal Year which is in excess of the sum of (i) the amount such Interest Holder is obligated to restore pursuant to any provision of the Operating Agreement, and (ii) the amount such Interest Holder is deemed to be obligated to restore pursuant to the penultimate sentences of Regulations Sections 1.704-2(g)(1) and 1.704-2(i)(5), each such Interest Holder shall be specially allocated items of Company income and gain in the amount of such excess as quickly as possible, provided that an allocation pursuant to this Section 3(d) shall be made only if and to the extent that such Interest Holder would have a deficit Capital Account in excess of such sum after all other allocations provided for in this Exhibit C have been made as if Section 3(c) and (d) of this Exhibit C were not in the Agreement.

e. Nonrecourse Deductions. Nonrecourse Deductions for any Fiscal Year shall be allocated to all of the Interest Holders on a Pro Rata Basis.

f. Member Nonrecourse Deductions. Any Member Nonrecourse Deductions for any Fiscal Year shall be specially allocated to the Interest Holder who bears the economic risk of loss with respect to the Member Nonrecourse Debt to which such Member Nonrecourse Deductions are attributable in accordance with Regulations Section 1.704-2(i)(1).

g. Section 754 Adjustments. To the extent an adjustment to the adjusted tax basis of any Company asset pursuant to Code Section 734(b) or Code Section 743(b), is required (pursuant to Regulations Sections 1.704-l(b)(2)(iv)(m)(2) or 1.704 -l(b)(2)(iv)(m)(4),) to be taken into account in determining Capital Accounts as the result of a distribution to an Interest Holder in complete liquidation of its interest in the Company, the amount of such adjustment to Capital Accounts shall be treated as an item of gain (if the adjustment increases the basis of the asset) or loss (if the adjustment decreases such basis) and such gain or loss shall be specially allocated to the Interest Holders on a Pro Rata Basis or in the event that Regulations Section 1.704-l(b)(2)(iv)(m)(2), applies, or to the Interest Holder to whom such distribution was made in the event that Regulations Section 1.704-l(b)(2)(iv)(m)(4), applies.

h. Preferred Return Allocations. In the event, at any time and for any reason, there arises a disproportion in the Capital Account balances of the Interest Holders, then prior to the liquidation of the Company, in accordance with Section 9 of the Operating Agreement, or at such earlier times and in such amounts as the Manager shall determine in its sole discretion, all or a portion of the remaining items of Company income or gain, if any, shall be specially allocated among the Interest Holders in such manner necessary to bring the Capital Account balances of the Interest Holders into proportion with their then existing Percentage Interests.

i. Allocations Relating to Taxable Issuance of Interests. Any income, gain, loss, or deduction realized as a direct or indirect result of the issuance of an Interest by the Company to an Interest Holder (the "Issuance Items") shall be allocated among the Interest Holders so that, to the extent possible, the net amount of such Issuance Items, together with all other allocations under the Operating Agreement to each Interest Holder, shall be equal to the net amount that would have been allocated to each such Interest Holder if the Issuance Items had not been realized.

Section 4. Curative Allocations. The allocations set forth in Sections 2(b), 3(a), 3(b), 3(c), 3(d), 3(e), 3(f) and 3(g) of this Exhibit C (the "Regulatory Allocations") are intended to comply with certain requirements of the Regulations. It is the intent of the Members that, to the extent possible, all Regulatory Allocations shall be offset either with other Regulatory Allocations or with special allocations of other items of Company income, gain, loss, or deduction pursuant to this Section 4.

Therefore, notwithstanding any other provision of this Exhibit C (other than the Regulatory Allocations), the Manager shall make such offsetting special allocations of Company income, gain, loss, or deduction in whatever manner it determines appropriate so that, after such offsetting allocations are made, each Interest Holder's Capital Account balance is, to the extent possible, equal to the Capital Account balance such Interest Holder would have had if the Regulatory Allocations were not part of the Agreement and all Company items were allocated pursuant to Sections 1, 2(a), and 3(h) hereof. In exercising its discretion under this Section 4, the Manager shall take into account future Regulatory Allocations under Sections 3(a) and 3(b) that, although not yet made, are likely to offset other Regulatory Allocations previously made under Sections 3(e) and 3(f).

Section 5. Other Allocation Rules.

   a. For purposes of determining the Net Profits, Net Losses, or any other items allocable to any period, Net Profits, Net Losses, and any such other items shall be determined on a daily, monthly or other basis, as determined by the Manager, using any permissible method under Code section 706 and the Regulations thereunder.

   b. All allocations to the Interest Holders pursuant to this Exhibit C, except as otherwise provided, shall be divided among them on a Pro Rata Basis.

   c. The Interest Holders are aware of the income tax consequences of the allocations made by this Exhibit C and hereby agree to be bound by the provisions of this Exhibit C in reporting their shares of Company income and loss for income tax purposes.

   d. Solely for purposes of determining an Interest Holder's proportionate share of the "excess nonrecourse liabilities" of the Company within the meaning of Regulations Section 1.752-3(a)(3), the Interest Holders' interests in Company profits shall be deemed to be on a Pro Rata Basis.

   e. To the extent permitted by Regulations Section 1.704-2(h)(3), the Manager shall endeavor to treat distributions of Net Available Cash Flow or Net Capital Proceeds as having been made from the proceeds of a Nonrecourse Liability or a Member Nonrecourse Debt only to the extent that such distributions would cause or increase an Adjusted Capital Account Deficit for any Interest Holder.

   f. Any income of the Company that is exempt from federal income tax and not otherwise taken into account in computing Net Profits or Net Losses pursuant to the terms of the Agreement or any Exhibits thereto shall be allocated separately to all of the Interest Holders on a Pro Rata Basis.

Section 6. Tax Allocations: Code Section 704 (c). In accordance with Code Section 704 (c) and the Regulations thereunder, income, gain, loss, and deduction with respect to any property contributed to the capital of the Company, solely for tax purposes, shall be allocated among the Interest Holders so as to take account of any variation between the adjusted basis of such property to the Company for federal income tax purposes and its initial Gross Asset Value (computed in accordance with Section 14(a) of Exhibit B to the Operating Agreement). In the event the Gross Asset Value of any Company asset is adjusted pursuant to Section 14(b) of Exhibit A to the Operating Agreement, subsequent allocations of income, gain, loss, and deduction with respect to such asset shall take account of any variation between the adjusted basis of such asset for federal income tax purposes and its Gross Asset Value in the same manner as under Code Section 704(c) and the Regulations thereunder. Any elections or other decisions relating to such allocations shall be made by the Manager in any manner that reasonably reflects the purpose and intention of the Operating Agreement. Allocations pursuant to this Section 6 are solely for purposes of federal, state, and local taxes and shall not affect, or in any way be taken into account in computing, any Person's Capital Account or share of Net Profits, Net Losses, other items or distributions pursuant to any provision of this Agreement.

The Limited Liability Company membership interests have not been registered under the Securities Act of 1933, as amended (the "Act"), any state securities laws, or the laws of any other nation or jurisdiction, and may not be sold or otherwise transferred unless the same have been included in an effective registration statement under the Act or such laws, or an opinion of counsel, satisfactory to the Manager of the Company, has been rendered to the Company, that an exemption from registration under applicable securities laws is available. In addition, transfer or other disposition of the Limited Liability Company membership interests is restricted as provided in the Operating Agreement.

EXECUTION PAGE
FOR THE OPERATING AGREEMENT OF
ANDERSON INDUSTRIES, LLC

IN WITNESS WHEREOF, the parties hereto have executed this Operating Agreement in multiple counterparts as of the day and in the year first above written, and each of such counterparts, when taken together, shall constitute one and the same instrument.

SIGNATURE OF THE MANAGER

BY: _____ DATE: _____
BOB ANDERSON, Initial Manager

SIGNATURE OF THE MEMBER

BY: _____ DATE: _____

_____
NAME OF MEMBER AND TITLE, IF APPLICABLE (Please print this response and those below)

_____
ADDRESS

_____
TELEPHONE NUMBER

_____
FACSIMILE NUMBER

_____
NAME OF TRUSTEE (IF APPLICABLE)

_____
ADDRESS OF TRUSTEE (IF APPLICABLE)

_____
NAME OF PLAN SPONSOR (IF APPLICABLE)

_____
ADDRESS OF PLAN SPONSOR (IF APPLICABLE)

_____
TAX ID

Index

LEGAL SURVIVAL IN BUSINESS

The Complete Book of Corporate Forms (2E)	$29.95
The Complete Hiring and Firing Handbook	$19.95
The Complete Home-Based Business Kit	$14.95
The Complete Limited Liability Company Kit	$24.95
The Complete Partnership Book	$24.95
The Complete Patent Book	$26.95
The Complete Patent Kit	$39.95
The Entrepreneur's Internet Handbook	$21.95
The Entrepreneur's Legal Guide	$26.95
Financing Your Small Business	$16.95
Fired, Laid-Off or Forced Out	$14.95
How to Buy a Franchise	$19.95
How to Form a Nonprofit Corporation (3E)	$24.95
How to Form Your Own Corporation (4E)	$26.95
How to Register Your Own Copyright (5E)	$24.95
HR for Small Business	$14.95
Incorporate in Delaware from Any State	$26.95
Incorporate in Nevada from Any State	$24.95
The Law (In Plain English)® for Small Business	$19.95
The Law (In Plain English)® for Writers	$14.95
Making Music Your Business	$18.95
Minding Her Own Business (4E)	$14.95
Most Valuable Business Legal Forms You'll Ever Need (3E)	$21.95
Profit from Intellectual Property	$28.95
Protect Your Patent	$24.95
The Small Business Owner's Guide to Bankruptcy	$21.95
Start Your Own Law Practice	$16.95
Tax Power for the Self-Employed	$17.95
Tax Smarts for Small Business	$21.95
Your Rights at Work	$14.95

LEGAL SURVIVAL IN COURT

Attorney Responsibilities & Client Rights	$19.95
Crime Victim's Guide to Justice (2E)	$21.95
Legal Research Made Easy (4E)	$24.95
Winning Your Personal Injury Claim (3E)	$24.95

LEGAL SURVIVAL IN REAL ESTATE

The Complete Kit to Selling Your Own Home	$18.95
The Complete Book of Real Estate Contracts	$18.95
Essential Guide to Real Estate Leases	$18.95
Homeowner's Rights	$19.95
How to Buy a Condominium or Townhome (2E)	$19.95
How to Buy Your First Home (2E)	$14.95
How to Make Money on Foreclosures	$16.95
The Mortgage Answer Book	$14.95
Sell Your Home Without a Broker	$14.95
The Weekend Landlord	$16.95
Working with Your Homeowners Association	$19.95

LEGAL SURVIVAL IN SPANISH

Cómo Comprar su Primera Casa	$8.95
Cómo Conseguir Trabajo en los Estados Unidos	$8.95
Cómo Hacer su Propio Testamento	$16.95
Cómo Iniciar su Propio Negocio	$8.95
Cómo Negociar su Crédito	$8.95
Cómo Organizar un Presupuesto	$8.95
Cómo Solicitar su Propio Divorcio	$24.95
Guía de Inmigración a Estados Unidos (4E)	$24.95
Guía de Justicia para Víctimas del Crimen	$21.95
Guía Esencial para los Contratos de Arrendamiento de Bienes Raices	$22.95 $16.95
Inmigración y Ciudadanía en los EE.UU. Preguntas y Respuestas	$16.95
Inmigración a los EE.UU. Paso a Paso (2E)	$24.95
Manual de Beneficios del Seguro Social	$18.95
El Seguro Social Preguntas y Respuestas	$16.95
¡Visas! ¡Visas! ¡Visas!	$9.95

LEGAL SURVIVAL IN PERSONAL AFFAIRS

101 Complaint Letters That Get Results	$18.95
The 529 College Savings Plan (2E)	$18.95
The 529 College Savings Plan Made Simple	$7.95
The Alternative Minimum Tax	$14.95
The Antique and Art Collector's Legal Guide	$24.95
The Childcare Answer Book	$12.95
Child Support	$18.95
The Complete Book of Insurance	$18.95
The Complete Book of Personal Legal Forms	$24.95
The Complete Credit Repair Kit	$18.95
The Complete Legal Guide to Senior Care	$21.95
Credit Smart	$18.95
The Easy Will and Living Will Kit	$16.95
Fathers' Rights	$19.95
The Frequent Traveler's Guide	$14.95
File Your Own Divorce (6E)	$24.95
Gay & Lesbian Rights	$26.95
Grandparents' Rights (4E)	$24.95
How to File Your Own Bankruptcy (6E)	$21.95
How to Make Your Own Simple Will (3E)	$18.95
How to Parent with Your Ex	$12.95
How to Write Your Own Living Will (4E)	$18.95
How to Write Your Own Premarital Agreement (3E)	$24.95
The Infertility Answer Book	$16.95
Law 101	$16.95
Law School 101	$16.95
The Living Trust Kit	$21.95
Living Trusts and Other Ways to Avoid Probate (3E)	$24.95
Mastering the MBE	$16.95
Nursing Homes and Assisted Living Facilities	$19.95
The Power of Attorney Handbook (5E)	$22.95
Quick Cash	$14.95
Seniors' Rights	$19.95
Sexual Harassment in the Workplace	$18.95
Sexual Harassment Your Guide to Legal Action	$18.95:
Sisters-in-Law	$16.95
The Social Security Benefits Handbook (4E)	$18.95
Social Security Q&A	$12.95
Starting Out or Starting Over	$14.95
Teen Rights (and Responsibilities) (2E)	$14.95
Unmarried Parents' Rights (and Responsibilities) (3E)	$16.95
U.S. Immigration and Citizenship Q&A	$18.95
U.S. Immigration Step by Step (2E)	$24.95
U.S.A. Immigration Guide (5E)	$26.95
What to Do—Before "I DO"	$14.95
The Wills, Estate Planning and Trusts Legal Kit	$26.95
Win Your Unemployment Compensation Claim (2E)	$21.95
Your Right to Child Custody, Visitation, & Support	$24.95

SPHINX® PUBLISHING ORDER FORM

BILL TO:		SHIP TO:	
Phone #	**Terms**	**F.O.B.** Chicago, IL	**Ship Date**

Charge my: ☐ VISA   ☐ MasterCard   ☐ American Express   ☐ **Money Order or Personal Check**

Credit Card Number   **Expiration Date**

Qty	ISBN	Title	Retail	Qty	ISBN	Title	Retail
		SPHINX PUBLISHING NATIONAL TITLES			1-57248-384-9	How to Buy a Franchise	$19.95
	1-57248-363-6	101 Complaint Letters That Get Results	$18.95		1-57248-497-7	How to Buy Your First Home (2E)	$14.95
	1-57248-361-X	The 529 College Savings Plan (2E)	$18.95		1-57248-472-1	How to File Your Own Bankruptcy (6E)	$21.95
	1-57248-483-7	The 529 College Savings Plan Made Simple	$7.95		1-57248-390-3	How to Form a Nonprofit Corporation (3E)	$24.95
	1-57248-460-8	The Alternative Minimum Tax	$14.95		1-57248-345-8	How to Form Your Own Corporation (4E)	$26.95
	1-57248-349-0	The Antique and Art Collector's Legal Guide	$24.95		1-57248-520-5	How to Make Money on Foreclosures	$16.95
	1-57248-347-4	Attorney Responsibilities & Client Rights	$19.95		1-57248-232-X	How to Make Your Own Simple Will (3E)	$18.95
	1-57248-482-9	The Childcare Answer Book	$12.95		1-57248-479-9	How to Parent with Your Ex	$12.95
	1-57248-382-2	Child Support	$18.95		1-57248-379-2	How to Register Your Own Copyright (5E)	$24.95
	1-57248-487-X	Cómo Comprar su Primera Casa	$8.95		1-57248-394-6	How to Write Your Own Living Will (4E)	$18.95
	1-57248-488-8	Cómo Conseguir Trabajo en los Estado Unidos	$8.95		1-57248-156-0	How to Write Your Own	$24.95
	1-57248-148-3	Cómo Hacer su Propio Testamento	$16.95			Premarital Agreement (3E)	
	1-57248-532-9	Cómo Iniciar su Propio Negocio	$8.95		1-57248-504-3	HR for Small Business	$14.95
	1-57248-462-4	Cómo Negociar su Crédito	$8.95		1-57248-230-3	Incorporate in Delaware from Any State	$26.95
	1-57248-463-2	Cómo Organizar un Presupuesto	$8.95		1-57248-158-7	Incorporate in Nevada from Any State	$24.95
	1-57248-147-1	Cómo Solicitar su Propio Divorcio	$24.95		1-57248-531-0	The Infertility Answer Book	$16.95
	1-57248-507-8	The Complete Book of Corporate Forms (2E)	$29.95		1-57248-474-8	Inmigración a los EE.UU. Paso a Paso (2E)	$24.95
	1-57248-383-0	The Complete Book of Insurance	$18.95		1-57248-400-4	Inmigración y Ciudadanía en los EE. UU.	$16.95
	1-57248-499-3	The Complete Book of Personal Legal Forms	$24.95			Preguntas y Respuestas	
	1-57248-528-0	The Complete Book of Real Estate Contracts	$18.95		1-57248-377-6	The Law (In Plain English)® for Small Business	$19.95
	1-57248-500-0	The Complete Credit Repair Kit	$19..95		1-57248-476-4	The Law (In Plain English)® for Writers	$14.95
	1-57248-458-6	The Complete Hiring and Firing Handbook	$19.95		1-57248-453-5	Law 101	$16.95
	1-57248-484-5	The Complete Home-Based Business Kit	$14.95		1-57248-374-1	Law School 101	$16.95
	1-57248-353-9	The Complete Kit to Selling Your Own Home	$18.95		1-57248-509-4	Legal Research Made Easy (4E)	$24.95
	1-57248-229-X	The Complete Legal Guide to Senior Care	$21.95		1-57248-449-7	The Living Trust Kit	$21.95
	1-57248-498-5	The Complete Limited Liability Company Kit	$24.95		1-57248-165-X	Living Trusts and Other Ways to	$24.95
	1-57248-391-1	The Complete Partnership Book	$24.95			Avoid Probate (3E)	
	1-57248-201-X	The Complete Patent Book	$26.95		1-57248-486-1	Making Music Your Business	$18.95
	1-57248-514-0	The Complete Patent Kit	$39.95		1-57248-186-2	Manual de Beneficios para el Seguro Social	$18.95
	1-57248-369-5	Credit Smart	$18.95		1-57248-220-6	Mastering the MBE	$16.95
	1-57248-163-3	Crime Victim's Guide to Justice (2E)	$21.95		1-57248-455-1	Minding Her Own Business, 4E	$14.95
	1-57248-251-6	The Entrepreneur's Internet Handbook	$21.95		1-57248-480-2	The Mortgage Answer Book	$14.95
	1-57248-235-4	The Entrepreneur's Legal Guide	$26.95		1-57248-167-6	Most Val. Business Legal Forms	$21.95
	1-57248-160-9	Essential Guide to Real Estate Leases	$18.95			You'll Ever Need (3E)	
	1-57248-375-X	Fathers' Rights	$19.95		1-57248-388-1	The Power of Attorney Handbook (5E)	$22.95
	1-57248-517-5	File Your Own Divorce (6E)	$24.95		1-57248-332-6	Profit from Intellectual Property	$28.95
	1-57248-553-1	Financing Your Small Business	$16.95		1-57248-329-6	Protect Your Patent	$24.95
	1-57248-459-4	Fired, Laid-Off or Forced Out	$14.95		1-57248-376-8	Nursing Homes and Assisted Living Facilities	$19.95
	1-57248-502-7	The Frequent Traveler's Guide	$14.95		1-57248-385-7	Quick Cash	$14.95
	1-57248-331-8	Gay & Lesbian Rights	$26.95		1-57248-350-4	El Seguro Social Preguntas y Respuestas	$16.95
	1-57248-526-4	Grandparents' Rights (4E)	$24.95		1-57248-386-5	Seniors' Rights	$19.95
	1-57248-475-6	Guía de Inmigración a Estados Unidos (4E)	$24.95		1-57248-527-2	Sexual Harassment in the Workplace	$18.95
	1-57248-187-0	Guía de Justicia para Víctimas del Crimen	$21.95		1-57248-217-6	Sexual Harassment: Your Guide to Legal Action	$18.95
	1-57248-253-2	Guía Esencial para los Contratos de	$22.95		1-57248-378-4	Sisters-in-Law	$16.95
		Arrendamiento de Bienes Raices			1-57248-219-2	The Small Business Owner's Guide to Bankruptcy	$21.95
	1-57248-334-2	Homeowner's Rights	$19.95		1-57248-529-9	Sell Your Home Without a Broker	$14.95
	1-57248-164-1	How to Buy a Condominium or Townhome (2E)	$19.95				

Form Continued on Following Page   **SubTotal** _____

Qty	ISBN	Title	Retail
_____	1-57248-395-4	The Social Security Benefits Handbook (4E)	$18.95
_____	1-57248-216-8	Social Security Q&A	$12.95
_____	1-57248-521-3	Start Your Own Law Practice	$16.95
_____	1-57248-328-8	Starting Out or Starting Over	$14.95
_____	1-57248-525-6	Teen Rights (and Responsibilities) (2E)	$14.95
_____	1-57248-457-8	Tax Power for the Self-Employed	$17.95
_____	1-57248-366-0	Tax Smarts for Small Business	$21.95
_____	1-57248-236-2	Unmarried Parents' Rights (and Responsibilities(3E)	$16.95
_____	1-57248-362-8	U.S. Immigration and Citizenship Q&A	$18.95
_____	1-57248-387-3	U.S. Immigration Step by Step (2E)	$24.95
_____	1-57248-392-X	U.S.A. Immigration Guide (5E)	$26.95
_____	1-57248-478-0	¡Visas! ¡Visas! ¡Visas!	$9.95
_____	1-57248-477-2	The Weekend Landlord	$16.95
_____	1-57248-451-9	What to Do — Before "I DO"	$14.95
_____	1-57248-330-X	The Wills, Estate Planning and Trusts Legal Kit	$26.95
_____	1-57248-473-X	Winning Your Personal Injury Claim (3E)	$24.95
_____	1-57248-225-7	Win Your Unemployment Compensation Claim (2E)	$21.95
_____	1-57248-333-4	Working with Your Homeowners Association	$19.95
_____	1-57248-380-6	Your Right to Child Custody, Visitation and Support (3E)	$24.95
_____	1-57248-505-1	Your Rights at Work	$14.95

CALIFORNIA TITLES

Qty	ISBN	Title	Retail
_____	1-57248-489-6	How to File for Divorce in CA (5E)	$26.95
_____	1-57248-464-0	How to Settle and Probate an Estate in CA (2E)	$28.95
_____	1-57248-336-9	How to Start a Business in CA (2E)	$21.95
_____	1-57248-194-3	How to Win in Small Claims Court in CA (2E)	$18.95
_____	1-57248-246-X	Make Your Own CA Will	$18.95
_____	1-57248-397-0	Landlords' Legal Guide in CA (2E)	$24.95
_____	1-57248-241-9	Tenants' Rights in CA	$21.95

FLORIDA TITLES

Qty	ISBN	Title	Retail
_____	1-57248-396-2	How to File for Divorce in FL (8E)	$28.95
_____	1-57248-356-3	How to Form a Corporation in FL (6E)	$24.95
_____	1-57248-490-X	How to Form a Limited Liability Co. in FL (3E)	$24.95
_____	1-57071-401-0	How to Form a Partnership in FL	$22.95
_____	1-57248-456-X	How to Make a FL Will (7E)	$16.95
_____	1-57248-354-7	How to Probate and Settle an Estate in FL (5E)	$26.95
_____	1-57248-339-3	How to Start a Business in FL (7E)	$21.95
_____	1-57248-204-4	How to Win in Small Claims Court in FL (7E)	$18.95
_____	1-57248-381-4	Land Trusts in Florida (7E)	$29.95
_____	1-57248-338-5	Landlords' Rights and Duties in FL (9E)	$22.95

GEORGIA TITLES

Qty	ISBN	Title	Retail
_____	1-57248-340-7	How to File for Divorce in GA (5E)	$21.95
_____	1-57248-493-4	How to Start a Business in GA (4E)	$21.95

ILLINOIS TITLES

Qty	ISBN	Title	Retail
_____	1-57248-244-3	Child Custody, Visitation, and Support in IL	$24.95
_____	1-57248-206-0	How to File for Divorce in IL (3E)	$24.95
_____	1-57248-170-6	How to Make an IL Will (3E)	$16.95
_____	1-57248-265-9	How to Start a Business in IL (4E)	$21.95
_____	1-57248-252-4	Landlord's Legal Guide in IL	$24.95

MARYLAND, VIRGINIA AND THE DISTRICT OF COLUMBIA

Qty	ISBN	Title	Retail
_____	1-57248-240-0	How to File for Divorce in MD, VA, and DC	$28.95
_____	1-57248-359-8	How to Start a Business in MD, VA, or DC	$21.95

MASSACHUSETTS TITLES

Qty	ISBN	Title	Retail
_____	1-57248-115-3	How to Form a Corporation in MA	$24.95
_____	1-57248-466-7	How to Start a Business in MA (4E)	$21.95
_____	1-57248-398-9	Landlords' Legal Guide in MA (2E)	$24.95

MICHIGAN TITLES

Qty	ISBN	Title	Retail
_____	1-57248-467-5	How to File for Divorce in MI (4E)	$24.95
_____	1-57248-182-X	How to Make a MI Will (3E)	$16.95
_____	1-57248-468-3	How to Start a Business in MI (4E)	$21.95

MINNESOTA TITLES

Qty	ISBN	Title	Retail
_____	1-57248-142-0	How to File for Divorce in MN	$21.95
_____	1-57248-179-X	How to Form a Corporation in MN	$24.95
_____	1-57248-178-1	How to Make a MN Will (2E)	$16.95

NEW JERSEY TITLES

Qty	ISBN	Title	Retail
_____	1-57248-512-4	File for Divorce in NJ	$24.95
_____	1-57248-448-9	How to Start a Business in NJ	$21.95

NEW YORK TITLES

Qty	ISBN	Title	Retail
_____	1-57248-193-5	Child Custody, Visitation and Support in NY	$26.95
_____	1-57248-351-2	File for Divorce in NY	$26.95
_____	1-57248-249-4	How to Form a Corporation in NY (2E)	$24.95
_____	1-57248-401-2	How to Make a NY Will (3E)	$16.95
_____	1-57248-468-1	How to Start a Business in NY (3E)	$21.95
_____	1-57248-198-6	How to Win in Small Claims Court in NY (2E)	$18.95
_____	1-57248-122-6	Tenants' Rights in NY	$21.95

NORTH CAROLINA AND SOUTH CAROLINA TITLES

Qty	ISBN	Title	Retail
_____	1-57248-508-6	How to File for Divorce in NC (4E)	$26.95
_____	1-57248-371-7	How to Start a Business in NC or SC	$24.95
_____	1-57248-091-2	Landlords' Rights & Duties in NC	$21.95

OHIO TITLES

Qty	ISBN	Title	Retail
_____	1-57248-503-5	How to File for Divorce in OH (3E)	$24.95
_____	1-57248-174-9	How to Form a Corporation in OH	$24.95
_____	1-57248-173-0	How to Make an OH Will	$16.95

PENNSYLVANIA TITLES

Qty	ISBN	Title	Retail
_____	1-57248-242-7	Child Custody, Visitation and Support in PA	$26.95
_____	1-57248-495-0	How to File for Divorce in PA (4E)	$26.95
_____	1-57248-358-X	How to Form a Corporation in PA	$24.95
_____	1-57248-094-7	How to Make a PA Will (2E)	$16.95
_____	1-57248-357-1	How to Start a Business in PA (3E)	$21.95
_____	1-57248-245-1	Landlords' Legal Guide in PA	$24.95

TEXAS TITLES

Qty	ISBN	Title	Retail
_____	1-57248-171-4	Child Custody, Visitation, and Support in TX	$22.95
_____	1-57248-399-7	How to File for Divorce in TX (4E)	$24.95
_____	1-57248-470-5	How to Form a Corporation in TX (3E)	$24.95
_____	1-57248-496-9	How to Probate and Settle an Estate in TX (4E)	$26.95
_____	1-57248-471-3	How to Start a Business in TX (4E)	$21.95
_____	1-57248-111-0	How to Win in Small Claims Court in TX (2E)	$16.95
_____	1-57248-355-5	Landlords' Legal Guide in TX	$24.95
_____	1-57248-513-2	Write Your Own TX Will (4E)	$16.95

WASHINGTON TITLES

Qty	ISBN	Title	Retail
_____	1-57248-522-1	File for Divorce in WA	$24.95

SubTotal This page _____

SubTotal previous page _____

Shipping — $5.00 for 1st book, $1.00 each additional _____

Illinois residents add 6.75% sales tax _____

Connecticut residents add 6.00% sales tax _____

Total _____